PRINCIPLES OF INDUSTRIAL PHARMACY-I

ESSENTIAL CONCEPTS IN DRUG MANUFACTURING

KONATHAM MOUNIKA, KUCHUKUNTLA MOUNIKA, RAJENDRA KUMAR JADI

Contents

AUTHORS   *v*

Preface   *vii*

Table of Contents   *ix*

  1. Preformulation Studies   1

  2. Tablets   71

  3. Liquid Orals   126

  4. Capsules   164

  5. Pellets   198

  6. Parenteral Products   223

  7. Cosmetics   258

  8. Pharmaceutical Aerosols   287

Authors

Konatham Mounika, M.Pharm., (Ph.D.)
Assistant Professor,
Department of Pharmaceutics,
Omega College of Pharmacy,
Edulabad (V), Ghatkesar, Medchal Dist.,
Telangana - 501301, India
Kuchukuntla Mounika, M.Pharm., (Ph.D.)
Assistant Professor,
Department of Pharmaceutics,
School of Pharmacy, Anurag University,
Venkatapur, Ghatkesar, Medchal-Malkajgiri,
Hyderabad - 500088, Telangana, India
Dr. Rajendra Kumar Jadi
Assistant Professor,
Department of Pharmaceutics,
School of Pharmacy, Anurag University,
Venkatapur, Ghatkesar, Medchal-Malkajgiri,
Hyderabad - 500088, Telangana, India

Preface

The pharmaceutical industry is a cornerstone of healthcare, providing essential medicines that improve and sustain human life. The field of **industrial pharmacy** bridges the gap between pharmaceutical sciences and manufacturing processes, ensuring that high-quality, safe, and effective medicines reach patients in need. **Principles of Industrial Pharmacy-I: Essential Concepts in Drug Manufacturing** has been written to provide a **comprehensive, structured, and application-oriented understanding** of the fundamental principles involved in drug manufacturing. This book serves as a **valuable academic and professional resource** for students, researchers, and industry professionals seeking to gain a deeper insight into the science and technology behind pharmaceutical production.

The book covers a wide range of topics, beginning with **preformulation studies**, which lay the foundation for understanding the physicochemical properties of drug substances and their impact on formulation stability. It then explores **the science of tablet and capsule formulation, liquid and parenteral dosage forms, and specialized drug delivery systems** such as pellets and aerosols. Each chapter is structured to provide **detailed theoretical concepts, manufacturing techniques, quality control parameters, and regulatory considerations**, ensuring a holistic approach to industrial pharmacy.

A key focus of this book is the **integration of pharmaceutical sciences with industrial applications**, highlighting the importance of **Good Manufacturing Practices (GMP), quality assurance, and process validation** in large-scale drug production. In addition, **advances in technology, innovations in drug formulation, and compliance with evolving regulatory frameworks** are discussed to prepare readers for the challenges and opportunities in pharmaceutical manufacturing.

This book is designed to be **student-friendly, academically rigorous, and industry-relevant**. The content is presented in **a clear, structured manner**, with **illustrations, case studies, and real-world examples** to aid comprehension. By maintaining a **balance between theoretical knowledge and practical applications**, this book aims to equip learners with the skills necessary to **understand, design, and optimize pharmaceutical formulations** in an industrial setting.

We extend our sincere gratitude to **academicians, researchers, and industry experts** whose contributions to the field of industrial pharmacy have paved the way for scientific advancements in drug manufacturing. Special thanks to our mentors, colleagues, and students whose feedback and insights have been invaluable in shaping this book.

We hope that **Principles of Industrial Pharmacy-I: Essential Concepts in Drug Manufacturing** serves as a **comprehensive reference** for students pursuing **B.Pharm and M.Pharm courses**, as well as **a practical guide** for professionals working in pharmaceutical formulation and manufacturing. We welcome **constructive feedback and suggestions** from readers to further enhance the content in future editions.

Konatham Mounika, Kuchukuntla **Mounika, Dr. Rajendra Kumar Jadi**

Table Of Contents

Chapter 1: Preformulation Studies

1.1 Introduction to Preformulation
  1.1.1 Goals and Objectives
  1.1.2 Importance in Pharmaceutical Development
    1.2 Physicochemical Characteristics of Drug Substances
  1.2.1 Physical Properties
    1.2.1.1 Crystalline and Amorphous Forms
    1.2.1.2 Polymorphism and Industrial Significance
    1.2.1.3 Particle Size and Shape
    1.2.1.4 Flow Properties
    1.2.1.5 Solubility Profile: pKa, pH, and Partition Coefficient
  1.2.2 Chemical Properties
    1.2.2.1 Hydrolysis
    1.2.2.2 Oxidation and Reduction
    1.2.2.3 Racemization
    1.2.2.4 Polymerization
  1.3 BCS Classification and Applications
  1.3.1 Classification of Drugs
  1.3.2 Applications in Preformulation Studies
    1.4 Impact on Dosage Form Stability
  1.4.1 Solid Dosage Forms
  1.4.2 Liquid Oral Dosage Forms
  1.4.3 Parenteral Dosage Forms

Chapter 2: Tablets

2.1 Introduction to Tablets
  2.1.1 Ideal Characteristics of Tablets
  2.1.2 Classification of Tablets
    2.2 Formulation and Manufacturing Techniques
  2.2.1 Excipients in Tablet Formulation
  2.2.2 Granulation Methods
    2.2.2.1 Wet Granulation

2.2.2.2 Dry Granulation

2.2.2.3 Direct Compression

2.2.3 Compression and Processing Problems

2.3 Tablet Coating

2.3.1 Types of Coating

2.3.1.1 Sugar Coating

2.3.1.2 Film Coating

2.3.1.3 Enteric Coating

2.3.2 Coating Materials and Composition

2.3.3 Defects in Coating and Remedies

2.4 Quality Control Tests

2.4.1 In-Process Tests

2.4.1.1 Weight Variation

2.4.1.2 Hardness

2.4.1.3 Friability

2.4.2 Finished Product Tests

2.4.2.1 Disintegration Time

2.4.2.2 Dissolution Testing

Chapter 3: Liquid Orals

3.1 Formulation and Manufacturing

3.1.1 Solutions

3.1.2 Suspensions

3.1.3 Emulsions

3.2 Filling and Packaging

3.3 Quality Control

3.3.1 Evaluation of Solutions

3.3.2 Evaluation of Suspensions

3.3.3 Evaluation of Emulsions

Chapter 4: Capsules

4.1 Hard Gelatin Capsules

4.1.1 Gelatin Extraction and Capsule Shell Production

4.1.2 Filling Techniques

4.1.2.1 Manual Filling

4.1.2.2 Semi-Automatic Filling

4.1.2.3 Automatic Filling

4.1.3 Finishing and Special Formulation Techniques

4.2 Soft Gelatin Capsules

4.2.1 Nature of Shell and Content

4.2.2 Base Adsorption and Minimum/Gram Factor

4.2.3 Filling and Sealing Techniques

4.3 Quality Control Tests

4.3.1 In-Process Tests

4.3.2 Finished Product Tests

Chapter 5: Pellets

5.1 Introduction to Pellets

5.1.1 Advantages of Pellets

5.1.2 Requirements for Formulation

5.2 Pelletization Process

5.2.1 Extrusion-Spheronization

5.2.2 Layering Techniques

5.2.3 Fluidized Bed Coating

5.3 Equipment for Pellet Manufacture

5.3.1 Working Principle of Fluidized Bed Coater (FBC)

Chapter 6: Parenteral Products

6.1 Introduction to Parenterals

6.1.1 Definition and Types

6.1.2 Advantages and Limitations

6.2 Preformulation Considerations

6.2.1 Vehicles and Additives

6.2.2 Importance of Isotonicity

6.3 Production and Quality Control

6.3.1 Sterilization Methods

6.3.1.1 Heat Sterilization

6.3.1.2 Filtration

6.3.1.3 Irradiation

6.3.2 Stability Testing

6.3.3 Evaluation of Parenterals

6.4 Ophthalmic Preparations
6.4.1 Eye Drops
6.4.2 Eye Ointments
6.4.3 Eye Lotions

Chapter 7: Cosmetics

7.1 Lip and Skin Products
7.1.1 Lipsticks
7.1.2 Cold Creams
7.1.3 Vanishing Creams
7.2 Hair Care Products
7.2.1 Shampoos
7.2.2 Hair Dyes
7.3 Sunscreens

Chapter 8: Pharmaceutical Aerosols

8.1 Introduction to Aerosols
8.1.1 Definition and Components
8.1.2 Propellants, Containers, and Valves
8.2 Formulation and Manufacture
8.2.1 Types of Aerosol Systems
8.3 Quality Control and Stability Studies

Chapter 9: Packaging Materials Science

9.1 Types of Packaging Materials
9.1.1 Glass
9.1.2 Plastic
9.1.3 Metal and Rubber
9.2 Factors Influencing Packaging Choice
9.3 Stability Considerations
9.4 Legal and Official Requirements

Preformulation Studies

1.1 Introduction to Preformulation

Preformulation is a critical and foundational phase in the pharmaceutical development process. It involves a systematic study of the physicochemical properties of a drug substance and its interaction with potential excipients. These studies lay the groundwork for designing and developing safe, effective, and stable pharmaceutical dosage forms. Preformulation ensures that a drug molecule transitions smoothly from the laboratory to the clinical and commercial stages. The information gathered during preformulation not only optimizes the drug formulation but also aids in meeting regulatory requirements and addressing potential challenges during manufacturing, storage, and distribution.

The scope of preformulation is vast, encompassing properties such as solubility, stability, particle size, polymorphism, hygroscopicity, and compatibility with excipients. Each of these properties influences critical aspects such as bioavailability, shelf life, and patient acceptability. By thoroughly understanding these factors, pharmaceutical scientists can predict and mitigate formulation challenges, thereby ensuring the success of the final product.

1.1.1 Goals and Objectives

The goals and objectives of preformulation studies are multi-faceted, aiming to optimize the development process while ensuring the safety and efficacy of the drug product. These objectives form the backbone of pharmaceutical development and are geared toward addressing both scientific and regulatory aspects.

Determining Physicochemical Properties of Drugs

One of the primary goals of preformulation is to determine the **physicochemical properties** of the drug substance. These properties significantly influence the drug's behavior during manufacturing and in vivo. Key parameters include:

Solubility: Solubility plays a crucial role in drug bioavailability. For example, poorly soluble drugs like **Griseofulvin** (aqueous solubility ~0.05 mg/mL at 25°C) often exhibit low bioavailability, necessitating solubility enhancement techniques. Solubility is tested in various solvents such as water, ethanol, and buffer solutions of different pH values to assess the drug's dissolution profile.

Stability Profiling: Stability studies identify conditions under which a drug remains stable, determining its shelf life and storage requirements. Parameters such as **temperature**, **humidity**, **light sensitivity**, and exposure to oxygen are studied. For instance, **Vitamin C** (ascorbic acid) degrades rapidly in the presence of oxygen, necessitating antioxidant additives.

Partition Coefficient (Log P): The partition coefficient indicates a drug's hydrophilicity or lipophilicity, influencing absorption and distribution. For example, **Diazepam**, with a Log P of ~2.8, demonstrates good lipophilicity, making it suitable for oral and parenteral formulations.

Polymorphism: Drugs like **Ritonavir** exhibit polymorphism, where different crystal forms have varied solubility and stability profiles. Identifying stable polymorphic forms is essential to avoid unexpected failures during production or storage.

Stability Profile

Stability profiling ensures the drug's integrity under various environmental conditions. For instance, **antibiotics** like amoxicillin are highly sensitive to humidity, which can degrade the active ingredient. Compatibility studies evaluate how the drug interacts with excipients. For example, **Aspirin** can undergo hydrolysis in the presence of magnesium stearate, leading to the formation of salicylic acid, which reduces efficacy. Such studies guide the selection of appropriate excipients and packaging materials.

Forced Degradation Studies: These studies expose the drug to extreme conditions, such as **40°C/75% RH**, to identify potential degradation pathways.

Excipient Compatibility Testing: Differential Scanning Calorimetry (DSC) is a common technique to evaluate interactions between drugs and excipients. For instance, **Paracetamol** shows compatibility with microcrystalline cellulose but not with lactose under certain conditions.

Formulation Optimization

Preformulation studies provide critical data to optimize the formulation. For instance, the **particle size** of a drug affects dissolution and bioavailability. Drugs like **Ibuprofen** require particle size reduction to improve solubility and absorption. Similarly, determining the drug's **pKa** ensures that the pH of the formulation is maintained in a range that maximizes stability and solubility. For example, the pKa of **Diclofenac sodium** is 4.0, so formulations are buffered at a pH above this value to ensure solubility and prevent precipitation.

1. **Designing Dosage Forms**: Data from preformulation studies guide the selection of dosage forms, such as tablets, capsules, or injectables. For example, poorly soluble drugs like **Itraconazole** are formulated as nanosuspensions to enhance absorption.
2. **Avoiding Stability Challenges**: Drugs sensitive to oxidation, like **Adrenaline**, are formulated with antioxidants like sodium metabisulfite to maintain stability.

Examples of Impact

1. **Solubility and Bioavailability**: Poorly water-soluble drugs such as **Bicalutamide** often require solubility enhancement techniques like solid dispersions or surfactant-based formulations to achieve therapeutic efficacy.
2. **Stability in Formulation**: **Amoxicillin trihydrate** requires careful stabilization in suspension formulations to prevent degradation over time. Formulating it with suitable buffers and preservatives ensures extended shelf life and efficacy.

By focusing on these goals and objectives, preformulation studies provide a scientific basis for successful drug development. They reduce risks, enhance formulation efficiency, and ensure that the final product meets quality and performance standards. This phase acts as a bridge between discovery and development, integrating scientific insights into practical pharmaceutical applications.

1.1.2 Importance in Pharmaceutical Development

Preformulation studies are an essential pillar in the pharmaceutical development process. These studies serve as the scientific foundation for transforming a drug molecule into a safe, effective, and stable dosage form. By investigating the physicochemical and biological characteristics of a drug, preformulation enables pharmaceutical scientists to identify potential challenges and devise strategies to overcome them. The importance of preformulation lies in its ability to enhance **drug delivery**, improve **bioavailability**, and promote **patient compliance**, ultimately bridging the gap between research and product development.

Role in Improving Drug Delivery, Bioavailability, and Patient Compliance

Enhancing Drug Delivery

Preformulation studies play a vital role in designing appropriate drug delivery systems. The **physicochemical properties** of a drug, such as **solubility**, **permeability**, and **stability**, directly impact its delivery to the site of action. For instance, drugs with poor solubility may require advanced drug delivery technologies like **liposomes**, **micelles**, or **nanoemulsions** to ensure effective therapeutic outcomes. An example is **Amphotericin B**, which was reformulated into liposomal preparations (AmBisome®) to reduce toxicity and improve targeted delivery.

Improving Bioavailability

Bioavailability, defined as the fraction of an administered drug that reaches systemic circulation, is heavily influenced by preformulation findings. Poorly water-soluble drugs like **Fenofibrate** (aqueous solubility < 10 µg/mL) suffer from low bioavailability. Through preformulation studies, techniques such as **particle size reduction**, **solid dispersion**, and **co-crystallization** are employed to improve solubility and dissolution rates. For instance, **Fenofibrate Nanocrystal®** formulations demonstrated enhanced bioavailability, enabling reduced dosing and improved patient outcomes.

Promoting Patient Compliance

Preformulation studies also contribute to patient-friendly formulations, ensuring ease of administration and adherence. Factors such as **taste masking**, **controlled release**, and **reduced dosing frequency** significantly enhance patient compliance. For example, **Metformin**, a widely used antidiabetic drug, is formulated as extended-release tablets to minimize gastrointestinal side effects and improve patient adherence by reducing the number of daily doses.

Case Studies: Success and Failure in Preformulation Studies
Successful Cases

1. **Atorvastatin (Lipitor®)**: Atorvastatin faced challenges related to poor solubility and stability during early development. Comprehensive preformulation studies identified the optimal crystalline form and excipients, leading to a stable and bioavailable formulation. Lipitor® became one of the best-selling drugs globally due to its robust preformulation efforts.
2. **Itraconazole (Sporanox®)**: Itraconazole is a poorly water-soluble antifungal drug. Preformulation studies revealed that traditional formulations would not provide adequate absorption. Consequently, the drug was reformulated as a **cyclodextrin inclusion complex**, significantly improving its bioavailability and therapeutic efficacy.

Failure Cases

1. **Ritonavir (Norvir®)**: During post-launch stability studies, Ritonavir unexpectedly exhibited **polymorphic instability**, leading to a significant drop in solubility and bioavailability. This failure highlighted the need for exhaustive preformulation studies to identify and stabilize the optimal polymorphic form during development.
2. **Cisapride**: This gastroprokinetic agent was withdrawn from the market due to serious cardiac side effects caused by excipient interactions that went undetected during preformulation. This failure emphasized the importance of comprehensive drug-excipient compatibility studies.

How Preformulation Bridges Research and Product Development

Preformulation serves as the critical link between drug discovery and product development. It translates laboratory findings into practical knowledge that informs the design of pharmaceutical formulations. Without robust preformulation studies, promising drug candidates may fail during development or post-market stages, leading to significant financial and time losses.

1. **Guiding Dosage Form Design**: Preformulation data provide insights into the selection of dosage forms (e.g., tablets, capsules, injectables) based on the drug's properties. For example, **Paclitaxel**, a poorly soluble anticancer drug, was successfully developed as an injectable formulation using **Cremophor EL®** to enhance solubility.
2. **Mitigating Risks**: By identifying potential stability issues, preformulation studies reduce the likelihood of product recalls. For instance, preformulation efforts identified the need for moisture-resistant packaging for **Aspirin**, ensuring product stability during storage.
3. **Facilitating Regulatory Approvals**: Regulatory agencies like the US FDA require comprehensive preformulation data as part of New Drug Applications (NDAs). These data demonstrate the safety, efficacy, and stability of the product, accelerating the approval process.
4. **Optimizing Manufacturing Processes**: Preformulation studies also inform manufacturing decisions by identifying suitable excipients, ensuring process compatibility, and optimizing conditions such as granulation, drying, and compression.

1.2 Physicochemical Characteristics of Drug Substances

Understanding the physicochemical characteristics of drug substances is fundamental to pharmaceutical development. These characteristics influence the drug's stability, solubility, bioavailability, and overall performance in a dosage form. Among these, the physical properties of a drug substance play a significant role in determining its behavior during formulation and delivery. One of the most critical aspects of physical properties is the distinction between crystalline and amorphous forms.

1.2.1 Physical Properties

The physical state of a drug substance—whether crystalline or amorphous—greatly impacts its solubility, stability, and bioavailability. Both forms have their own advantages and challenges, and their selection depends on the specific requirements of the formulation.

1.2.1.1 Crystalline and Amorphous Forms

The crystalline and amorphous forms of drugs represent two distinct physical states. Their differences lie in molecular arrangement, stability, solubility, and overall pharmaceutical performance.

A crystalline drug is characterized by a highly ordered molecular structure, where molecules are arranged in a repeating three-dimensional lattice. This ordered arrangement results in well-defined melting points and high physical stability.

Examples

Paracetamol exists in crystalline form, exhibiting excellent stability.

Ritonavir in its crystalline form is stable but has reduced solubility.

Significance:

Stability: Crystalline forms are generally more stable than amorphous forms due to the strong intermolecular forces within the lattice.

Solubility: These forms often have lower solubility compared to their amorphous counterparts, as the strong lattice structure resists dissolution.

Bioavailability: Lower solubility can translate into reduced bioavailability, especially for poorly water-soluble drugs.

In amorphous forms, molecules are arranged randomly without a defined crystalline lattice. This lack of order results in unique physical and chemical properties.

Examples:

Atorvastatin calcium in its amorphous form exhibits higher solubility and bioavailability compared to its crystalline counterpart.

Cefuroxime axetil is an amorphous drug known for improved absorption.

Significance:

Stability: Amorphous forms are less stable, prone to recrystallization over time, and may require stabilization techniques such as polymer addition.

Solubility: They exhibit higher solubility due to the absence of a rigid lattice, which allows easier interaction with solvents.

Analytical Techniques for Characterization

Characterizing the crystalline or amorphous nature of a drug is essential to ensure optimal formulation and performance. Various advanced analytical techniques are employed for this purpose:

X-Ray Diffraction (XRD)

Principle: XRD measures the diffraction patterns of X-rays passing through the sample. Crystalline substances produce sharp, distinct peaks, while amorphous substances generate broad, diffuse halos.

Application: Used to identify and quantify crystalline phases in a drug. For example, XRD can distinguish between the polymorphic forms of **Carbamazepine.**

Differential Scanning Calorimetry (DSC)

Principle: DSC measures the heat flow associated with phase transitions as the sample is heated. Crystalline forms exhibit sharp endothermic peaks corresponding to melting points, while amorphous forms show a broad glass transition.

Application: Used to determine the thermal stability and polymorphic transitions of drugs. For example, DSC can analyze the glass transition temperature ($T_gT\_gT_g$) of **Amorphous Indomethacin.**

Fourier-Transform Infrared Spectroscopy (FTIR)

Principle: FTIR measures molecular vibrations to identify functional groups and molecular arrangements. Crystalline and amorphous forms often exhibit differences in peak intensities and positions.

Application: Helps in identifying polymorphic forms and confirming the presence of amorphous content.

Scanning Electron Microscopy (SEM)

Principle: SEM provides detailed images of the sample's surface morphology. Crystalline forms show uniform, geometric shapes, while amorphous forms exhibit irregular, disordered structures.

Application: Used for visual confirmation of the structural form of a drug substance.

Impact on Pharmaceutical Development

Solubility and Bioavailability

The selection of amorphous or crystalline forms is guided by the desired solubility and bioavailability profile. For example, converting **Nifedipine** to its amorphous form improved its bioavailability.

Stability Challenges

Stabilizing amorphous forms requires careful formulation strategies. Techniques like **spray drying** and **solid dispersions** are often employed. For instance, **Voriconazole** is stabilized in its amorphous form using polymer carriers.

Processing and Manufacturing

The crystalline or amorphous nature of a drug influences its behavior during manufacturing processes such as granulation and compression. Crystalline forms generally exhibit better flow properties, while amorphous forms may require excipient modifications.

1.2.1.2 Polymorphism and Industrial Significance

Polymorphism is the ability of a compound to exist in more than one crystalline form, with each form having a distinct arrangement of molecules within the crystal lattice. These different forms, known as **polymorphs**, exhibit unique physicochemical properties such as solubility, stability, melting point, and mechanical strength. Polymorphism is especially significant in the pharmaceutical industry because these variations can profoundly impact a drug's bioavailability, manufacturability, and stability.

Role of Polymorphism in pharmaceuticals

Definition and Relevance in Industry

Polymorphism plays a critical role in drug development and production. Different polymorphs of the same drug can exhibit varying dissolution rates, influencing the drug's bioavailability and therapeutic efficacy. For instance, **Chloramphenicol palmitate** has multiple polymorphic forms, but only one of them demonstrates adequate bioavailability for therapeutic use. The selection of the appropriate polymorph is crucial to ensure consistent performance of the final product throughout its shelf life.

In addition to bioavailability, polymorphism affects the drug's behavior during manufacturing. Differences in polymorphic forms can lead to challenges in tableting, powder flow, and stability. For example, **Theophylline** exists in an anhydrous crystalline form and a monohydrate form, with significant differences in compressibility and stability, necessitating precise control during production.

Polymorph-Dependent Solubility Differences

The solubility of a drug often varies between its polymorphs due to differences in lattice energy. A notable example is **Ritonavir**, an antiretroviral drug. During its commercial production, a new polymorphic form (Form II) unexpectedly emerged, exhibiting much lower solubility compared to the original marketed polymorph (Form I). This change drastically reduced the drug's bioavailability, leading to product recalls and a halt in production until the issue was resolved by reformulating the drug. Such cases highlight the necessity of robust polymorph screening during preformulation to anticipate and prevent similar challenges.

Another example is **Carbamazepine**, an anticonvulsant that exists in multiple polymorphic forms. The metastable polymorph of Carbamazepine exhibits higher solubility than its stable counterpart, making it more suitable for applications where rapid drug release is desired. However, the metastable form can spontaneously convert to the stable form, necessitating careful formulation strategies to maintain its properties.

Methods to Identify and Control Polymorphs

Identifying and controlling polymorphic forms are critical tasks in pharmaceutical development. Advanced analytical techniques are employed to distinguish between polymorphs and monitor transitions during formulation and manufacturing.

X-Ray Diffraction (XRD): XRD is a primary tool for polymorph characterization. It identifies the unique diffraction patterns associated with each polymorphic form. For

example, the polymorphs of **Sulphathiazole** produce distinct XRD peaks, enabling accurate differentiation.

Differential Scanning Calorimetry (DSC): DSC measures the heat flow associated with phase transitions, providing insights into the melting points and thermal stability of polymorphs. For instance, the polymorphic forms of **Indomethacin** can be characterized by their distinct melting behaviors using DSC.

Infrared Spectroscopy (IR): IR spectroscopy detects differences in molecular vibrations that arise from variations in crystal packing. For example, polymorphs of **Cefuroxime axetil** exhibit characteristic IR peaks, aiding in their identification.

Thermogravimetric Analysis (TGA): TGA is used to monitor weight changes during heating, providing valuable information about polymorphic transitions. It is especially useful for identifying hydrate or solvate forms.

Control Strategies for Polymorphs

Controlling polymorphic forms requires meticulous attention during the synthesis, crystallization, and storage of a drug substance. Techniques such as solvent selection, temperature control, and the use of crystallization inhibitors are commonly employed to ensure the production of the desired polymorph.

For instance, the polymorphs of **Paracetamol** can be selectively crystallized by adjusting solvent polarity and cooling rates during crystallization. Similarly, the polymorphs of **Glycine** are controlled by modifying the pH of the crystallization medium. Moreover, excipients like polymers or surfactants are sometimes added to formulations to stabilize the desired polymorphic form and prevent unwanted transitions.

Case Studies Highlighting Industrial Significance

Several examples from the pharmaceutical industry underscore the critical importance of polymorphism:

Abacavir sulfate: During its development, polymorph screening identified a stable form with higher bioavailability than the initially discovered polymorph, significantly enhancing the drug's therapeutic efficacy.

Cimetidine: Polymorphism caused issues with compressibility during tableting, leading to the development of a polymorph-specific manufacturing process to ensure consistent quality.

Sulindac: Polymorphic screening revealed a metastable form with enhanced solubility. Stabilizing this form using excipients enabled the development of a fast-acting formulation for pain relief.

Industrial and Regulatory Implications

Regulatory agencies such as the **US FDA** and **EMA** mandate polymorphic characterization as part of drug development. Comprehensive polymorphic studies are essential for filing New Drug Applications (NDAs) and ensuring product consistency. For instance, in the case of **Lamivudine**, extensive polymorphic analysis during development ensured a robust supply chain by identifying the most stable form for commercial production.

1.2.1.3 Particle Size and Shape

The **particle size and shape** of a drug substance are crucial physical parameters that significantly influence its performance in pharmaceutical formulations. These properties affect key factors such as **dissolution rate**, **bioavailability**, and **flow properties**, ultimately determining the efficacy and manufacturability of the final product. Understanding and controlling particle size and shape are essential for developing formulations with predictable performance and stability.

Impact on Dissolution Rate, Bioavailability, and Flow Properties

Dissolution Rate and Bioavailability

The dissolution rate of a drug is directly influenced by its particle size. Smaller particles have a larger surface area relative to their volume, leading to faster dissolution. This is especially critical for **poorly water-soluble drugs**, where dissolution is the rate-limiting step in absorption. As the particle size decreases, the surface area (A) increases, leading to an enhanced dissolution rate. For example:

Griseofulvin, a poorly soluble antifungal drug, demonstrated a twofold increase in bioavailability when its particle size was reduced to the micronized range (~2-3 μm).

Nanoparticles of **Paclitaxel**, with sizes below 100 nm, showed improved solubility and bioavailability, enabling effective delivery in injectable formulations.

Flow Properties and Manufacturability

Particle size and shape also affect the **flowability** of powders, a critical property for processes like mixing, granulation, and compression during tablet manufacturing. Uniform, spherical particles exhibit better flow properties than irregularly shaped ones. For instance:

Fine powders (<50 μm) often show poor flowability due to increased cohesion between particles.

Larger, spherical particles (~250 μm) exhibit excellent flow characteristics, making them suitable for direct compression.

Poor flow properties can lead to uneven filling of tablet dies, resulting in weight variability and compromised product quality. To address these issues, granulation techniques or excipients like glidants (e.g., talc or colloidal silicon dioxide) are often employed.

Particle Size Ranges for Various Dosage Forms

Different dosage forms require specific particle size ranges to optimize their performance and manufacturability. Some examples include:

1. **Oral Tablets**: Particle sizes typically range between **50-150 µm** to ensure adequate flow and compressibility during tablet formation.
2. **Inhalation Powders**: To target the respiratory system effectively, particle sizes must be in the **1-5 µm** range to penetrate the alveoli.
3. **Suspensions**: Particle sizes between **1-10 µm** prevent sedimentation and provide uniform dosing.
4. **Injectables**: Injectable suspensions require particle sizes below **5 µm** to avoid clogging needles and ensure stability.

Topical Formulations: Particle sizes between **10-100 µm** ensure smooth texture and avoid grittiness.

Examples and Case Studies

1. **Effect of Particle Size on Bioavailability**

   The bioavailability of **Fenofibrate**, a poorly water-soluble lipid-lowering agent, was significantly enhanced by reducing its particle size. The micronized formulation of Fenofibrate demonstrated up to 30% higher bioavailability compared to its non-micronized counterpart.
2. **Flow Properties in Manufacturing**

   During the development of **Paracetamol** tablets, irregular particle shapes led to poor flowability, causing uneven weight distribution in tablets. Spheroidizing the particles through granulation improved flow properties and ensured consistent tablet quality.
3. **Dissolution Rate Enhancement**

   Ibuprofen, a non-steroidal anti-inflammatory drug, faced challenges with dissolution in its coarse form. By reducing its particle size to approximately **20 µm**, the dissolution rate improved significantly, enabling rapid onset of action.

Control and Measurement of Particle Size and Shape

Controlling particle size and shape is a critical step in pharmaceutical development. Advanced techniques are employed to measure and regulate these properties:

Techniques for Particle Size Measurement

Laser Diffraction: Widely used for particle size analysis, offering rapid and accurate measurements across a broad size range (0.1 μm to 3 mm).

Dynamic Light Scattering (DLS): Ideal for nanoparticles, measuring sizes in the range of **1-1000 nm**.

Microscopy: Scanning Electron Microscopy (SEM) and Optical Microscopy are used to visually inspect particle shape and size.

Particle Size Reduction Techniques

Micronization: High-pressure jet milling reduces particle size to the micron range (~1-10 μm).

Nanotechnology: Techniques like **wet milling** and **nanoprecipitation** create nanoparticles (<100 nm), improving solubility and bioavailability

1.2.1.4 Flow Properties

The **flow properties** of powders are critical in pharmaceutical manufacturing, as they influence processes like mixing, granulation, compression, and encapsulation. Poor flowability can lead to inconsistent weight and content uniformity of tablets and capsules, equipment blockages, and reduced manufacturing efficiency. Flow properties are primarily governed by factors such as particle size, shape, surface texture, and moisture content. Understanding and optimizing these properties is essential for ensuring the quality and performance of pharmaceutical products.

Impact of Flow Properties on Manufacturing

1. **Uniform Mixing and Blending**
   Good flow properties are necessary to achieve uniform mixing of drug substances and excipients. Irregular or cohesive powders may segregate during mixing, leading to variability in drug content.

2. **Tablet Compression and Encapsulation**
   During tablet compression and capsule filling, powders with poor flow can cause inconsistent filling of tablet dies or capsules, resulting in weight variation and non-uniform dosing.

3. **Operational Efficiency**
   Powders with excellent flow properties reduce equipment blockages, minimize downtime, and improve production efficiency. For example, free-flowing granules exhibit better handling in automated machinery compared to fine powders prone to clumping.

Flow Characterization and Formulas

Several methods are used to characterize the flow properties of powders, with key parameters including the **angle of repose, Carr's index**, and **Hausner ratio.**

Angle of Repose

The angle of repose (θ) is the maximum angle at which a pile of powder remains stable without sliding. It provides a quick assessment of powder flowability.

Threshold Values:

1. **25°-30°**: Excellent flow
2. **30°-40°**: Good to fair flow
3. **>40°**: Poor flow

Carr's Index (Compressibility Index)

Carr's index (C) measures the compressibility of a powder, indicating its flowability based on bulk and tapped densities.

Threshold Values:

1. **<10%**: Excellent flow
2. **10%-20%**: Good flow
3. **20%-30%**: Poor flow
4. **>30%**: Very poor flow

Hausner Ratio
Threshold Values:

1. **1.0-1.2**: Excellent flow
2. **1.2-1.4**: Fair to passable flow
3. **>1.4**: Poor flow

The Hausner ratio (H) is the ratio of tapped density to bulk density, providing another indicator of powder flowability.

Examples of Flow Property Challenge

1. **Paracetamol**: The fine particle size and irregular shape of raw paracetamol powder result in poor flow properties. Granulation is used to improve flow, enabling consistent die filling during tablet compression.
2. **Aspirin**: The cohesive nature of aspirin powder requires the addition of glidants like colloidal silicon dioxide to enhance flowability in tablet formulations.
3. **Inhalation Powders**: Dry powders for inhalation (e.g., salbutamol sulfate) must have specific flow properties to ensure uniform dosing and aerosolization. Particle sizes in the range of 1–5 μm can lead to poor flow, necessitating carrier particles like lactose to improve handling.

Techniques to Improve Flow Propertie

1. **Granulation**
   Granulation transforms fine powders into larger, free-flowing granules. Wet granulation and dry granulation are commonly employed to improve flow properties.
2. **Addition of Glidants**
   Glidants like talc, magnesium stearate, or colloidal silicon dioxide reduce interparticle friction, enhancing flowability.
3. **Particle Size Optimization**
   Increasing particle size through milling or sieving improves flow, as larger particles exhibit reduced cohesion.
4. **Moisture Control**
   Reducing moisture content in powders prevents clumping and improves flow. Hygroscopic materials, like lactose, require desiccation or the addition of drying agents to maintain optimal flow properties.

1.2.1.5 Solubility Profile: pKa, pH, and Partition Coefficient

Solubility, pKa, and the partition coefficient are critical parameters that determine a drug's behavior in biological systems and its performance in pharmaceutical formulations. These characteristics influence the drug's absorption, distribution, and overall bioavailability, making them essential considerations in the development of effective drug delivery systems.

Solubility and Its Relevance in Drug Absorption

Solubility refers to the maximum amount of a substance that can dissolve in a given solvent under specified conditions, such as temperature and pressure. In drug development, solubility is crucial because it determines the rate and extent of dissolution, which directly impacts drug absorption in the gastrointestinal tract.

Importance in Drug Absorption:

Drugs must dissolve in biological fluids to cross membranes and reach systemic circulation. Poorly soluble drugs often exhibit low bioavailability, limiting their therapeutic effectiveness.

For example, **Griseofulvin** (aqueous solubility ~0.05 mg/mL) requires formulation strategies like particle size reduction or use of surfactants to enhance solubility.

pKa and Solubility-pH Relationships

The **pKa** of a drug is the pH at which 50% of the drug exists in its ionized form, and 50% remains unionized. The ionization state significantly influences solubility and permeability, as unionized forms are more lipid-soluble and readily cross cell membranes.

Henderson-Hasselbalch Equation:

The solubility-pH relationship for weak acids and bases can be described using the Henderson-Hasselbalch equation:

Application in Formulation:

Weakly acidic drugs like **Aspirin** (pKa ~3.5) are more soluble in alkaline environments, as they predominantly exist in the ionized form.

Weakly basic drugs like **Lidocaine** (pKa ~7.9) are more soluble in acidic environments, as they are predominantly ionized at lower pH.

Partition Coefficient and Lipid Solubility

The **partition coefficient (Log P)** is the ratio of a drug's concentration in a lipid phase (e.g., octanol) to its concentration in an aqueous phase (e.g., water) when the two phases are at equilibrium. It reflects the drug's lipophilicity and predicts its ability to cross lipid membranes.

Relevance in Drug Absorption:

Drugs with high Log P values are more lipid-soluble, enabling them to easily cross cell membranes. However, excessively high Log P values may lead to poor aqueous solubility and reduced bioavailability.

Drugs with low Log P values are more water-soluble but may struggle to cross lipid membranes, limiting their absorption.

Examples:

Diazepam (Log P ~2.8): Highly lipophilic, easily crosses the blood-brain barrier, making it suitable for treating anxiety.

Metformin (Log P ~ -1.43): Hydrophilic, absorbed via specific transport mechanisms in the gut.

Optimal Log P Range for Oral Drugs: Most orally active drugs have a Log P between 1 and 3, balancing lipid solubility for membrane permeability and aqueous solubility for dissolution in biological fluids.

Examples of Solubility Profiles in Drugs

Ibuprofen:
Solubility: Poorly water-soluble (~21 mg/L).

pKa: ~4.9, indicating that it becomes more soluble in alkaline pH.

Log P: ~3.5, making it lipophilic and readily absorbed through lipid membranes.

Propranolol:
Solubility: Moderate in water (~60 mg/L).

pKa: ~9.4, soluble in acidic pH where it exists in ionized form.

Log P: ~3.48, suitable for oral administration and lipid membrane permeability.

Warfarin:
Solubility: Very poor aqueous solubility (~0.17 mg/L).

pKa: ~5.0, better solubility at alkaline pH.

Log P: ~3.1, enabling lipid membrane permeability but requiring solubility enhancers for formulation.

1.2.2 Chemical Properties

Chemical properties of drug substances, such as hydrolysis, oxidation, and photodegradation, play a vital role in determining their stability, efficacy, and shelf life. Among these, **hydrolysis** is one of the most common pathways of chemical degradation, particularly for drugs containing ester, amide, lactone, or lactam functional groups. Understanding the mechanisms of hydrolysis is essential for predicting and mitigating chemical instability in pharmaceutical formulations.

1.2.2.1 Hydrolysis

Hydrolysis refers to the chemical breakdown of a compound due to its reaction with water. This process is a significant cause of drug instability, especially in formulations exposed to moisture or aqueous environments. Hydrolysis can lead to the loss of drug potency and the formation of potentially harmful degradation products.

Role of Hydrolysis in Chemical Instability

1. **Mechanism**:
   Hydrolysis involves the cleavage of covalent bonds in the presence of water, typically catalyzed by acids, bases, or enzymes. Drugs containing ester, amide, lactone, or lactam bonds are particularly susceptible to hydrolysis. The rate of hydrolysis depends on factors such as **pH, temperature, moisture content**, and the **presence of catalysts.**

2. **Impact on Pharmaceutical Stability**:

   Hydrolysis can render the drug inactive, reducing its therapeutic efficacy.

   Degradation products formed via hydrolysis may be toxic or cause adverse effects.

   Moisture-sensitive drugs require specialized packaging and storage conditions to prevent hydrolysis.

Examples of Hydrolysis in Drugs

1. **Aspirin (Acetylsalicylic Acid)**:
   Aspirin undergoes hydrolysis in the presence of moisture, leading to the formation of salicylic acid and acetic acid, both of which reduce the drug's efficacy. The reaction is accelerated by heat and humidity.

2. **Beta-Lactam Antibiotics (e.g., Penicillins and Cephalosporins)**:
   Beta-lactam drugs are highly prone to hydrolysis due to the strained four-membered lactam ring. Hydrolysis leads to the opening of the lactam ring, rendering the antibiotic inactive.

3. **Procaine:**
   Procaine, a local anesthetic containing an ester bond, undergoes hydrolysis to produce **p-aminobenzoic acid (PABA)** and ethanol.

Factors Influencing Hydrolysis

1. **pH:**
   Hydrolysis is typically catalyzed under extreme pH conditions (acidic or basic). For instance, **Aspirin** is more stable at neutral pH but rapidly hydrolyzes in alkaline conditions.
2. **Temperature:**
   Elevated temperatures accelerate hydrolytic reactions. For example, penicillins degrade faster at higher temperatures, necessitating refrigeration for storage.
3. **Moisture Content:**
   Hygroscopic drugs, such as **Amoxicillin**, readily absorb moisture, increasing their susceptibility to hydrolysis.
4. **Catalysts:**
   Presence of metal ions, enzymes, or excipients can enhance hydrolysis. For example, **enzymatic hydrolysis** by esterases significantly contributes to the breakdown of ester-containing prodrugs.

Strategies to Minimize Hydrolysis

1. **Formulation Adjustments:**

   - Use of **buffer systems** to maintain optimal pH levels and prevent acid/base catalysis.
   - Incorporation of **stabilizers** such as antioxidants or chelating agents to inhibit catalytic activity.

2. **Packaging:**

   - Use of moisture-resistant packaging materials like **aluminum foil blister packs** for drugs prone to hydrolysis.

- Storage in low-humidity environments or desiccant-containing containers.

3. **Prodrug Design**:

- Conversion of hydrolysis-prone drugs into more stable prodrugs. For example, the prodrug **enalapril** is designed to resist hydrolysis, converting to its active form, **enalaprilat**, only in vivo.

1.2.2.2 Oxidation and Reduction

Oxidation and **reduction** are chemical reactions that significantly influence the stability of pharmaceutical compounds. Oxidative degradation, in particular, is a common pathway for the chemical instability of drugs. Both oxidation and reduction reactions can compromise drug efficacy, safety, and shelf life, making it essential to understand their mechanisms and implement strategies for stabilization.

Oxidative Degradation

Oxidative degradation involves the loss of electrons from a drug molecule, often facilitated by the presence of oxygen, light, heat, or metal ions. It is one of the most common causes of chemical instability, particularly in drugs containing functional groups like phenols, ethers, amines, and unsaturated hydrocarbons.

Mechanism of Oxidation:
Oxidation typically occurs in a stepwise manner:

Initiation: Formation of free radicals, often triggered by heat, light, or trace metal ions.

Propagation: Free radicals react with oxygen to form peroxides, which further degrade the drug.

Termination: Free radicals combine to form stable products, halting the chain reaction.

Example:

Ascorbic Acid (Vitamin C): Oxidized to dehydroascorbic acid in the presence of oxygen, leading to loss of potency:

Factors Influencing Oxidation:

Oxygen: The presence of oxygen accelerates oxidative degradation. For example, **epinephrine** is readily oxidized to adrenochrome in the presence of air.

Light: Photochemical reactions can initiate oxidation. For instance, **riboflavin** degrades rapidly when exposed to light.

Metal Ions: Trace amounts of iron or copper catalyze oxidation, as seen in the degradation of **ascorbic acid** and **methionine.**

Examples of Common Oxidizable Drugs:

Epinephrine: Oxidizes to pink-colored adrenochrome.

Simvastatin: Undergoes oxidative degradation, forming less active or inactive by-products.

Vitamin E (Tocopherol): Oxidized to quinone derivatives, losing its antioxidant properties.

Reduction Reactions

Reduction reactions involve the gain of electrons, often leading to changes in the chemical structure of drugs. While less common than oxidation, reduction can occur under certain conditions, such as in the presence of reducing agents or anaerobic environments.

Mechanism of Reduction:

Reduction involves the addition of hydrogen atoms or electrons to a molecule, altering its chemical properties.

Example:

Nitro Compounds: Reduction of **chloramphenicol**, a nitroaromatic drug, can lead to the formation of inactive or toxic metabolites.

Examples of Drugs Prone to Reduction:

Metronidazole: Reduced to active metabolites in anaerobic environments.

Chloramphenicol: Nitro group reduction can lead to degradation.

Use of Antioxidants in Formulations

Antioxidants are added to pharmaceutical formulations to prevent or minimize oxidative degradation by scavenging free radicals, reducing oxidizing agents, or forming inert complexes with catalysts like metal ions.

Types of Antioxidants:

Free Radical Scavengers: Interrupt propagation by neutralizing free radicals. Examples include **butylated hydroxyanisole (BHA)** and **butylated hydroxytoluene (BHT).**

Reducing Agents: Donate electrons to oxidized species, regenerating the active drug. Examples include **ascorbic acid** and **sodium bisulfite.**

Chelating Agents: Bind metal ions to prevent catalytic oxidation. Common examples include **EDTA** and **citric acid.**

Examples of Antioxidant Use:

Vitamin C Tablets: Stabilized with EDTA and sodium metabisulfite to prevent oxidation.

Adrenaline Injections: Contain sodium bisulfite to inhibit oxidation to adrenochrome.

Antioxidant Efficacy and Doses:

Ascorbic Acid: Effective at concentrations of **0.1%-1% w/v.**

BHT: Used at levels of **0.01%-0.02% w/w** in lipid-based formulations.

Strategies to Mitigate Oxidation and Reduction

Formulation Adjustments:

Use of antioxidants, as mentioned above.

Incorporation of inert gases (e.g., nitrogen) in packaging to minimize oxygen exposure.

Packaging Solutions:

Use of amber glass or UV-resistant containers to protect photosensitive drugs.

Vacuum-sealed or airtight packaging for oxidation-prone drugs like **Simvastatin.**

Storage Conditions:

Controlled storage in cool, dry places to reduce the rate of oxidation.

Avoidance of light exposure for sensitive drugs like **riboflavin.**

1.2.2.3 Racemization

Racemization refers to the conversion of an optically active compound into an equimolar mixture of its enantiomers, resulting in a racemic mixture. Enantiomers are mirror-image forms of a chiral molecule, often denoted as RRR and SSS. In pharmaceutical sciences, racemization is a critical concern because enantiomers of a drug may exhibit different biological activities, with one enantiomer being therapeutically active and the other potentially inactive or harmful.

Relevance in Chiral Drugs

Chirality plays a vital role in drug efficacy and safety. Many drugs are chiral, and their pharmacological and toxicological properties are often enantiomer-specific. Racemization can alter the enantiomeric composition of a drug during manufacturing, storage, or in vivo, potentially leading to reduced efficacy or adverse effects.

Therapeutic Impact:

1. **Active vs. Inactive Enantiomers**: For example, **ibuprofen** is marketed as a racemic mixture, but only the SSS-enantiomer exhibits anti-inflammatory activity.
2. **Active vs. Harmful Enantiomers**: The most infamous example is **thalidomide**, where the RRR-enantiomer has sedative effects, but the SSS-enantiomer is teratogenic, causing severe birth defects. Racemization of thalidomide in vivo led to tragic consequences in the 1960s.
3. **Stability Concerns**:
   Racemization can compromise the stability of optically active drugs, affecting their shelf life and therapeutic reliability.

Factors Affecting Racemization

Temperature:

Higher temperatures accelerate racemization.

Example: The racemization rate of **pilocarpine**, an ophthalmic drug, increases significantly at elevated temperatures.

pH:

Racemization is often catalyzed by acidic or basic conditions, depending on the drug's chemical structure.

Example: Epinephrine undergoes rapid racemization in basic conditions, leading to the formation of less active or inactive enantiomers.

Solvent Polarity:

Polar solvents can stabilize intermediates or transition states, influencing the racemization rate.

Catalysts:

Metal ions or specific excipients can act as catalysts, accelerating the racemization process.

Examples of Racemization

1. **Thalidomide:**
   Thalidomide racemizes rapidly under physiological conditions (pH ~7.4), converting between its RRR- and SSS-enantiomers. This racemization contributed to its teratogenic effects, as the harmful SSS-enantiomer was generated from the therapeutic RRR-enantiomer.
2. **Lactic Acid**:
   Lactic acid exists as DDD- and LLL-enantiomers. In aqueous solutions, racemization occurs, producing a racemic mixture. The rate depends on temperature and pH, with faster racemization observed under alkaline conditions.
3. **Pilocarpine**:
   Pilocarpine, used to treat glaucoma, undergoes racemization in aqueous solutions, particularly under heat. The racemic mixture has reduced therapeutic activity compared to the SSS-enantiomer.

Strategies to Mitigate Racemization

Formulation Adjustments:

Maintaining optimal pH to minimize racemization. For instance, buffer systems are used to stabilize chiral drugs like **epinephrine**.

Incorporating stabilizers such as cyclodextrins to protect chiral drugs from racemization.

Storage Conditions:

Storing drugs at low temperatures to reduce the racemization rate.

Using moisture-proof packaging to prevent hydrolysis, which may facilitate racemization.

Chemical Modifications:

Prodrug strategies can be employed to prevent racemization. For example, designing derivatives with reduced racemization tendencies.

1.2.2.4 Polymerization

Polymerization is a chemical reaction in which small molecules, known as monomers, combine to form larger macromolecules called polymers. In the context of pharmaceuticals, polymerization can occur unintentionally as a degradation mechanism, leading to undesirable changes in drug stability and performance. Such reactions are often triggered by environmental factors like light, heat, pH, or the presence of reactive impurities.

Polymerization as a Degradation Mechanism

Mechanism:
Polymerization occurs through various pathways, including **free radical polymerization**, **condensation polymerization**, and **addition polymerization**. In free radical polymerization, reactive free radicals initiate chain reactions that lead to the formation of polymeric chains.

Condensation Polymerization: This involves the combination of monomers with the elimination of small molecules like water or methanol.

Triggers for Polymerization:

Light: UV or visible light can initiate free radical polymerization in light-sensitive drugs.

Impurities: Presence of peroxides or trace metals catalyzes polymerization reactions.

Heat: Elevated temperatures increase the energy of molecular collisions, promoting polymerization.

Examples of Polymerization in Pharmaceuticals

Formaldehyde Polymerization:

Formaldehyde, sometimes used as a preservative, can undergo

polymerization to form **paraformaldehyde**, reducing its effectiveness and altering the formulation properties.

Epoxide-Containing Drugs:

Epoxides, like those found in some antibiotics, are highly reactive and can polymerize, leading to loss of drug potency.

Acrylic Monomers:

Acrylic-based compounds used in dental materials or certain drug delivery systems may undergo polymerization when exposed to light or heat, affecting their intended properties.

Catecholamines (e.g., Dopamine and Epinephrine):

Catecholamines can polymerize through oxidative coupling, forming dark-colored polymers that reduce drug efficacy and aesthetic acceptability.

Impacts of Polymerization on Drug Stability and Performance

Reduced Potency:

Polymerization consumes the active drug molecules, leading to a reduction in their availability for therapeutic action.

Example: Polymerization of dopamine in solution decreases its therapeutic efficacy in treating Parkinson's disease.

Altered Physical Properties:

Formation of polymeric products can change the physical characteristics of a drug formulation, such as increased viscosity or precipitation.

Example: Polymerization in ophthalmic solutions can lead to turbidity, affecting patient compliance and dosing accuracy.

Formation of Toxic Byproducts:

Some polymerization reactions produce harmful byproducts, posing safety concerns.

Example: Peroxide-initiated polymerization in lipid-based formulations can generate cytotoxic compounds.

Color Changes and Stability Issues:

Polymerization often results in discoloration of the drug product, which can affect its appearance and stability.

Example: Catecholamine polymerization results in a dark brown or black coloration, reducing product acceptability.

Strategies to Prevent Polymerization

Incorporation of Stabilizers:

Antioxidants like **butylated hydroxytoluene (BHT)** or **ascorbic acid** can scavenge free radicals and inhibit polymerization reactions.

Packaging Solutions:

Use of light-resistant containers to prevent photoinitiated polymerization.

Airtight or vacuum-sealed packaging to minimize exposure to oxygen, which can initiate oxidative polymerization.

Control of Storage Conditions:

Low-temperature storage slows down polymerization kinetics.

Avoiding moisture exposure in hygroscopic formulations reduces the likelihood of polymerization in aqueous environments.

Chelating Agents:

Adding chelating agents like **EDTA** can neutralize metal ions that catalyze polymerization.

1.3 BCS Classification and Applications

The **Biopharmaceutical Classification System (BCS)** is a scientific framework used to classify drug substances based on their **solubility** and **intestinal permeability**. Developed by Amidon et al. in 1995, the BCS plays a pivotal role in predicting the drug absorption process, guiding formulation development, and determining regulatory requirements for bioequivalence studies.

1.3.1 Classification of Drugs

The BCS categorizes drugs into four distinct classes based on their solubility and permeability characteristics. These classifications help pharmaceutical scientists assess a drug's oral absorption potential and identify challenges in formulation development.

Definition of Solubility and Permeability in BCS

The Four BCS Classes

Class I: High Solubility, High Permeability

Drugs in Class I exhibit both high solubility and high permeability. They dissolve rapidly in the gastrointestinal tract and are efficiently absorbed, making them the most straightforward candidates for oral formulations.

Characteristics:

1. Rapid dissolution in aqueous environments.
2. Minimal absorption challenges.
3. Bioavailability is primarily influenced by drug release from the dosage form.

Examples:
Paracetamol: A common analgesic and antipyretic drug with excellent solubility and absorption.

Propranolol: A beta-blocker used to treat hypertension.

Class II: Low Solubility, High Permeability

Drugs in Class II have high permeability but low solubility, meaning their absorption is limited by the rate of dissolution. Strategies to enhance solubility, such as particle size reduction or the use of surfactants, are critical for improving bioavailability.

Characteristics:

1. Absorption is dissolution-limited.
2. Bioavailability can be enhanced using solubility-improving techniques.

Examples:
Ibuprofen: A nonsteroidal anti-inflammatory drug (NSAID) with poor aqueous solubility but high intestinal permeability.

Ketoconazole: An antifungal agent with low solubility requiring pH-dependent solubility enhancement.

Class III: High Solubility, Low Permeability

Drugs in Class III dissolve readily in the gastrointestinal tract but have limited permeability, often due to their hydrophilic nature or interaction with efflux transporters. Absorption is primarily permeability-limited, and strategies such as permeability enhancers or prodrug approaches are employed to overcome these challenges.

Characteristics:
Rapid dissolution in the gastrointestinal tract.

Limited ability to cross intestinal membranes.

Examples:
Atenolol: A beta-blocker with high solubility but poor permeability.

Cimetidine: An H2-receptor antagonist used for acid reflux.

Class IV: Low Solubility, Low Permeability

Drugs in Class IV pose the greatest formulation challenges due to their poor solubility and permeability. These drugs often exhibit low oral bioavailability and require advanced delivery systems like nanoparticles or lipid-based formulations.

Characteristics:

Poor solubility and limited absorption potential.

Bioavailability enhancement requires complex formulation strategies.

Examples:

Amphotericin B: An antifungal drug with extremely poor solubility and permeability.

Paclitaxel: An anticancer drug requiring advanced formulations like liposomes for delivery.

Significance of BCS in Drug Development

1. **Guidance for Formulation Development**:
   The BCS classification provides a clear understanding of the challenges associated with solubility and permeability, guiding the selection of appropriate formulation strategies. For example, Class II drugs benefit from solubility enhancement techniques like solid dispersions or nanocrystals.
2. **Bioavailability Prediction**:
   The BCS helps predict the oral bioavailability of a drug, aiding in early decision-making during drug discovery and development.
3. **Regulatory Applications**:
   Regulatory authorities like the **US FDA** and **EMA** use BCS to determine **biowaivers** for bioequivalence studies. Class I drugs with rapid dissolution profiles may not require in vivo bioequivalence testing, reducing the time and cost of drug development.

1.3.2 Applications in Preformulation Studies

The **Biopharmaceutical Classification System (BCS)** plays a pivotal role in preformulation studies by providing a framework to understand the solubility and permeability characteristics of drug substances. This understanding guides the development of effective formulation strategies, ensuring optimal drug performance in vivo. The BCS not only informs solubility and permeability enhancement approaches but also has significant regulatory implications, such as waivers for bioequivalence studies in certain cases.

Guiding Solubility and Permeability Enhancement Strategies

Class I (High Solubility, High Permeability)

For Class I drugs, preformulation studies focus on ensuring rapid drug release from the dosage form, as their absorption is not limited by solubility or permeability. Simple formulations, such as immediate-release tablets, are typically sufficient.

Example: Paracetamol, a Class I drug, requires no complex formulation modifications. Conventional tablets or liquid formulations ensure effective drug delivery.

Class II (Low Solubility, High Permeability)

Class II drugs face absorption challenges due to their low solubility, making solubility enhancement a primary focus in preformulation studies. Strategies include:

Particle Size Reduction: Micronization or nanocrystal technology increases the surface area for dissolution.

Example: Ibuprofen formulations use micronization to enhance solubility and dissolution rates.

Solid Dispersions: Combining the drug with hydrophilic carriers like polyvinylpyrrolidone (PVP) to improve solubility.

Example: Ketoconazole is formulated as a solid dispersion to address its solubility limitations.

Use of Surfactants: Incorporating surfactants like sodium lauryl sulfate facilitates wetting and dissolution.

Example: Fenofibrate is formulated with surfactants to improve its bioavailability.

Class III (High Solubility, Low Permeability)

For Class III drugs, preformulation focuses on enhancing permeability, as solubility is not a limiting factor. Strategies include:

Permeability Enhancers: Use of excipients like bile salts or fatty acids to improve membrane permeability.

Example: Atenolol formulations may include excipients to enhance intestinal absorption.

Prodrug Approaches: Modifying the drug chemically to improve permeability while maintaining solubility.

Example: Valacyclovir is a prodrug of acyclovir designed to enhance intestinal absorption.

Class IV (Low Solubility, Low Permeability)

Class IV drugs present the greatest challenge, requiring both solubility and permeability enhancement. Advanced delivery systems are often employed:

Lipid-Based Formulations: Self-emulsifying drug delivery systems (SEDDS) enhance solubility and permeability.

Example: Paclitaxel is delivered using lipid-based carriers like liposomes to overcome its poor solubility and permeability.

Nanotechnology: Nanoparticles and polymeric carriers improve solubility and facilitate transport across biological membranes.

Example: Amphotericin B liposomal formulations enhance bioavailability while reducing toxicity.

Formulation Changes Based on BCS

Solubility Enhancers for Class II Drugs:

Poorly soluble drugs like **Carbamazepine** and **Ritonavir** are formulated with surfactants or as amorphous solid dispersions to improve their dissolution profiles and bioavailability.

Permeability Enhancers for Class III Drugs:

Drugs like **Metformin**, which exhibit low permeability, are often combined with absorption enhancers or modified chemically into more permeable prodrugs to improve systemic absorption.

Complex Formulations for Class IV Drugs:

Drugs such as **Itraconazole** require innovative approaches, such as cyclodextrin complexes or lipid-based formulations, to address both solubility and permeability challenges.

Regulatory Implications

The BCS has significant regulatory implications, particularly for the approval of generic drugs, where it is used to determine whether **in vivo bioequivalence (BE) studies** can be waived in favor of **in vitro testing**.

Biowaivers for Class I Drugs:

Regulatory agencies like the **US FDA** and **EMA** grant biowaivers for Class I drugs if they meet the following criteria:

Rapid dissolution in aqueous media.

High solubility and high permeability verified through standardized tests.

Example: Generic versions of **Propranolol** can be approved without in vivo bioequivalence studies if dissolution profiles match the reference product.

Class III Drugs and Biowaivers:
Recent guidelines extend biowaivers to certain Class III drugs, provided the formulation ensures rapid dissolution and no permeability-limiting excipients are added.

Example: Generic formulations of **Cimetidine** may qualify for biowaivers under specific conditions.

Challenges for Class II and IV Drugs:
For Class II and IV drugs, biowaivers are rarely granted because their absorption depends heavily on in vivo factors such as solubility and permeability. These drugs often require extensive bioequivalence testing.

1.4 Impact on Dosage Form Stability

The stability of pharmaceutical dosage forms is crucial to maintaining their efficacy, safety, and quality throughout their shelf life. For solid dosage forms, such as tablets and capsules, stability is influenced by various physicochemical properties of the drug and excipients, including **hygroscopicity**, **polymorphism**, and other factors. Understanding these properties and their effects is vital for designing stable formulations and ensuring proper storage conditions.

1.4.1 Solid Dosage Forms

Solid dosage forms are the most commonly used pharmaceutical formulations due to their convenience, stability, and ease of manufacturing. However, their stability can be compromised by environmental factors and intrinsic properties of the drug.

Physicochemical Properties Affecting Tablet Stability

Hygroscopicity:
Hygroscopic drugs absorb moisture from the environment, which can lead to chemical degradation, physical changes, or dissolution problems.

Impact:

Hydrolysis: Absorbed moisture can accelerate hydrolytic degradation of susceptible drugs. For example, **aspirin** degrades into salicylic acid and acetic acid in the presence of moisture.

Physical Changes: Excessive moisture absorption can cause caking, clumping, or softening of tablets, affecting their integrity.

Examples:

Sodium valproate: A highly hygroscopic drug that requires protective packaging, such as blister packs with desiccants, to maintain stability.

Amoxicillin: Absorbs moisture, leading to reduced efficacy; therefore, it is often formulated as a dry powder for reconstitution.

Real-World Data:

Stability studies of **aspirin** show that tablets stored at **40°C/75% RH** lose up to 25% potency within 6 months due to hydrolysis.

Polymorphism:

Drugs exhibiting polymorphism can exist in multiple crystalline forms, each with distinct physical and chemical properties, such as solubility, stability, and compressibility.

Impact:

Phase Transformation: During manufacturing or storage, a metastable polymorphic form may convert to a more stable form, leading to changes in dissolution rates or loss of bioavailability.

Stability Issues: The unstable polymorphic form may degrade faster under stress conditions.

Examples:

Ritonavir: Polymorphic instability caused the drug to crystallize in an insoluble form during storage, necessitating reformulation.

Carbamazepine: Exhibits four polymorphic forms, with differences in solubility and bioavailability. Stability studies showed a 30% reduction in dissolution for the metastable form stored under high humidity.

Storage Conditions and Their Impact

Proper storage conditions are critical for maintaining the stability of solid dosage forms. Environmental factors such as temperature, humidity, and light significantly influence the degradation and stability of tablets and capsules.

Temperature:

High temperatures accelerate chemical degradation reactions, such as hydrolysis and oxidation, reducing the drug's shelf life.

Examples:

Ibuprofen tablets stored at 50°C for 6 months showed 15% degradation due to increased oxidation.

Levothyroxine is highly temperature-sensitive, requiring storage below 25°C to prevent potency loss.

Humidity:

Elevated humidity levels exacerbate hygroscopicity-related issues, leading to moisture absorption and physical changes.

Examples:

Effervescent tablets degrade rapidly in humid conditions due to premature activation of effervescent agents like citric acid and sodium bicarbonate.

Aspirin stability is significantly reduced in high-humidity environments, necessitating the use of desiccants or low-humidity storage.

Light:

Photochemical reactions induced by light exposure can degrade sensitive drugs. Solid dosage forms often require light-protective packaging.

Examples:

Riboflavin: Degrades rapidly when exposed to light, necessitating the use of amber glass bottles or opaque blisters.

Nifedipine tablets require storage in light-resistant containers to prevent photodegradation.

Strategies for Enhancing Stability

Protective Packaging:

Use of **blister packs** with desiccants to control moisture exposure for hygroscopic drugs.

Storage in **amber or opaque containers** to prevent light-induced degradation.

Formulation Modifications:

Incorporation of **stabilizers** such as antioxidants (e.g., butylated hydroxytoluene) or moisture scavengers.

Use of **anhydrous excipients** to reduce hydrolytic degradation.

Controlled Storage Conditions:

Maintaining **cool, dry storage** conditions (e.g., 25°C/60% RH or lower) for sensitive drugs.

Refrigeration for temperature-sensitive formulations like insulin tablets.

Polymorphic Screening:

Identification and stabilization of the most suitable polymorphic form during development. For example, **indomethacin** formulations are stabilized in their alpha form to ensure consistent performance.

1.4.2 Liquid Oral Dosage Forms

Liquid oral dosage forms, such as syrups and suspensions, offer advantages like ease of swallowing and dose flexibility. However, these formulations are often more susceptible to stability challenges compared to solid dosage forms. Issues like **solubility, pH**, and **chemical stability** must be carefully addressed to maintain drug efficacy and shelf life.

Solubility Issues in Liquid Oral Dosage Forms

Solubility Challenges:

Many drugs exhibit poor aqueous solubility, leading to difficulties in achieving therapeutic concentrations in liquid formulations. Solubility challenges are particularly evident in suspensions, where the drug remains dispersed as insoluble particles.

Example: Phenytoin suspension contains the poorly soluble drug in a finely dispersed form, requiring careful stabilization to prevent sedimentation or aggregation.

Solubilization Techniques:

Use of **cosolvents** like ethanol or propylene glycol to enhance drug solubility.

Incorporation of **surfactants** like polysorbates to improve wetting and dissolution.

Formation of **salt forms** or **complexes** to increase solubility.

Example: Erythromycin ethylsuccinate is used in oral suspensions due to its enhanced solubility compared to the parent compound.

pH and Stability in Liquid Dosage Forms

The pH of a liquid formulation plays a critical role in solubility and chemical stability. Many drugs exhibit pH-dependent solubility and degradation profiles, necessitating precise pH adjustments during formulation.

pH-Dependent Solubility:

Weakly acidic or basic drugs exhibit varying solubility across different pH ranges.

Example: Ibuprofen syrup is formulated at an alkaline pH (~7-8) to enhance solubility, as the drug is a weak acid (pKa ~4.9).

pH-Dependent Stability:

Many drugs degrade rapidly under extreme pH conditions due to hydrolysis, oxidation, or other chemical reactions.

Case Study: The stability of **chloramphenicol** in aqueous solutions depends on pH. It is most stable at pH 6.0, while rapid degradation occurs at pH < 4 or > 7. This knowledge guides buffer selection for maintaining optimal stability.

Chemical Stability Issues

Hydrolysis:

Drugs with ester or amide groups are particularly prone to hydrolysis in aqueous environments.

Example: Aspirin syrup undergoes hydrolysis to salicylic acid and acetic acid in the presence of water, reducing efficacy.

Oxidation:

Liquid formulations are more susceptible to oxidation due to increased exposure to dissolved oxygen.

Example: Vitamin C syrups degrade rapidly due to oxidation, forming dehydroascorbic acid.

Preservative Instability:

Preservatives in syrups, such as benzoic acid or parabens, can degrade at extreme pH levels, reducing their antimicrobial efficacy.

Formulas for Stability Adjustments

Buffer Systems:

Buffer systems are employed to maintain the optimal pH for stability.

Example: For **paracetamol syrups**, a citrate buffer is used to maintain pH around 4.5, where the drug is chemically stable.

Antioxidants:

Incorporating antioxidants like **sodium metabisulfite** or **ascorbic acid** prevents oxidative degradation.

Example: Antioxidants are added to **ferrous sulfate syrup** to maintain the stability of the iron ions and prevent discoloration.

Surfactants and Stabilizers:

Surfactants like polysorbates are used to stabilize suspensions by reducing interparticle attraction.

Example: Nystatin suspension is stabilized with polysorbates to ensure uniformity and prevent aggregation.

Examples of Stability Challenges in Liquid Forms

Amoxicillin Suspension:

The reconstituted suspension is stable for only 7-14 days due to hydrolytic degradation of the drug. Refrigeration slows this degradation, preserving potency.

Aspirin Syrup:

Hydrolysis is a significant challenge, necessitating formulation adjustments such as low moisture content and pH control to minimize degradation.

Cough Syrups Containing Codeine:

Codeine is susceptible to oxidation, requiring the addition of antioxidants and storage in light-resistant containers to maintain stability.
Storage Conditions and Their Impact

1. **Temperature:**
   Elevated temperatures accelerate chemical degradation reactions. For example, **amoxicillin suspensions** degrade rapidly at temperatures above 25°C, necessitating refrigeration.
2. **Light:**
   Exposure to light can trigger photodegradation of sensitive drugs like **riboflavin** in liquid formulations. Amber glass or opaque containers are used to prevent this.

   Humidity:
Humidity can lead to microbial growth in improperly sealed syrups or suspensions, compromising their stability. Proper packaging and preservatives mitigate this risk.

1.4.3 Parenteral Dosage Forms

Parenteral dosage forms, such as injections, infusions, and sterile solutions, deliver drugs directly into the bloodstream or tissues, ensuring rapid therapeutic action. However, their formulation and storage present unique stability challenges due to their reliance on aqueous environments, stringent sterility requirements, and sensitivity to environmental factors. Key stability concerns include **precipitation, hydrolysis,** and **oxidation,** which can compromise the drug's efficacy, safety, and shelf life.

Stability Challenges in Parenteral Dosage Forms
Precipitation:
Cause: Precipitation occurs when the drug's solubility is exceeded due to changes in pH, temperature, or the presence of incompatible excipients. Precipitation can lead to drug inactivation and pose a risk of embolism in intravenous administration.
Example: Phenytoin sodium injection precipitates when the pH drops below 10. The drug is formulated in an alkaline vehicle to maintain solubility.
Prevention Strategies:
Use of **cosolvents** (e.g., ethanol, propylene glycol) to enhance solubility.

Adjusting **pH** to maintain the drug in its soluble form.

Hydrolysis:

Cause: Hydrolysis is a common degradation pathway in aqueous parenteral formulations, particularly for drugs with ester or amide bonds. Elevated temperatures or extreme pH values accelerate this process.

Example: **Amphotericin B** undergoes hydrolysis in aqueous solutions, requiring lyophilization to enhance stability.

Prevention Strategies:

Lyophilization: Converting the drug into a freeze-dried powder that is reconstituted before use.

Buffer Systems: Maintaining optimal pH to minimize hydrolytic degradation. For example, **penicillin G injections** use phosphate buffers to stabilize the drug.

Oxidation:

Cause: Oxidation involves the loss of electrons, often catalyzed by oxygen, light, or trace metal ions. Oxidative degradation can result in loss of potency and the formation of toxic by-products.

Example: **Epinephrine injections** oxidize to adrenochrome, a reddish-brown compound, reducing potency.

Prevention Strategies:

Use of **antioxidants**: Sodium metabisulfite is added to **adrenaline injections** to prevent oxidation.

Packaging in **oxygen-impermeable ampoules** or under inert gases like nitrogen.

Formulation Adjustments for Stability

pH Adjustments:

The solubility and stability of drugs in parenteral formulations are often pH-dependent. Buffer systems are used to maintain a pH range that minimizes degradation.

Example:

Dobutamine injection: Stabilized at a pH range of 2.5–5.5 to prevent oxidative degradation.

Insulin injections: Formulated at pH 7.4 to match physiological pH and maintain stability.

Stabilizers:

Stabilizers are added to parenteral formulations to prevent chemical degradation or physical changes.

Examples:

Antioxidants: Sodium metabisulfite or ascorbic acid to prevent oxidation.

Chelating Agents: EDTA binds metal ions to inhibit oxidation.

Cryoprotectants: Sucrose or trehalose is used in freeze-dried formulations to protect the drug during lyophilization.

Cosolvents:

Cosolvents enhance drug solubility and prevent precipitation in aqueous solutions.

Example:

Diazepam injection: Contains ethanol and propylene glycol as cosolvents to maintain the drug in solution.

Surfactants:

Surfactants reduce interfacial tension, stabilizing emulsions or suspensions in parenteral formulations.

Example: Paclitaxel injection uses polysorbate 80 to improve drug solubility and stability.

Examples of Stability Challenges and Solutions

Oxidation of Vitamin C (Ascorbic Acid):

Challenge: Oxidation leads to the formation of dehydroascorbic acid and discoloration.

Solution: Antioxidants like sodium bisulfite are added, and the injection is packaged in amber vials to block light.

Hydrolysis of Penicillin G:

Challenge: Rapid hydrolytic degradation in aqueous solutions.

Solution: Formulated as a lyophilized powder to be reconstituted before administration, and phosphate buffers are used to stabilize the pH.

Precipitation of Phenytoin:

Challenge: Precipitation in intravenous lines due to pH shifts.

Solution: The injection is prepared at an alkaline pH (~11) and diluted with compatible solvents like saline before administration.

Photodegradation of Riboflavin:

Challenge: Light exposure causes photodegradation, reducing potency.

Solution: Packaging in light-protective amber vials and storing away from light.

Storage and Packaging for Stability

1. **Temperature Control**:

Parenteral formulations are often stored at refrigerated temperatures

(2–8°C) to reduce the rate of hydrolysis and oxidation. For example, **insulin** requires cold storage to maintain potency.

2. **Oxygen-Resistant Packaging**:
    Ampoules, vials with rubber stoppers, or sealed containers under an inert gas (e.g., nitrogen) prevent oxygen exposure. For instance, **adrenaline injections** are sealed in oxygen-impermeable containers.

3. **Light Protection**:
    Light-sensitive drugs like **amphotericin B** and **riboflavin** are packaged in amber or opaque containers to prevent photodegradation.

REVIEW QUESTIONS

1. What is preformulation in pharmaceutical development?

Answer: Preformulation is the systematic study of the physicochemical properties of a drug substance and its interaction with excipients to optimize the drug's formulation, stability, and bioavailability.

2. Why is preformulation important in drug development?

Answer: Preformulation ensures that a drug transitions smoothly from the laboratory to clinical and commercial stages, optimizing formulation, stability, bioavailability, and addressing potential manufacturing challenges.

3. What are the main properties studied during preformulation?

Answer: Properties studied include solubility, stability, particle size, polymorphism, hygroscopicity, and compatibility with excipients.

4. What is the goal of determining physicochemical properties of drugs in preformulation studies?

Answer: The goal is to understand how a drug behaves during manufacturing and in vivo, optimizing bioavailability, stability, and effectiveness of the final dosage form.

5. What role does solubility play in drug formulation?

Answer: Solubility affects the bioavailability of the drug; poorly soluble drugs may require solubility enhancement techniques to improve absorption.

6. Why is stability profiling important in preformulation studies?

Answer: Stability profiling helps identify conditions under which a drug remains stable, thus determining its shelf life, storage requirements, and suitability for formulation.

7. What is a partition coefficient (Log P)?

Answer: Log P is the ratio of a drug's concentration in a lipid phase to its concentration in an aqueous phase, influencing its ability to be absorbed and distributed in the body.

8. What is polymorphism in pharmaceuticals?

Answer: Polymorphism refers to the ability of a drug to exist in different crystalline forms, each with unique solubility, stability, and bioavailability profiles.

9. How does forced degradation study contribute to preformulation?

Answer: Forced degradation studies help identify potential degradation pathways under extreme conditions, allowing for better formulation and packaging choices.

10. What is the role of excipient compatibility testing?

Answer: Excipients must not interact with the drug in a way that affects its stability or efficacy. Compatibility testing ensures safe interaction between the drug and excipients.

11. Why is particle size reduction important in drug formulations?

Answer: Reducing particle size increases the surface area for dissolution, improving the solubility and bioavailability of poorly soluble drugs.

12. What is the significance of a drug's pKa in formulation design?

Answer: The pKa determines the drug's ionization at different pH levels, guiding the pH adjustment of the formulation to enhance solubility and stability.

13. What is the role of preformulation in formulation optimization?

Answer: Preformulation provides essential data that informs the design of stable, effective, and bioavailable drug formulations.

14. How do preformulation studies help in dosage form design?

Answer: They provide data on solubility, stability, and compatibility, guiding the selection of dosage forms like tablets, capsules, or injectables.

15. What is the impact of solubility on bioavailability?

Answer: Poorly soluble drugs exhibit low bioavailability, which can be improved by techniques like solid dispersions, micronization, or surfactant use.

16. How does stability in formulation impact the shelf life of drugs?

Answer: Stable formulations maintain drug efficacy and safety over time, ensuring extended shelf life and compliance with regulatory standards.

17. What are forced degradation studies?

Answer: These studies expose the drug to extreme conditions (e.g., high temperature, humidity) to assess potential degradation pathways and ensure stability.

18. What are the common excipients used in pharmaceutical formulations?

Answer: Common excipients include binders, fillers, lubricants, stabilizers, and preservatives, all chosen based on their compatibility with the drug.

19. How is solubility tested in preformulation studies?

Answer: Solubility is tested in various solvents such as water, ethanol, and buffer solutions of different pH values to assess the drug's dissolution profile.

20. Why is compatibility testing essential for excipients in preformulation?

Answer: Compatibility testing ensures that excipients do not interact with the drug in a way that could reduce its effectiveness or stability.

21. What is the importance of forced degradation in preformulation?

Answer: Forced degradation helps identify potential degradation products, guiding formulation strategies to ensure the drug's stability.

22. How does preformulation ensure effective drug delivery?

Answer: By analyzing a drug's physicochemical properties, preformulation optimizes drug release profiles, ensuring effective delivery to the site of action.

23. What role does preformulation play in regulatory submissions?

Answer: Preformulation data support regulatory submissions by demonstrating the drug's stability, safety, and efficacy, helping secure approvals.

24. What is the significance of determining the pKa of a drug in formulation development?

Answer: pKa helps predict the drug's ionization at different pH levels, guiding the pH adjustments to optimize solubility and absorption.

25. What is the impact of polymorphism on drug development?

Answer: Polymorphism affects solubility, stability, and bioavailability, so identifying and stabilizing the appropriate polymorph is crucial for consistent drug performance.

26. How are stability studies conducted in preformulation?

Answer: Stability studies are conducted by exposing drugs to various environmental conditions like temperature, light, and humidity to identify degradation pathways.

27. What is the role of preformulation in bioavailability enhancement?

Answer: Preformulation helps identify solubility and permeability challenges and provides strategies to enhance bioavailability, such as particle size reduction and formulation modifications.

28. Why is it necessary to understand the crystalline and amorphous forms of a drug?

Answer: Understanding the form helps predict solubility, stability, and bioavailability, as amorphous forms generally exhibit higher solubility but lower stability than crystalline forms.

29. What is the role of preformulation in controlling drug stability?

Answer: Preformulation identifies potential stability issues and allows for the design of formulations that minimize degradation and improve shelf life.

30. What are the key goals of preformulation studies?

Answer: The primary goals include determining physicochemical properties, optimizing formulations, ensuring stability, and supporting regulatory compliance.

31. What are solubility enhancement techniques?

Answer: Techniques like solid dispersions, co-crystallization, and the use of surfactants are used to enhance the solubility of poorly water-soluble drugs.

32. How does preformulation contribute to patient compliance?

Answer: Preformulation helps design formulations that are easier for patients to take, such as by enhancing taste, reducing dosing frequency, and minimizing side effects.

33. Why is the partition coefficient important in drug design?

Answer: The partition coefficient predicts a drug's ability to cross cell membranes, influencing its absorption and distribution in the body.

34. How does polymorphism impact drug bioavailability?

Answer: Different polymorphs of a drug can have varying solubility and bioavailability profiles, influencing the drug's therapeutic efficacy.

35. What is the significance of excipient compatibility testing in preformulation?

Answer: Compatibility testing ensures that excipients do not interact with the drug in a way that could cause instability or reduce efficacy.

36. What factors influence a drug's solubility?

Answer: Factors include the drug's chemical structure, the pH of the solvent, temperature, and the presence of excipients that can enhance solubility.

37. Why is particle size reduction important in drug formulation?

Answer: Reducing particle size increases surface area, which can enhance dissolution rate and bioavailability, especially for poorly soluble drugs.

38. What role does preformulation play in formulation optimization?

Answer: Preformulation studies provide data that inform the selection of excipients, dosage form, and manufacturing process to optimize the final formulation.

39. How does preformulation help in predicting and mitigating formulation challenges?

Answer: By understanding the drug's physicochemical properties, preformulation helps anticipate issues like instability, poor solubility, and bioavailability challenges.

40. What is the role of excipients in pharmaceutical formulations?

Answer: Excipients are inactive substances that help stabilize, preserve, and facilitate the administration of the active drug ingredient.

41. How does the pH affect drug stability?

Answer: Extreme pH values can lead to chemical degradation, such as hydrolysis or oxidation, so maintaining an optimal pH range is critical for stability.

42. What is the significance of forced degradation studies?

Answer: These studies help identify how a drug degrades under extreme conditions, providing insights into the drug's stability and helping optimize formulation and storage conditions.

43. What are the factors affecting drug stability in formulations?

Answer: Factors include temperature, humidity, light exposure, pH, and interactions with excipients.

44. How are solubility challenges addressed during preformulation?

Answer: Solubility challenges are addressed through techniques like particle size reduction, co-solvents, and surfactants to enhance the drug's dissolution rate.

45. How does preformulation support the regulatory process?

Answer: Preformulation data provide essential evidence of a drug's safety, efficacy, and stability, helping meet regulatory requirements for new drug applications.

46. What is the impact of hygroscopicity on drug stability?

Answer: Hygroscopic drugs absorb moisture, which can lead to hydrolytic degradation and affect the drug's stability and integrity.

47. What role does preformulation play in determining optimal dosage forms?

Answer: Preformulation provides data that help select the best dosage form (e.g., tablet, capsule, injectable) based on the drug's properties.

48. How does preformulation contribute to the success of drug development?

Answer: By ensuring that drugs are stable, bioavailable, and manufacturable, preformulation helps mitigate risks and ensures the success of the final product.

49. Why is polymorphism screening critical in drug development?

Answer: Polymorphism screening ensures the selection of the most stable and bioavailable polymorph, reducing the risk of formulation failures.

50. How does preformulation optimize drug manufacturing?

Answer: Preformulation data guide manufacturing decisions by identifying suitable excipients, optimizing conditions, and ensuring compatibility with manufacturing processes.

MCQS

1. What is preformulation in pharmaceutical development?

a) The study of drug release profiles
b) The study of drug stability under extreme conditions
c) The study of physicochemical properties of a drug and its interaction with excipients
d) The study of packaging and storage conditions
  Answer: c) The study of physicochemical properties of a drug and its interaction with excipients

2. Why is preformulation critical in drug development?

a) It improves patient compliance
b) It ensures the drug is compatible with excipients and stable under storage conditions
c) It determines the market price of the drug
d) It reduces the cost of drug marketing
  Answer: b) It ensures the drug is compatible with excipients and stable under storage conditions

3. Which of the following properties is NOT part of preformulation studies?

a) Solubility
b) Stability
c) Drug efficacy
d) Polymorphism
  Answer: c) Drug efficacy

4. Which technique is commonly used to evaluate drug-excipient compatibility?

a) HPLC
b) Differential Scanning Calorimetry (DSC)

c) X-ray Diffraction (XRD)

d) Fourier Transform Infrared Spectroscopy (FTIR)

Answer: b) Differential Scanning Calorimetry (DSC)

5. What is the primary focus of stability profiling in preformulation?

a) To determine the pKa of the drug

b) To assess the drug's shelf life under various conditions

c) To measure the solubility in different solvents

d) To determine the melting point of the drug

Answer: b) To assess the drug's shelf life under various conditions

6. The partition coefficient (Log P) primarily helps in determining a drug's:

a) Toxicity

b) Hydrophilicity or lipophilicity

c) Stability

d) Solubility in different solvents

Answer: b) Hydrophilicity or lipophilicity

7. What is polymorphism in drug substances?

a) The ability of a drug to exist in multiple crystal forms

b) The study of drug metabolism

c) The variation in a drug's solubility over time

d) The process of drug absorption in the gastrointestinal tract

Answer: a) The ability of a drug to exist in multiple crystal forms

8. Why is particle size reduction crucial in formulation development?

a) It improves drug solubility and bioavailability

b) It increases the drug's shelf life

c) It makes the drug tasteless

d) It reduces the cost of manufacturing

Answer: a) It improves drug solubility and bioavailability

9. Which of the following is the most likely result of polymorphic instability?

a) Improved solubility
b) Increased bioavailability
c) Decreased solubility and bioavailability
d) Enhanced patient compliance
   Answer: c) Decreased solubility and bioavailability

10. What does preformulation data provide for dosage form design?

a) Data for patient preferences
b) Guidelines for regulatory compliance
c) Insights into excipient selection, formulation techniques, and stability
d) Financial cost predictions
   Answer: c) Insights into excipient selection, formulation techniques, and stability

11. How does the solubility of a drug affect its bioavailability?

a) Solubility is not related to bioavailability
b) High solubility generally increases bioavailability
c) High solubility decreases bioavailability
d) Bioavailability is determined solely by particle size
   Answer: b) High solubility generally increases bioavailability

12. What is the primary objective of forced degradation studies?

a) To identify the drug's therapeutic effect
b) To examine potential degradation pathways under extreme conditions
c) To evaluate the drug's packaging
d) To determine the drug's molecular weight
   Answer: b) To examine potential degradation pathways under extreme conditions

13. What does the pKa value of a drug indicate?

a) The melting point of the drug
b) The solubility of the drug in water
c) The pH at which 50% of the drug is ionized
d) The drug's ability to cross the blood-brain barrier
   Answer: c) The pH at which 50% of the drug is ionized

14. Which type of drug is most affected by solubility enhancement techniques?

a) Drugs with high aqueous solubility
b) Drugs with low bioavailability due to poor solubility
c) Drugs that are highly lipophilic
d) Drugs with high stability
   Answer: b) Drugs with low bioavailability due to poor solubility

15. Which of the following is a method used to improve the solubility of poorly soluble drugs?

a) Reducing the molecular weight
b) Formulating with surfactants
c) Decreasing the surface area
d) Increasing particle size
   Answer: b) Formulating with surfactants

16. What is the significance of excipient compatibility testing?

a) It ensures that excipients improve the drug's solubility
b) It guarantees that excipients do not interfere with drug stability
c) It helps in reducing the drug's cost
d) It eliminates the need for regulatory approval
   Answer: b) It guarantees that excipients do not interfere with drug stability

17. What is a common method for measuring particle size in preformulation studies?

a) X-ray Diffraction (XRD)
b) Scanning Electron Microscopy (SEM)
c) Differential Scanning Calorimetry (DSC)
d) Infrared Spectroscopy (IR)
   Answer: b) Scanning Electron Microscopy (SEM)

18. What is the primary focus of stability studies?

a) To assess the solubility of the drug
b) To determine the optimal excipient
c) To predict the drug's shelf life under various conditions
d) To evaluate the drug's bioavailability
   Answer: c) To predict the drug's shelf life under various conditions

19. What is the significance of studying polymorphism in drug development?

a) Polymorphism affects only the drug's color
b) Polymorphic forms influence the drug's bioavailability and stability
c) Polymorphism has no impact on the drug's formulation
d) It determines the drug's expiration date
   Answer: b) Polymorphic forms influence the drug's bioavailability and stability

20. How does preformulation ensure drug stability?

a) By selecting the appropriate excipients and optimizing storage conditions
b) By reducing the drug's molecular weight
c) By adding flavor to the formulation
d) By increasing the drug's solubility in water
   Answer: a) By selecting the appropriate excipients and optimizing storage conditions
   I will continue generating the rest of the questions in the next message to meet your requirement of 100 MCQs.
   Here are the next set of MCQs:

21. What is the role of excipients in pharmaceutical formulations?

a) To provide stability and improve the drug's bioavailability
b) To increase the cost of the drug
c) To replace the active pharmaceutical ingredient (API)
d) To enhance the drug's color
   Answer: a) To provide stability and improve the drug's bioavailability

22. How does preformulation aid in optimizing dosage forms?

a) By enhancing patient comfort
b) By ensuring that the drug is stable, effective, and well-absorbed
c) By improving the color and appearance of the drug
d) By ensuring the drug is cheap to produce
   Answer: b) By ensuring that the drug is stable, effective, and well-absorbed

23. Which of the following is NOT typically tested during preformulation studies?

a) Drug solubility
b) Drug metabolism
c) Particle size
d) Drug-excipient compatibility
   Answer: b) Drug metabolism

24. How does the solubility of a drug influence its formulation?

a) It determines the drug's color
b) It affects how quickly the drug dissolves and is absorbed in the body
c) It affects only the drug's taste
d) It impacts the drug's packaging only
   Answer: b) It affects how quickly the drug dissolves and is absorbed in the body

25. What type of drug stability is most commonly tested in preformulation?

a) Chemical stability
b) Visual appearance
c) Marketability
d) Excipients cost-effectiveness
   Answer: a) Chemical stability

26. Which of the following is a potential outcome of forced degradation studies?

a) Identification of possible drug degradation products
b) Enhanced drug taste
c) Reduced manufacturing costs
d) Improved drug potency
   Answer: a) Identification of possible drug degradation products

27. What is the role of a drug's pKa value in its formulation?

a) It helps determine the solubility and absorption at different pH levels
b) It determines the drug's visual appearance
c) It defines the drug's therapeutic effect
d) It has no impact on formulation
   Answer: a) It helps determine the solubility and absorption at different pH levels

28. What is an essential consideration in preformulation when developing oral dosage forms?

a) The drug's solubility and stability in the gastrointestinal tract
b) The drug's taste
c) The drug's ability to change color in the formulation
d) The speed at which the drug is metabolized
   Answer: a) The drug's solubility and stability in the gastrointestinal tract

29. How is solubility typically tested in preformulation studies?

a) By mixing the drug with different solvents and measuring dissolution rates
b) By measuring the molecular weight of the drug
c) By calculating the drug's absorption rate
d) By determining the drug's bioavailability directly
   Answer: a) By mixing the drug with different solvents and measuring dissolution rates

30. What is the primary purpose of determining the stability of a drug in preformulation studies?

a) To determine the cost of production
b) To identify the shelf life and ideal storage conditions
c) To predict how patients will react to the drug
d) To assess the drug's efficacy against specific diseases
   Answer: b) To identify the shelf life and ideal storage conditions

31. Why is particle size important in the formulation of solid dosage forms?

a) It determines the drug's color
b) It affects the surface area for dissolution and, consequently, bioavailability
c) It impacts only the drug's texture
d) It has no effect on bioavailability
   Answer: b) It affects the surface area for dissolution and, consequently, bioavailability

32. How can polymorphism influence the formulation of a drug?

a) It has no effect on the drug's effectiveness
b) It can alter the drug's solubility, stability, and bioavailability
c) It changes the color of the drug
d) It reduces the drug's price

Answer: b) It can alter the drug's solubility, stability, and bioavailability

33. What is the primary goal of drug-excipient compatibility testing?

a) To increase the drug's solubility
b) To ensure that excipients do not negatively affect the drug's stability or efficacy
c) To reduce the cost of production
d) To improve the appearance of the drug
   Answer: b) To ensure that excipients do not negatively affect the drug's stability or efficacy

34. What is the importance of knowing a drug's partition coefficient (Log P) in formulation development?

a) It determines the drug's solubility in water
b) It helps predict the drug's ability to be absorbed across cell membranes
c) It defines the drug's toxicity
d) It has no relevance to formulation
   Answer: b) It helps predict the drug's ability to be absorbed across cell membranes

35. Which method is used to measure the crystalline structure of a drug?

a) X-ray diffraction (XRD)
b) HPLC
c) IR spectroscopy
d) DSC
   Answer: a) X-ray diffraction (XRD)

36. How does the pKa of a drug affect its absorption?

a) It determines the drug's taste
b) It impacts the drug's solubility at different pH levels, affecting absorption
c) It has no effect on the drug's absorption
d) It influences the drug's visual appearance

Answer: b) It impacts the drug's solubility at different pH levels, affecting absorption

37. Why is stability testing a critical part of preformulation?

a) To determine the color of the drug
b) To ensure that the drug will remain effective and safe over time
c) To enhance the drug's taste
d) To reduce the drug's cost
　　Answer: b) To ensure that the drug will remain effective and safe over time

38. What does forced degradation testing involve?

a) Testing the drug's effect on different diseases
b) Exposing the drug to harsh conditions to identify possible degradation products
c) Reducing the drug's molecular size
d) Measuring the drug's solubility in different solvents
　　Answer: b) Exposing the drug to harsh conditions to identify possible degradation products

39. How does the solubility of a drug affect its formulation?

a) It only affects the appearance of the drug
b) It affects the absorption rate and bioavailability
c) It influences the drug's taste and color
d) It has no effect on the formulation
　　Answer: b) It affects the absorption rate and bioavailability

40. What is the significance of knowing a drug's melting point in preformulation?

a) It helps determine the drug's solubility
b) It assists in predicting the drug's stability and ease of processing
c) It defines the drug's toxicity
d) It impacts the drug's bioavailability

Answer: b) It assists in predicting the drug's stability and ease of processing

I will continue generating additional questions in the next response to meet the 100 MCQ requirement.

Here is the continuation of the MCQs:

41. Why is the study of drug stability important during preformulation?

a) To ensure the drug is affordable
b) To predict how long the drug will remain effective and safe in storage
c) To improve the drug's taste
d) To determine the drug's color
Answer: b) To predict how long the drug will remain effective and safe in storage

42. What does the solubility of a drug directly affect?

a) Its taste
b) Its absorption and bioavailability
c) Its shelf life
d) Its packaging design
Answer: b) Its absorption and bioavailability

43. What is the effect of excipient incompatibility in a formulation?

a) It enhances drug bioavailability
b) It can cause degradation or reduced efficacy of the drug
c) It improves the drug's color
d) It makes the formulation less expensive
Answer: b) It can cause degradation or reduced efficacy of the drug

44. What is the role of particle size in oral dosage form formulation?

a) It determines the drug's color
b) It affects the drug's dissolution rate, which impacts bioavailability

c) It determines the shelf life of the drug

d) It impacts the drug's price

Answer: b) It affects the drug's dissolution rate, which impacts bioavailability

45. Why is it essential to study a drug's crystalline form?

a) It affects the manufacturing process and drug stability

b) It determines the drug's therapeutic effect

c) It changes the drug's taste

d) It has no effect on formulation

Answer: a) It affects the manufacturing process and drug stability

46. How does preformulation aid in the regulatory approval of a drug?

a) By determining the drug's market price

b) By providing data on drug stability, solubility, and efficacy to meet regulatory standards

c) By reducing the time to market

d) By enhancing the drug's taste

Answer: b) By providing data on drug stability, solubility, and efficacy to meet regulatory standards

47. What does an increase in a drug's solubility typically lead to?

a) Decreased absorption

b) Improved bioavailability

c) Reduced shelf life

d) Increased manufacturing cost

Answer: b) Improved bioavailability

48. What is the primary goal of conducting forced degradation studies on a drug?

a) To determine the drug's color

b) To identify potential degradation products that may form under stress conditions

c) To measure the drug's bioavailability

d) To reduce the drug's cost

Answer: b) To identify potential degradation products that may form under stress conditions

49. Which of the following is a benefit of using surfactants in drug formulations?

a) They enhance the drug's color

b) They improve the solubility of poorly water-soluble drugs

c) They increase the drug's toxicity

d) They affect only the drug's packaging

Answer: b) They improve the solubility of poorly water-soluble drugs

50. Why is it important to assess the compatibility of excipients with the drug during preformulation?

a) To ensure the formulation is cost-effective

b) To ensure that the excipients do not cause degradation or instability in the drug

c) To improve the drug's taste

d) To determine the drug's color

Answer: b) To ensure that the excipients do not cause degradation or instability in the drug

51. What does the term 'bioavailability' refer to in pharmaceutical formulations?

a) The ability of a drug to dissolve in water

b) The proportion of the drug that reaches systemic circulation in an active form

c) The drug's shelf life

d) The drug's taste and appearance

Answer: b) The proportion of the drug that reaches systemic circulation in an active form

52. What is the significance of studying a drug's pH solubility profile?

a) To enhance drug taste
b) To identify the pH range where the drug is most soluble, aiding in formulation design
c) To determine the molecular weight of the drug
d) To predict the drug's color change in the body
   Answer: b) To identify the pH range where the drug is most soluble, aiding in formulation design

53. Which of the following techniques is used to study drug degradation pathways?

a) Differential Scanning Calorimetry (DSC)
b) Forced degradation studies
c) HPLC
d) Microscopy
   Answer: b) Forced degradation studies

54. What is the key benefit of preformulation studies for drug manufacturers?

a) They help design more effective and stable drug formulations
b) They reduce the cost of raw materials
c) They eliminate the need for clinical trials
d) They enhance the drug's taste and flavor
   Answer: a) They help design more effective and stable drug formulations

55. What does the melting point of a drug help determine in preformulation?

a) The drug's solubility
b) The drug's stability and processing requirements
c) The drug's absorption rate
d) The drug's color
   Answer: b) The drug's stability and processing requirements

56. What is the effect of polymorphs on drug solubility?

a) Different polymorphs can have different solubility profiles, affecting bioavailability
b) Polymorphs have no effect on drug solubility
c) Polymorphs increase drug toxicity
d) Polymorphs improve drug taste
   Answer: a) Different polymorphs can have different solubility profiles, affecting bioavailability

57. What role does preformulation play in the cost of drug manufacturing?

a) It helps identify excipients that reduce production costs without compromising quality
b) It increases the cost of manufacturing
c) It has no effect on manufacturing costs
d) It enhances the drug's taste, which reduces cost
   Answer: a) It helps identify excipients that reduce production costs without compromising quality

58. What is the purpose of conducting solubility studies on drugs?

a) To determine the drug's color
b) To identify the solvent that enhances the drug's absorption
c) To reduce the cost of formulation
d) To evaluate the drug's stability under various conditions
   Answer: b) To identify the solvent that enhances the drug's absorption

59. What is one of the main concerns when developing solid oral dosage forms?

a) Ensuring the drug's solubility and stability under gastrointestinal conditions
b) Enhancing the drug's taste
c) Reducing the drug's price

d) Ensuring the drug changes color upon ingestion

Answer: a) Ensuring the drug's solubility and stability under gastrointestinal conditions

60. Why is excipient selection crucial in formulation development?

a) Excipients help in improving the drug's solubility, stability, and bioavailability
b) Excipients affect only the drug's taste
c) Excipients have no impact on drug formulation
d) Excipients are selected to reduce production costs only

Answer: a) Excipients help in improving the drug's solubility, stability, and bioavailability

61. What is the primary purpose of preformulation studies in pharmaceutical development?

a) To assess the drug's cost
b) To determine the drug's packaging requirements
c) To understand the drug's physicochemical properties and interactions with excipients
d) To test the drug on animals

Answer: c) To understand the drug's physicochemical properties and interactions with excipients

62. Which of the following is NOT a typical property studied during preformulation?

a) Solubility
b) Stability
c) Drug efficacy
d) Polymorphism

Answer: c) Drug efficacy

63. Why is solubility a key factor in drug formulation?

a) It determines the color of the drug
b) It affects the absorption rate and bioavailability
c) It defines the drug's toxicity
d) It impacts the drug's price
   Answer: b) It affects the absorption rate and bioavailability

64. Which of the following is a method used to measure drug stability?

a) HPLC
b) Forced degradation studies
c) IR spectroscopy
d) Scanning electron microscopy
   Answer: b) Forced degradation studies

65. What is the role of excipients in pharmaceutical formulations?

a) To improve the taste of the drug
b) To stabilize the drug and enhance its bioavailability
c) To increase the manufacturing cost
d) To change the color of the drug
   Answer: b) To stabilize the drug and enhance its bioavailability

66. How does particle size reduction impact drug formulations?

a) It decreases the drug's solubility
b) It increases the surface area for dissolution, improving bioavailability
c) It makes the drug taste better
d) It reduces the drug's cost
   Answer: b) It increases the surface area for dissolution, improving bioavailability

67. Why is it important to study the polymorphic forms of a drug?

a) Polymorphs affect the drug's solubility, stability, and bioavailability
b) Polymorphs change the drug's color
c) Polymorphs have no effect on the drug's formulation
d) Polymorphs reduce the cost of manufacturing
   Answer: a) Polymorphs affect the drug's solubility, stability, and bioavailability

68. What is the significance of the partition coefficient (Log P) in drug formulation?

a) It determines the drug's stability
b) It helps predict the drug's ability to pass through biological membranes
c) It defines the drug's solubility in water
d) It has no impact on the formulation
   Answer: b) It helps predict the drug's ability to pass through biological membranes

69. Which of the following methods is commonly used to measure particle size in preformulation studies?

a) Differential Scanning Calorimetry (DSC)
b) X-ray diffraction (XRD)
c) Scanning Electron Microscopy (SEM)
d) High-Performance Liquid Chromatography (HPLC)
   Answer: c) Scanning Electron Microscopy (SEM)

70. What is the primary goal of preformulation studies?

a) To reduce the cost of drug production
b) To determine the drug's marketability
c) To ensure the drug is stable, bioavailable, and manufacturable
d) To enhance the drug's taste
   Answer: c) To ensure the drug is stable, bioavailable, and manufacturable

71. Which of the following is a potential outcome of forced degradation studies?

a) Identification of possible degradation products
b) Improved drug stability
c) Increased drug absorption
d) Reduced manufacturing cost
Answer: a) Identification of possible degradation products

72. How does the pKa value of a drug influence its formulation?

a) It helps determine the drug's solubility at different pH levels
b) It impacts the drug's color
c) It defines the drug's toxicity
d) It has no relevance in formulation
Answer: a) It helps determine the drug's solubility at different pH levels

73. Why is the study of drug solubility critical in formulation development?

a) It determines how quickly the drug will dissolve in the gastrointestinal tract
b) It defines the drug's color
c) It impacts the drug's manufacturing cost
d) It has no relevance to the drug's bioavailability
Answer: a) It determines how quickly the drug will dissolve in the gastrointestinal tract

74. What is the role of excipient compatibility testing?

a) To ensure excipients do not interact with the drug to reduce its stability or efficacy
b) To reduce the cost of excipients
c) To improve the taste of the drug
d) To change the drug's appearance
Answer: a) To ensure excipients do not interact with the drug to reduce its stability or efficacy

75. What does preformulation help determine regarding drug dosage forms?

a) The cost of manufacturing
b) The stability and suitability of the drug for different dosage forms
c) The packaging requirements
d) The legal requirements for drug approval
   Answer: b) The stability and suitability of the drug for different dosage forms

CHAPTER TWO

Tablets

2.1 Introduction to Tablets

Tablets are one of the most widely used pharmaceutical dosage forms, offering several advantages such as portability, stability, and ease of administration. They are solid unit dosage forms prepared by compressing active pharmaceutical ingredients (APIs) with excipients into a defined shape and size. To ensure efficacy, safety, and patient compliance, tablets must meet specific **ideal characteristics** that encompass physical, mechanical, chemical, and pharmacological attributes.

2.1.1 Ideal Characteristics of Tablets

An **ideal tablet** should meet stringent criteria for uniformity, mechanical strength, stability, ease of administration, and bioavailability. These characteristics ensure the tablet's performance from manufacturing to patient use.

1. Uniformity in Weight, Size, and Content

Uniformity ensures consistent dosing and therapeutic efficacy across a batch of tablets.

Weight Uniformity:

Tablets should meet pharmacopoeial standards for weight variation. For example, the **United States Pharmacopeia (USP)** specifies:

For tablets weighing **<80 mg**, the acceptable weight variation is **±10%**.

For tablets weighing **80–250 mg**, the variation is **±7.5%**.

For tablets weighing **>250 mg**, the variation is **±5%**.

Example:

Paracetamol tablets (500 mg): Typically meet weight variation limits due to precise manufacturing processes.

Aspirin tablets (50 mg): May fail weight uniformity if the granulation process is inconsistent.

Content Uniformity:

The active drug content in individual tablets should lie within **85–115%** of the label claim, with a relative standard deviation (RSD) of ≤6%.

- Example: **Digoxin tablets**, a potent drug with a narrow therapeutic index, require stringent content uniformity.

2. Mechanical Strength

Mechanical strength refers to the tablet's ability to withstand physical stress during handling, packaging, and transportation.

Hardness:

Measured in kiloponds (kp) or Newtons (N), ideal tablets have sufficient hardness to resist breaking but are not so hard that they hinder disintegration.

Typical hardness: **4–8 kp** for standard tablets.

Friability:

Friability is the measure of tablet resistance to abrasion. The **acceptable friability limit** is **≤1% weight loss** after 100 rotations in a friability tester.

Example:

Metformin tablets meet friability requirements due to robust excipient binding.

Poorly compressed tablets of **vitamin C** may exhibit excessive friability.

3. Ease of Swallowing

Tablets should have an optimal size, shape, and coating to enhance patient compliance, especially for pediatric and geriatric populations.

Size and Shape:

Smaller, oval tablets are generally easier to swallow compared to large, round ones.

Example: Cetirizine tablets (10 mg) are small and easy to swallow.

Coating:

Film or sugar coatings improve swallowing, mask unpleasant tastes, and protect the drug.

Example: Ibuprofen tablets are often film-coated for ease of swallowing and taste masking.

4. Stability

Stability ensures that tablets retain their potency and physical integrity throughout their shelf life. Stability is influenced by factors like moisture, temperature, and light.

Chemical Stability:

Active ingredients should not degrade significantly over time. For example, **ascorbic acid tablets** are prone to oxidative degradation, requiring moisture-resistant packaging.

Physical Stability:

Tablets should resist cracking, chipping, or color changes.

- **Example: Aspirin tablets** stored in humid conditions may hydrolyze, resulting in a vinegar odor (acetic acid formation).

5. Bioavailability

Bioavailability refers to the rate and extent of drug absorption into systemic circulation. Tablets should disintegrate and dissolve efficiently to release the active ingredient for absorption.

Disintegration:

The USP specifies a **disintegration time of ≤30 minutes** for uncoated tablets.

Example: Paracetamol tablets disintegrate quickly to ensure rapid onset of action.

Dissolution:

At least **85% of the drug** should dissolve within **30 minutes** under specified conditions.

Example: Immediate-release ibuprofen tablets exhibit rapid dissolution, whereas poorly formulated **phenytoin tablets** may fail dissolution tests, leading to bioavailability issues.

Examples of Specific Drugs

Drugs Meeting Ideal Characteristics:

Paracetamol (500 mg): Uniform in weight and content, with high mechanical strength and rapid disintegration, making it a widely used analgesic.

Cetirizine (10 mg): Small, easy-to-swallow tablets with robust stability and bioavailability.

Drugs Failing Ideal Characteristics:

Aspirin: Hygroscopic and prone to hydrolysis under humid conditions, leading to stability issues.

Digoxin: Narrow therapeutic index demands precise content uniformity; deviations can cause toxicity or subtherapeutic effects.

2.1.2 Classification of Tablets

Tablets are versatile dosage forms that can be classified based on various criteria, including their **route of administration**, **release pattern**, and **special purposes**. This classification enables pharmaceutical scientists to design tablets that meet specific therapeutic needs, enhance patient compliance, and optimize drug delivery.

Classification Based on Route of Administration

Oral Tablets:

Swallowed whole, disintegrating in the gastrointestinal tract for drug absorption.

Examples: Paracetamol tablets for fever and pain relief.

Sublingual Tablets:

Placed under the tongue for rapid systemic absorption through the sublingual mucosa.

Examples: Nitroglycerin tablets for angina relief.

Buccal Tablets:

Placed in the buccal cavity (cheek pouch) for prolonged release and absorption.

Examples: Prochlorperazine tablets for nausea and vomiting.

Classification Based on Release Pattern

Immediate-Release Tablets:

Designed to disintegrate and release the drug rapidly upon ingestion.

Purpose: Quick therapeutic action.

Examples: Ibuprofen tablets for pain relief.

Industrial Usage: ~60% of the tablet market.

Controlled-Release Tablets:

Release the drug at a predetermined rate to maintain consistent plasma levels over time.

Purpose: Reduced dosing frequency and enhanced compliance.

Examples: Metformin XR tablets for diabetes.

Sustained-Release Tablets:

Gradually release the drug over an extended period to prolong its therapeutic effect.

Purpose: Long-lasting effects with fewer doses.

Examples: Diltiazem SR tablets for hypertension.

Delayed-Release Tablets:

Release the drug after a specified lag time, often to target specific regions of the gastrointestinal tract.

Purpose: Protect the drug from gastric acid or minimize gastrointestinal side effects.

Examples: Pantoprazole EC tablets for acid reflux.

Classification Based on Special Types

Effervescent Tablets:

Contain effervescent agents (e.g., citric acid and sodium bicarbonate) that release carbon dioxide upon contact with water, creating a fizzy solution.

Purpose: Rapid dissolution and easy administration.

Examples: Vitamin C tablets.

Chewable Tablets:

Designed to be chewed before swallowing; often flavored for pediatric or geriatric patients.

Purpose: Ease of administration for patients who struggle with swallowing.

Examples: Calcium tablets.

Orally Disintegrating Tablets (ODTs):

Dissolve rapidly in the mouth without the need for water.

Purpose: Convenient for patients with swallowing difficulties.

Examples: Ondansetron ODT tablets for nausea.

Layered Tablets:

Contain two or more layers to separate incompatible drugs or provide sequential drug release.

Purpose: Multiple therapeutic effects in a single dose.

Examples: Ambien CR tablets for insomnia.

Film-Coated Tablets:

Coated with a thin polymer layer to mask taste, enhance stability, or modify drug release.

Purpose: Improved patient acceptability and drug protection.

Examples: Erythromycin tablets.

Industrial Usage of Tablet Types

Immediate-Release Tablets:
Constitute **~60% of the tablet market** due to their simplicity, cost-effectiveness, and rapid therapeutic action.

Controlled-Release and Sustained-Release Tablets:
Together account for **~25–30%** of the market, gaining popularity for chronic conditions requiring consistent plasma drug levels.

Specialty Tablets (Effervescent, ODTs, etc.):
Represent **~10–15%** of the market, targeting niche applications and patient populations like pediatrics and geriatrics.

2.2 Formulation and Manufacturing Techniques

Tablet formulation involves combining active pharmaceutical ingredients (APIs) with excipients to produce a stable, effective, and manufacturable product. Excipients play a critical role in the formulation, influencing the physical and chemical properties of tablets, including stability, bioavailability, and manufacturability. Proper selection and optimization of excipients are essential to achieve desired tablet characteristics.

2.2.1 Excipients in Tablet Formulation

Excipients are inert substances added to tablet formulations to enhance manufacturability, stability, and therapeutic efficacy. Each excipient serves a specific purpose, and their interactions with APIs must be carefully studied to ensure consistent performance.

Role of Excipients in Tablet Formulation

Binders:
Binders are used to provide cohesiveness to the powder blend, ensuring the formation of mechanically strong tablets. They enhance particle adhesion during compression, improving the structural integrity of tablets.

Examples of binders include polyvinylpyrrolidone (PVP) at 1–5% w/w, hydroxypropyl methylcellulose (HPMC) at 2–6% w/w, and starch paste at 5–10% w/w. Excess binder can lead to reduced tablet disintegration and dissolution, negatively impacting bioavailability.

Fillers:
Fillers, or diluents, are added to increase the bulk of the tablet when the API

is present in low doses. They improve the flowability and compressibility of the formulation.

Common fillers include lactose (30–60% w/w), microcrystalline cellulose (10–40% w/w), and dibasic calcium phosphate (20–50% w/w). For instance, lactose provides excellent compressibility, but its interaction with amines can lead to Maillard reactions, compromising stability.

Disintegrants:

Disintegrants facilitate the breakup of tablets into smaller particles upon contact with gastrointestinal fluids, promoting rapid dissolution and drug absorption.

Examples of disintegrants include sodium starch glycolate (2–8% w/w), crospovidone (2–5% w/w), and croscarmellose sodium (2–5% w/w). Overuse of disintegrants may cause tablets to lose mechanical strength, leading to friability issues.

Lubricants:

Lubricants reduce friction between the tablet surface and the die wall during compression and ejection, preventing sticking and ensuring smooth manufacturing.

Magnesium stearate (0.25–2% w/w), stearic acid (0.5–2% w/w), and talc (1–5% w/w) are commonly used lubricants. However, excessive lubricant can hinder tablet disintegration and dissolution by forming a hydrophobic film around particles.

Glidants:

Glidants enhance the flow properties of the powder blend, ensuring uniform filling of tablet dies during manufacturing.

Silicon dioxide (0.1–0.5% w/w) and talc (1–2% w/w) are typical glidants. Their inclusion minimizes weight variation and improves uniformity. However, overuse may impair tablet hardness due to reduced particle bonding.

Interactions Between Excipients and APIs

Excipients can interact with APIs, affecting the stability, bioavailability, or manufacturability of the tablet. These interactions must be identified and mitigated during preformulation studies.

Chemical Interactions:

Lactose, a common filler, may undergo Maillard reactions with APIs containing primary or secondary amines, leading to discoloration and reduced potency. For example, formulations with amlodipine require alternative fillers to avoid this issue.

Magnesium stearate, a widely used lubricant, can react with acidic APIs, reducing stability and causing degradation.

Physical Interactions:

Excipients like microcrystalline cellulose may adsorb moisture, accelerating the hydrolysis of hygroscopic APIs such as aspirin.

Over-lubrication with magnesium stearate can inhibit API dissolution, particularly for poorly water-soluble drugs like carbamazepine.

Functional Interactions:

Excessive binder concentration may retard disintegration, reducing the bioavailability of APIs like ibuprofen.

Incompatible disintegrants can lead to incomplete disintegration, affecting the dissolution of APIs such as paracetamol.

2.2.2 Granulation Methods

Granulation is a crucial step in tablet manufacturing, transforming fine powders into larger, uniform aggregates called granules. Granulation enhances flow properties, compressibility, and content uniformity, making it easier to produce high-quality tablets. Wet granulation is the most widely used granulation technique due to its versatility and ability to improve the properties of challenging formulations.

2.2.2.1 Wet Granulation

Wet granulation involves adding a liquid binder to the powder blend to create granules. The process can accommodate a wide range of drugs and excipients, particularly those with poor flow or compressibility. The following steps outline the wet granulation process:

1. Mixing

In the initial step, the API and excipients (fillers, disintegrants, etc.) are blended to ensure uniform distribution.

Objective: Homogeneous distribution of ingredients for uniform drug content in tablets.

Equipment: High-shear mixers or ribbon blenders are commonly used.

Example: Blending lactose (filler), croscarmellose sodium (disintegrant), and the API such as metformin.

2. Wetting

A liquid binder solution is added to the powder blend to moisten the particles. The binder provides cohesiveness, enabling the formation of granules during subsequent mixing.

Binder Solutions: Typically aqueous or hydroalcoholic solutions of binders like polyvinylpyrrolidone (PVP, 2–5% w/w), starch paste (5–10% w/w), or hydroxypropyl methylcellulose (HPMC, 2–6% w/w).

Equipment: Peristaltic pumps for controlled binder addition in high-shear granulators.

3. Granulation

The moistened powder is subjected to mechanical mixing, forming granules as particles adhere to one another. The extent of granule formation depends on binder concentration, mixing intensity, and liquid distribution.

Key Considerations:

Excess binder can cause hard, non-disintegrating granules, while insufficient binder results in weak granules.

Overwetting can lead to lump formation or sticky masses.

Equipment:

High-Shear Mixers: Efficient for rapid granulation.

Planetary Mixers: Suitable for smaller-scale operations.

Example: Paracetamol formulations benefit from wet granulation to improve compressibility and uniformity.

4. Drying

The granules are dried to remove excess moisture and achieve a stable moisture content, critical for preventing degradation and ensuring compressibility.

Moisture Content After Drying: Ideally, 2–10% w/w, depending on the formulation requirements.

Example: If granules weigh 1000 g before drying and 950 g after drying, the moisture content is 5%.

Equipment:

Fluid Bed Dryers: Provide uniform drying and shorter processing times.

Tray Dryers: Used for small-scale production.

5. Sieving

After drying, granules are passed through a sieve to break down large lumps and achieve uniform granule size.

Objective: Ensure uniform particle size distribution for improved flow and compression.

Mesh Size: Commonly used mesh sizes range from 16–30 mesh (1–0.5 mm).

Equipment:

Vibratory Sifters: Provide precise control over particle size.

Oscillating Granulators: Break large lumps into smaller granules.

Equipment for Wet Granulation

Examples of Drugs/Formulations Suited for Wet Granulation

Paracetamol: Poor compressibility necessitates granulation to improve flow and compactibility.

Metformin: High-dose formulations benefit from wet granulation to ensure uniform distribution and compressibility.

Ibuprofen: Wet granulation enhances the handling of fine, poorly flowing powders.

Amoxicillin: Granulation prevents segregation of drug and excipients in powder blends.

Advantages of Wet Granulation

Improves the flowability and compressibility of powders.

Enhances content uniformity, especially for low-dose drugs.

Reduces dust generation, improving occupational safety during production.

2.2.2.2 Dry Granulation

Dry granulation is a granulation technique that forms granules without the use of solvents or heat, making it ideal for **moisture-sensitive** or **thermally labile APIs**. The process involves compressing powders into larger aggregates, followed by size reduction to achieve the desired granule size. Dry granulation is preferred for APIs or excipients that are poorly flowable or have limited compressibility.

Methods of Dry Granulation

Dry granulation is primarily achieved through two methods: **slugging** and **roller compaction**. Both methods involve applying high pressure to compact powders into aggregates, but they differ in equipment and process design.

1. Slugging Method

Slugging involves compressing powders into large compacts (slugs) using a tablet press, followed by milling to break the slugs into granules of uniform size.

Process Steps:

Powder blend (API and excipients) is compressed into slugs using a heavy-duty tablet press.

The slugs are typically flat or disk-shaped, with dimensions suitable for subsequent milling.

The slugs are milled or sieved to produce granules of uniform size.

Compression Force:

High pressures of approximately **10,000–20,000 psi** are required to form durable slugs.

Advantages:

Suitable for batch processes.

No specialized equipment is needed beyond a standard tablet press and milling system.

Disadvantages:

Time-intensive compared to roller compaction.

Higher wastage due to the need for multiple milling steps.

Examples:

Aspirin: Slugging improves its flow properties and compressibility.

Ibuprofen: The method is used to process its moisture-sensitive formulation.

2. Roller Compaction Method

In roller compaction, powders are compressed into ribbons or sheets using a roller compactor. These ribbons are then milled into granules.

Process Steps:

Powder blend is fed into the roller compactor.

Rollers apply a continuous high pressure, compacting the powders into dense ribbons or sheets.

The ribbons are milled to obtain granules of uniform size.

Compression Force:

Roller compaction typically operates at forces ranging from **5–15 kN/cm** of roller width, depending on the material properties.

Advantages:

Continuous process suitable for large-scale production.

Reduced material loss compared to slugging.

Lower dust generation improves occupational safety.

Disadvantages:

Requires specialized roller compaction equipment.

Higher initial equipment cost compared to slugging.

Examples:

Aspirin: Roller compaction ensures uniform granule size for consistent tablet quality.

Ibuprofen: Used to handle its poor flow properties and prevent segregation of powder blends.

Key Advantages of Dry Granulation

Absence of Solvents:

Unlike wet granulation, dry granulation eliminates the use of solvents, making it suitable for APIs sensitive to moisture or those prone to hydrolysis, such as aspirin.

Thermal Stability:

The absence of drying steps makes dry granulation ideal for thermally sensitive drugs like ibuprofen.

Improved Flow and Compressibility:

Dry granulation enhances the flow properties and compressibility of powders, enabling uniform die filling during tableting.

Examples of Drugs Suitable for Dry Granulation

Aspirin:

Aspirin is highly moisture-sensitive and undergoes hydrolysis in the presence of water, forming salicylic acid and acetic acid.

Dry granulation improves its flow and compressibility without exposing it to moisture.

Ibuprofen:

Ibuprofen has poor flow properties and compressibility.

Roller compaction enhances its handling characteristics for high-dose formulations.

Metformin:

High-dose metformin formulations benefit from dry granulation to prevent segregation and improve uniformity.

Vitamin C (Ascorbic Acid):

Ascorbic acid is sensitive to moisture and oxidation, making dry granulation a suitable method for its processing

2.2.2.3 Direct Compression

Direct compression is a tablet manufacturing process in which powders, including the active pharmaceutical ingredient (API) and excipients, are directly compressed into tablets without any intermediate granulation steps. This method is simpler and more time-efficient than granulation-based techniques, as it eliminates wetting, drying, and sieving stages.

Advantages of Direct Compression

Simplicity:
Direct compression reduces the number of processing steps, making it more cost-effective and faster than wet or dry granulation.

Suitability for Heat- or Moisture-Sensitive APIs:
Since it avoids the use of heat or solvents, direct compression is ideal for APIs like aspirin, which are prone to hydrolysis or thermal degradation.

Enhanced Uniformity:
The absence of granulation minimizes the risk of content uniformity issues, particularly for low-dose APIs.

Scalability:
Direct compression is well-suited for high-throughput manufacturing, reducing production time and operational costs.

Critical Factors in Direct Compression
The success of direct compression depends on the physical properties of the powders used, including flowability and compressibility.

Flow Properties of Powders:
Good flowability is essential to ensure uniform die filling during tablet compression, preventing weight variation and content inconsistencies. Poor flow properties can lead to segregation and non-uniform tablets.

Enhancers: Glidants such as silicon dioxide (0.1–0.5% w/w) improve flowability in direct compression formulations.

Compressibility:
Powders must deform plastically or fragment under compression to form strong, cohesive tablets. Compressibility issues can lead to weak, friable tablets or sticking problems during compression.

Enhancers: Excipients like microcrystalline cellulose (MCC) are added to improve compressibility.

Frequently Used Excipients in Direct Compression

Excipients play a crucial role in ensuring the flowability, compressibility, and stability of direct compression formulations.

Fillers:

Microcrystalline Cellulose (MCC): A widely used filler with excellent compressibility and binding properties. Typical concentration: 20–40% w/w.

Lactose: Used as a filler in formulations with good flow and solubility properties. Typical concentration: 30–60% w/w.

Binders:

Pregelatinized Starch: Provides additional cohesiveness. Typical concentration: 5–10% w/w.

Disintegrants:

Croscarmellose Sodium: Ensures rapid tablet disintegration. Typical concentration: 2–5% w/w.

Sodium Starch Glycolate: Commonly used for quick-release formulations. Typical concentration: 2–8% w/w.

Glidants:

Colloidal Silicon Dioxide: Improves powder flow. Typical concentration: 0.1–0.5% w/w.

Lubricants:

Magnesium Stearate: Reduces friction during tablet ejection. Typical concentration: 0.25–2% w/w.

Examples of APIs Suitable for Direct Compression

Direct compression is suitable for APIs with inherent good flowability and compressibility or for those that can be processed with appropriate excipients.

Paracetamol:

Directly compressible grades of paracetamol can be processed without granulation, provided excipients like MCC are included for binding and flow.

Ibuprofen:

Its compressibility can be enhanced with fillers like lactose or MCC, making it suitable for direct compression.

Ascorbic Acid:

Often combined with MCC and pregelatinized starch to achieve adequate flow and compressibility.

Lactose-Based Formulations:

Lactose, being naturally flowable and compressible, is frequently used in direct compression formulations for APIs like cetirizine and aspirin.

Challenges in Direct Compression

Segregation:

APIs and excipients may segregate due to differences in particle size or density, leading to content uniformity issues.

Lack of Compatibility:

APIs with poor flow or compressibility cannot be processed using direct compression without significant excipient modification.

Capping or Lamination:

Weak tablets may delaminate or cap under excessive compression forces. Adjusting lubricant levels or using cohesive fillers can mitigate this.

2.2.3 Compression and Processing Problems

Tablet compression is a critical step in pharmaceutical manufacturing that can encounter several challenges, leading to defective tablets. Common issues such as **capping**, **lamination**, **sticking**, **picking**, and **mottling** not only affect the appearance but also the functionality and stability of the tablets. Identifying the root causes and implementing appropriate remedies ensures the production of high-quality tablets.

Common Compression Problems

Capping:

Capping occurs when the upper or lower surface of a tablet separates from the body, resembling a cap.

Root Causes:

Excessive compression force, leading to trapped air.

Poor plasticity of the powder blend.

Insufficient binder concentration or over-drying of granules.

Remedies:

Reduce compression force to prevent air entrapment.

Add binders like polyvinylpyrrolidone (2–5% w/w) to enhance cohesiveness.

Optimize granule moisture content to 2–5% w/w.

Lamination:

Lamination refers to the horizontal splitting of a tablet into distinct layers during or after compression.

Root Causes:

Entrapped air due to improper granule size distribution.

Over-compression, causing reduced tablet elasticity.

Use

of poorly compressible materials or insufficient binder concentration.

Remedies:

Use pre-compression to allow trapped air to escape before final compression.

Adjust granule size by sieving to ensure uniform particle distribution.

Incorporate cohesive excipients like microcrystalline cellulose (10–40% w/w) to improve compressibility.

Sticking:

Sticking occurs when the powder blend adheres to the surfaces of the punches, leading to uneven tablet surfaces.

Root Causes:

High moisture content in the granules.

Insufficient lubrication during compression.

Use of hygroscopic materials prone to sticking under pressure.

Remedies:

Dry the granules to a moisture content of 2–5% w/w.

Increase the concentration of lubricants like magnesium stearate (0.25–2% w/w).

Apply anti-adherent coatings to punches to minimize sticking.

Picking:

Picking is a localized form of sticking, where particles adhere to specific areas of the punch, often the engraving.

Root Causes:

Improper drying of granules, leading to tacky surfaces.

Excessively sticky APIs or excipients.

Insufficient lubricant distribution in the blend.

Remedies:

Ensure uniform drying of granules to optimal moisture levels.

Increase the concentration of anti-adherents like talc (1–5% w/w).

Use smoother punch surfaces or modify engraving to reduce particle adherence.

Mottling:

Mottling refers to uneven color distribution on the tablet surface, resulting in a spotted or marbled appearance.

Root Causes:

Uneven distribution of colorants in the blend.

Color degradation due to heat, light, or moisture.

Variations in particle size between the API and excipients.

Remedies:

Premix colorants with excipients to ensure uniform distribution before blending.

Use stable, non-degradable colorants.

Ensure consistent particle sizes of components to prevent segregation.

2.3 Tablet Coating

Tablet coating is a critical process in pharmaceutical manufacturing that enhances the appearance, stability, and functionality of tablets. Coatings protect the active pharmaceutical ingredient (API) from environmental factors, mask unpleasant tastes or odors, and facilitate patient compliance. One of the oldest and most traditional methods is **sugar coating**, which creates an aesthetically pleasing and protective shell around the tablet.

2.3.1 Types of Coating

Tablet coatings can be broadly categorized into sugar coating, film coating, and specialized coatings like enteric or controlled-release coatings. This section focuses on sugar coating, a method that involves the application of multiple layers of a sugar-based solution to tablets.

2.3.1.1 Sugar Coating

Sugar coating is a multi-step process that results in tablets with a smooth, glossy, and sweet outer shell. The process enhances the visual appeal of tablets and masks any unpleasant taste or odor associated with the API. However, it is labor-intensive and increases the tablet's weight significantly (by 30–50%).

Steps in Sugar Coating

Sealing:

Purpose: To protect the core tablet from moisture and prevent interaction with the aqueous sugar-coating solutions.

Process: A sealing coat is applied using shellac or polymer-based solutions like hydroxypropyl methylcellulose (HPMC).

Challenges: Incomplete sealing can lead to tablet degradation due to moisture penetration.

Subcoating:

Purpose: To build up the tablet size and provide mechanical strength for subsequent coating layers.

Process: A mixture of gum (e.g., acacia) and sugar syrup is applied, followed by dusting with powdered materials like calcium carbonate or talc. Repeated applications ensure uniformity.

Challenges: Uneven application can lead to non-uniform tablet sizes and cracking.

Smoothing:

Purpose: To smoothen the surface of the subcoated tablet in preparation for the coloring step.

Process: A series of sugar syrup applications are made to eliminate any roughness from the subcoating layer.

Challenges: Overuse of syrup can lead to excess weight gain and extended drying times.

Coloring:

Purpose: To provide the tablet with a uniform, attractive color for identification and branding.

Process: Dyes or pigments are added to the sugar syrup, which is sprayed or layered onto the tablet.

Challenges: Achieving uniform color distribution requires precise mixing and application techniques.

Polishing:

Purpose: To provide the final glossy finish to the coated tablets.

Process: Tablets are polished in rotating pans using waxes like carnauba wax or beeswax.

Challenges: Over-polishing can result in sticking or loss of the gloss effect.

Challenges in Sugar Coating

Tablet Weight Gain:

Sugar coating significantly increases the weight of the tablet (30–50%), which can affect dosing and packaging requirements.

Example: A tablet weighing 500 mg before coating may weigh 750 mg after sugar coating.

Labor and Time Intensive:

The multi-step process requires prolonged drying and handling times, increasing manufacturing costs.

Moisture Sensitivity:

The use of aqueous sugar solutions can lead to degradation of moisture-sensitive APIs if the sealing step is insufficient.

Fragility of Coating:

Poor adhesion or over-drying can lead to cracking or chipping of the coating layer.

Examples of Sugar-Coated Drugs

Antacids:

Traditional antacid tablets, such as calcium carbonate or magnesium hydroxide formulations, are sugar-coated to mask their chalky taste.

Vitamins:

Multivitamin and mineral tablets are often sugar-coated to enhance their palatability and appearance.

Certain Antibiotics:

Sugar coating is used for antibiotics like erythromycin to mask the bitter taste and ensure patient compliance.

2.3.1.2 Film Coating

Film coating is a modern tablet coating method that involves applying a thin, polymer-based layer over the tablet core. It provides multiple benefits over traditional sugar coating, such as enhanced protection, faster processing, and improved dissolution control. This process has become the preferred method for coating tablets due to its versatility and efficiency.

Description of Film Coating

Film coating involves the application of a polymer solution or suspension to the tablet surface using spraying techniques. The polymer forms a thin, uniform film that adheres tightly to the tablet, providing protection and desired functional properties. The solution may also contain plasticizers, colorants, and other excipients to enhance film properties.

Polymers Used:

Polymers are the key components of the film coat and determine its physical and functional properties.

Hydroxypropyl Methylcellulose (HPMC): A widely used polymer due to its solubility in both water and organic solvents, forming clear and smooth films.

Methacrylic Acid Copolymers: Used for enteric or controlled-release coatings.

Polyvinyl Alcohol (PVA): Known for its high tensile strength and ability to form glossy films.

Plasticizers:

Plasticizers such as polyethylene glycol (PEG) or glycerin are added to improve the flexibility and elasticity of the film, reducing the risk of cracking.

Other Components:

Colorants: To provide aesthetic appeal and identification.

Opacifiers: Such as titanium dioxide, to protect light-sensitive APIs.

Advantages of Film Coating over Sugar Coating

Thinner Coating Layers:

Film coatings are typically **20–100 microns thick**, compared to sugar coatings, which add significant bulk and increase tablet weight by **30–50%**.

This thinner layer ensures minimal impact on tablet size and weight.

Faster Processing:

Film coating is a quicker process, reducing production time and costs compared to the labor-intensive sugar coating.

Improved Stability:

The polymer film provides better protection against environmental factors like moisture, oxygen, and light.

Controlled Dissolution Profiles:

Film coatings can be designed to achieve immediate, delayed, or extended-release profiles.

Better Mechanical Strength:

The thin yet robust film resists cracking, chipping, or abrasion during handling and transportation.

Examples of Film Coating Applications

Immediate-Release Tablets:

Film coatings are commonly used to mask unpleasant tastes or odors while providing protection.

Example: Ibuprofen film-coated tablets mask the bitter taste and improve swallowing.

Controlled-Release Tablets:

Polymers like **ethylcellulose** are used to regulate drug release over time.

Example: Metformin XR film-coated tablets maintain steady plasma levels for extended periods.

Enteric-Coated Tablets:
Film coatings protect APIs from degradation in acidic gastric environments and enable drug release in the intestine.

Example: Pantoprazole enteric-coated tablets resist gastric acid and release the drug in the duodenum.

Dissolution Profiles for Film-Coated Tablets
The dissolution profile of film-coated tablets depends on the coating composition and intended release pattern:

Immediate-Release Film Coating:
Dissolution begins rapidly upon contact with aqueous media.

Example: Ibuprofen tablets exhibit **85% dissolution within 30 minutes** in simulated gastric fluid.

Controlled-Release Film Coating:
The release rate is modulated by the thickness and permeability of the polymer coat.

Example: Metformin XR tablets release the drug over **8–12 hours**, achieving sustained plasma concentrations.

Enteric Film Coating:
Designed to delay dissolution until reaching the higher pH of the intestine.

Example: Pantoprazole enteric-coated tablets remain intact in gastric fluid (pH 1.2) but dissolve rapidly at intestinal pH (6.8).

2.3.1.3 Enteric Coating

Enteric coating is a specialized tablet coating technique designed to protect the drug from degradation in the acidic environment of the stomach and ensure its release in the more neutral or alkaline conditions of the intestines. This type of coating is particularly important for drugs that are acid-sensitive, irritate the gastric mucosa, or need to be absorbed in the intestine for therapeutic effectiveness.

Definition and Role of Enteric Coating
Definition:
Enteric coatings are pH-sensitive polymeric layers applied to tablets or capsules that resist dissolution in the stomach (pH 1–3) and dissolve only at higher pH levels, typically in the small intestine (pH > 5.5).

Role:

Protect acid-sensitive drugs (e.g., omeprazole) from degradation in the stomach.

Minimize gastric irritation caused by certain APIs (e.g., aspirin).

Facilitate site-specific drug release, particularly for drugs intended to act in the intestines (e.g., mesalamine for inflammatory bowel disease).

Materials Used for Enteric Coating

Enteric coatings are made from polymers that remain intact in acidic pH and dissolve at higher, alkaline pH levels. Common materials include:

Cellulose Acetate Phthalate (CAP):

A widely used enteric polymer known for its excellent acid resistance and rapid dissolution in the intestine.

Hydroxypropyl Methylcellulose Phthalate (HPMCP):

A versatile polymer with adjustable dissolution profiles based on its phthalate content, suitable for both gastric protection and delayed release.

Methacrylic Acid Copolymers:

Polymers such as Eudragit L100 and Eudragit S100 are popular due to their customizable pH-dissolution characteristics.

Eudragit L dissolves at pH > 6.0 (duodenum).

Eudragit S dissolves at pH > 7.0 (ileum).

Polyvinyl Acetate Phthalate (PVAP):

Offers stability against hydrolysis and light, making it suitable for long-term formulations.

Shellac:

A natural polymer providing acid resistance, though less commonly used due to variability in properties.

Examples of Enteric-Coated Drugs

Omeprazole:

A proton pump inhibitor used for conditions like gastroesophageal reflux disease (GERD).

Enteric coating protects it from degradation in the stomach, allowing effective absorption in the intestine.

Aspirin (Low-Dose):

Enteric-coated aspirin minimizes gastric irritation while maintaining its antiplatelet activity.

Mesalamine:

Used for inflammatory bowel diseases like ulcerative colitis, mesalamine tablets are enteric-coated to ensure drug release in the colon.

Pancrelipase:

An enzyme supplement for pancreatic insufficiency, enteric coating ensures the enzymes remain active after passing through the stomach.

Diclofenac:

An enteric-coated nonsteroidal anti-inflammatory drug (NSAID) to reduce gastrointestinal side effects.

Advantages of Enteric Coating

Protection of Acid-Sensitive APIs:

Prevents degradation of drugs like omeprazole, which is unstable in gastric acid.

Reduction of Gastric Side Effects:

Avoids direct irritation of the gastric mucosa caused by APIs like aspirin or diclofenac.

Site-Specific Drug Delivery:

Ensures therapeutic action in the intestines, as required for drugs like mesalamine.

2.3.2 Coating Materials and Composition

Tablet coatings rely on carefully selected materials to achieve the desired functionality, such as protection from environmental factors, improved aesthetics, or controlled drug release. The composition of the coating mixture, including **polymers**, **plasticizers**, and **pigments**, is tailored to meet specific formulation and performance requirements.

Key Components of Coating Formulations

1. Polymers

Polymers form the structural backbone of the coating and determine its physical and functional properties. The choice of polymer depends on the type of coating (e.g., film, enteric, or controlled release) and the intended drug release profile.

Common Polymers and Applications:

Hydroxypropyl Methylcellulose (HPMC):

Water-soluble polymer for immediate-release film coatings.

Typical concentration: **2–5% w/w** in the coating solution.

Example: Used in **ibuprofen film-coated tablets** to mask taste and improve appearance.

Ethylcellulose:

Water-insoluble polymer for controlled-release coatings.

Example: Found in **theophylline sustained-release tablets** to regulate drug release over 12–24 hours.

Cellulose Acetate Phthalate (CAP):

Acid-resistant polymer for enteric coatings.

Typical concentration: **5–10% w/w** in the coating formula.

Example: Used in **omeprazole enteric-coated tablets** to protect the API from stomach acid.

Methacrylic Acid Copolymers (Eudragit):

Tailored for enteric (Eudragit L100) or controlled-release (Eudragit RS/RL) coatings.

Example: Found in **mesalamine tablets** for site-specific drug delivery in the colon.

Polyvinyl Alcohol (PVA):

High-strength polymer used for durable film coatings.

Example: Used in **paracetamol tablets** for added stability.

2. Plasticizers

Plasticizers enhance the flexibility, elasticity, and durability of the polymer film, reducing the risk of cracking or brittleness.

Common Plasticizers:

Polyethylene Glycol (PEG):

Typical concentration: **1–2% w/w.**

Example: Improves flexibility in HPMC-based film coatings.

Glycerin:

Enhances film elasticity.

Example: Used in enteric-coated **aspirin tablets** to prevent cracking.

Triacetin:

Suitable for sustained-release formulations.

Example: Found in ethylcellulose-coated controlled-release tablets.

Dibutyl Sebacate:

Provides excellent plasticizing effects in controlled-release and enteric coatings.

3. Pigments and Opacifiers

Pigments and opacifiers provide color, enhance tablet appearance, and protect light-sensitive APIs.

Common Pigments and Opacifiers:

Titanium Dioxide:

Widely used as an opacifier for light-sensitive drugs.

Example: Used in **riboflavin-coated tablets** to prevent photodegradation.

Iron Oxides:

Provide vibrant colors and improve branding.

Example: Found in multivitamin tablets for aesthetic appeal.

FD&C Dyes:

Water-soluble colorants used in immediate-release film coatings.

Example: Adds color to HPMC-coated **paracetamol tablets.**

A batch passes the test if no more than 2 tablets deviate from the specified limits and none deviate by more than twice the allowed.

Importance of Weight Variation Testing

Ensures Uniformity:

Weight variation directly impacts dose uniformity, which is critical for low-dose formulations.

Compliance with Standards:

Meeting pharmacopoeial criteria ensures regulatory approval and consistency in manufacturing quality.

Indicator of Manufacturing Issues:

Weight variation can indicate problems in processes like powder flow, die filling, or tablet press settings.

2.4.1.2 Hardness

Tablet **hardness** refers to the ability of a tablet to withstand mechanical stress during handling, packaging, transportation, and storage without breaking or chipping. Hardness is a critical parameter for ensuring the physical integrity of tablets and maintaining their quality from production to patient use.

Definition and Importance

Definition:

Tablet hardness is the measure of the force required to break a tablet along its diameter. It reflects the mechanical strength of the tablet and its resistance to pressure.

Importance:

Packaging and Transportation: Adequate hardness prevents tablets from breaking or crumbling during handling, storage, and distribution.

Disintegration and Dissolution: While hardness contributes to mechanical strength, excessive hardness can delay disintegration and reduce bioavailability.

Product Uniformity: Ensures consistent mechanical strength across the batch, maintaining quality and compliance with standards.

Equipment for Measuring Hardness

Tablet hardness is typically measured using instruments designed to apply force until the tablet fractures. Common equipment includes:

Monsanto Hardness Tester:

A manually operated device that applies force via a spring. The tablet is placed between two anvils, and the spring tension is adjusted until the tablet breaks.

Advantages: Simple and cost-effective for small-scale or routine testing.

Limitations: Operator-dependent results due to manual operation.

Pfizer Hardness Tester:

Similar to the Monsanto tester but uses a plunger system to apply force.

Erweka Hardness Tester:

A motorized and automated device that ensures precise application of force. The instrument records the force required to break the tablet.

Advantages: High accuracy and repeatability, making it suitable for large-scale operations.

Example: Used in pharmaceutical industries for routine quality control.

Schleuniger Hardness Tester:

A modern, automated device that measures hardness with high precision and consistency. It can record and store data for analysis.

Procedure for Measuring Hardness

Sample Selection:

Select **10 tablets** randomly from the batch for testing.

Placement:

Place the tablet between the anvils of the hardness tester.

Application of Force:

Gradually apply force until the tablet fractures. Record the force required to break the tablet in **kilograms per square centimeter (kg/cm²)** or **Newtons (N).**

Results Interpretation:

Compare the measured hardness with the specified range for the product.

Factors Affecting Tablet Hardness

Formulation:

Higher binder concentrations increase hardness.

Insufficient lubricants may reduce cohesion and compromise hardness.

Compression Force:

Increased force during tablet compression enhances hardness but may delay disintegration.

Granule Properties:

Uniform granule size distribution contributes to consistent hardness.

2.4.1.3 Friability

Friability testing evaluates the tablet's ability to withstand mechanical stresses such as handling, packaging, and transportation without crumbling or breaking. This test measures the tablet's resistance to abrasion and is a crucial parameter for ensuring product durability and quality.

Friability Testing Using Roche Friabilator

Equipment:

The **Roche Friabilator** is the standard apparatus used for friability testing. It consists of a rotating drum with a curved baffle inside.

Procedure:

Sample Preparation: Select **10–20 tablets** randomly from the batch and dedust them. Weigh the tablets accurately (**initial weight, W^0**).

Testing: Place the tablets in the drum and rotate it at **25 revolutions per minute (rpm)** for **4 minutes**, completing a total of **100 revolutions**. The baffles inside the drum lift and drop the tablets repeatedly to simulate mechanical stress.

Post-Test Weighing: Remove the tablets, dedust them again, and weigh them (**final weight, W_1**).

Acceptance Criteria

Limits:

According to pharmacopoeial standards, tablets should have a friability of **≤1% weight loss**.

Exceptions:

Friability testing is not required for chewable tablets or tablets with very high mechanical strength, such as effervescent tablets.

Interpretation:

If the friability is **>1%**, the formulation or manufacturing process may need adjustments to improve mechanical strength.

Importance of Friability Testing

Mechanical Integrity: Ensures tablets can withstand handling during manufacturing, packaging, and transportation.

Product Quality: Minimizes the risk of chipped or broken tablets reaching the end user.

Indicator of Manufacturing Issues: High friability may indicate inadequate binder concentration, insufficient compression force, or poor granule quality.

Example of Friability Testing

Factors Affecting Friability

Formulation:

Low binder concentration or poor binder quality increases friability.

The presence of hygroscopic excipients may lead to moisture absorption, reducing tablet strength.

Manufacturing Process:

Inadequate compression force results in weak tablets.

Over-lubrication with agents like magnesium stearate can reduce interparticle bonding, increasing friability.

Granule Properties:

Poorly sized or non-uniform granules contribute to fragile tablets.

2.4.2 Finished Product Tests

Finished product tests are conducted on completed tablets to ensure they meet pharmacopoeial standards for efficacy, safety, and quality. Among these, **disintegration time** is a critical parameter that evaluates how quickly a tablet breaks down into smaller particles to facilitate drug release and absorption.

2.4.2.1 Disintegration Time

Definition and Importance

Definition:

Disintegration time is the duration required for a tablet to disintegrate into small particles under specified test conditions. The test determines whether a tablet breaks down appropriately in the gastrointestinal tract to release the drug for absorption.

Importance:

Drug Release: Ensures the timely release of the active pharmaceutical ingredient (API) for therapeutic action.

Bioavailability: For immediate-release tablets, rapid disintegration is critical for optimal drug absorption.

Compliance with Standards: Helps verify that the formulation meets regulatory requirements.

Pharmacopoeial Limits

The acceptable disintegration time varies by tablet type and intended use, as per pharmacopoeial standards:

Equipment and Method

Equipment:

The **disintegration apparatus** consists of a basket rack assembly with six cylindrical glass tubes, each fitted with a wire mesh at the bottom. The rack is suspended in a water bath maintained at the required temperature (usually **37 ± 2°C**) to simulate physiological conditions.

Testing Procedure:

Sample Preparation: Select six tablets randomly from the batch.

Setup: Place one tablet in each tube of the basket assembly.

Medium: Fill the water bath with the specified medium:

For uncoated/film-coated tablets: Use water or simulated gastric fluid.

For enteric-coated tablets: Use simulated gastric fluid for 2 hours, followed by simulated intestinal fluid.

Operation: The basket assembly is moved up and down in the medium at a frequency of **30 strokes per minute**.

End Point: Note the time at which the last tablet completely disintegrates into particles small enough to pass through the mesh.

Criteria for Passing:

All six tablets must disintegrate within the specified time limit.

If one or two tablets fail, repeat the test with 12 additional tablets. A batch passes if at least 16 of the 18 tablets meet the specified limit.

Factors Influencing Disintegration Time

Formulation Factors:

Disintegrants: Higher concentrations of disintegrants like croscarmellose sodium (2–5%) promote faster disintegration.

Binders: Excessive binders can slow disintegration by increasing tablet hardness.

Manufacturing Factors:

Compression force: Excessive force during compression can reduce porosity, delaying disintegration.

Granule properties: Uniform granule size ensures consistent disintegration.

Example of Disintegration Testing

Sample Data:

Six uncoated tablets are tested in water at 37°C.

Tablets disintegrate in 12, 14, 13, 15, 14, and 13 minutes.

Interpretation:

The mean disintegration time is within the limit of **≤15 minutes** for uncoated tablets, and all tablets pass the test.

2.4.2.2 Dissolution Testing

Principle and Importance of Dissolution Testing

Dissolution testing measures the rate and extent at which the active pharmaceutical ingredient (API) is released from a solid dosage form into a dissolution medium under standardized conditions. It is a crucial quality control test that predicts the drug's in vivo performance by simulating the conditions in the gastrointestinal tract.

Principle: The test assesses how quickly and efficiently a tablet releases its API into a liquid medium. It involves placing the tablet in a specified volume of dissolution medium and measuring the amount of drug dissolved over time.

Importance:

Quality Control: Ensures batch-to-batch consistency in manufacturing.

Predicting Bioavailability: Helps establish in vitro-in vivo correlations (IVIVC).

Formulation Development: Assists in optimizing drug release profiles.

Regulatory Compliance: Required by pharmacopoeias and regulatory agencies for product approval.

Dissolution Apparatus Types (USP I and II)

The United States Pharmacopeia (USP) specifies several types of dissolution apparatus. The most commonly used are **USP Apparatus I (Basket Method)** and **USP Apparatus II (Paddle Method)**.

USP Apparatus I: Basket Method

Description: Consists of a cylindrical basket made of stainless steel mesh attached to a rotating shaft. The tablet is placed inside the basket.

Operation:

The basket rotates at a specified speed (usually 50–100 rpm).

The basket is immersed in a dissolution medium (typically 900 mL) maintained at **37±0.5°C**.

Applications:

Suitable for capsules and dosage forms that tend to float.
Ideal for drugs with slow dissolution rates.

USP Apparatus II: Paddle Method

Description: Features a paddle attached to a rotating shaft. The tablet rests at the bottom of a vessel containing the dissolution medium.

Operation:

The paddle rotates at a specified speed (usually 50–75 rpm).

The vessel contains 900 mL of dissolution medium at $37 \pm 0.5°$C.

Applications:

Widely used for tablets and immediate-release formulations.

Preferred when the dosage form sinks and does not disintegrate slowly.

Examples of Dissolution Profiles

Immediate-Release Tablets

Characteristics: Designed to disintegrate and dissolve rapidly for quick drug absorption.

Dissolution Profile:

Typical Specification: Not less than 80% of the labeled amount dissolved within 30 minutes.

Review Questions

1. What are tablets, and why are they considered one of the most widely used dosage forms?

Answer:

Tablets are solid unit dosage forms containing active pharmaceutical ingredients (APIs) and excipients, compressed into a defined shape and size. They are widely used due to their portability, stability, and ease of administration, making them a convenient option for both patients and manufacturers.

2. What are the ideal characteristics of an ideal tablet?

Answer:

An ideal tablet should have uniformity in weight, size, and content; adequate mechanical strength to withstand physical stress; stability under various environmental conditions; ease of swallowing, especially for pediatric and geriatric patients; and bioavailability that ensures efficient drug release and absorption.

3. What is the significance of uniformity in weight, size, and content in tablet formulations?

Answer:

Uniformity ensures consistent dosing and therapeutic efficacy. Weight and content uniformity ensure that each tablet contains the correct amount of the active drug, which is crucial for maintaining drug potency and avoiding under or overdosing.

4. What is weight uniformity, and how is it regulated?

Answer:

Weight uniformity refers to the consistency in the weight of individual tablets within a batch. The United States Pharmacopeia (USP) specifies acceptable weight variations depending on tablet weight. For tablets weighing less than 80 mg, the weight variation should be ±10%; for tablets weighing between 80–250 mg, it should be ±7.5%; and for tablets weighing over 250 mg, it should be ±5%.

5. What is content uniformity, and what are its acceptable limits?

Answer:
Content uniformity refers to the consistency of active drug content in individual tablets. The active drug content in each tablet should lie within 85–115% of the label claim, with a relative standard deviation (RSD) of ≤6%, ensuring that the drug's therapeutic effect is reliable.

6. What is mechanical strength in tablet formulations, and why is it important?

Answer:
Mechanical strength refers to a tablet's ability to withstand physical stress during handling, packaging, and transportation without breaking or chipping. It is crucial for ensuring the tablet remains intact throughout its journey from manufacturing to patient use.

7. What is the role of hardness in tablet formulation?

Answer:
Hardness refers to the force required to break a tablet. Ideal tablets should have sufficient hardness to resist breaking but should not be so hard that they hinder disintegration, which is important for the drug's dissolution and absorption.

8. What is friability, and what is the acceptable limit for tablet friability?

Answer:
Friability measures a tablet's resistance to abrasion during handling, packaging, and transportation. The acceptable friability limit for tablets is ≤1% weight loss after 100 rotations in a friability tester, indicating that the

tablet is durable enough for the manufacturing and distribution process.

9. Why is the ease of swallowing an important characteristic of tablets?

Answer:
The ease of swallowing is essential to enhance patient compliance, especially for pediatric and geriatric populations. Tablet size, shape, and coating can all influence how easy it is for patients to swallow the tablet.

10. What is the role of film or sugar coating in tablets?

Answer:
Coating can enhance the swallowing ease of tablets, mask unpleasant tastes or odors, and protect the drug from environmental factors like moisture or light. Film coatings are also used to control drug release and improve tablet aesthetics.

11. What is stability in the context of tablet formulation?

Answer:
Stability refers to a tablet's ability to retain its potency, physical integrity, and appearance throughout its shelf life. Stability is influenced by environmental factors such as moisture, temperature, and light.

12. How does bioavailability relate to tablet formulation?

Answer:
Bioavailability refers to the extent and rate at which the active drug is absorbed into systemic circulation. Tablets must disintegrate and dissolve efficiently to release the active ingredient for absorption. Ensuring rapid disintegration and dissolution is crucial for effective bioavailability.

13. What is disintegration, and how does it impact bioavailability?

Answer:
Disintegration refers to the breakdown of a tablet into smaller particles

when exposed to gastrointestinal fluids. Rapid disintegration is essential for the timely release of the active ingredient for absorption, thus ensuring effective bioavailability.

14. What is the role of dissolution in tablet formulations?

Answer:
Dissolution refers to the process by which a drug is released from the tablet and dissolves in the gastrointestinal fluid. A tablet should dissolve rapidly to allow the drug to be absorbed efficiently, impacting both the onset of action and overall therapeutic effect.

15. How are tablets classified based on their route of administration?

Answer:
Tablets can be classified as oral tablets, which are swallowed and absorbed in the gastrointestinal tract, sublingual tablets, which are placed under the tongue for rapid absorption, and buccal tablets, which are placed in the cheek pouch for prolonged release and absorption.

16. How are tablets classified based on their release pattern?

Answer:
Tablets can be classified into immediate-release, controlled-release, sustained-release, and delayed-release tablets, depending on how the drug is released after ingestion. Immediate-release tablets disintegrate and release the drug rapidly, while controlled-release tablets maintain consistent plasma levels over time.

17. What are effervescent tablets, and how do they work?

Answer:
Effervescent tablets contain effervescent agents such as citric acid and sodium bicarbonate, which release carbon dioxide when they come into contact with water. This reaction creates a fizzy solution, aiding in rapid dissolution and ease of administration.

18. What are chewable tablets, and who are they intended for?

Answer:

Chewable tablets are designed to be chewed before swallowing. They are often flavored and intended for patients, particularly pediatric and geriatric populations, who have difficulty swallowing standard tablets.

19. What are orally disintegrating tablets (ODTs)?

Answer:

Orally disintegrating tablets dissolve rapidly in the mouth without the need for water. They are convenient for patients with swallowing difficulties and are often used for medications that require quick onset of action.

20. How are layered tablets used in tablet formulation?

Answer:

Layered tablets contain two or more layers, which can be used to separate incompatible drugs or to provide sequential drug release. These tablets allow multiple therapeutic effects in a single dose.

21. What is the importance of excipients in tablet formulation?

Answer:

Excipients are inactive substances that are added to tablet formulations to enhance manufacturability, stability, and therapeutic efficacy. They help improve properties such as tablet hardness, dissolution rate, and bioavailability.

22. What is the role of binders in tablet formulation?

Answer:

Binders provide cohesiveness to the powder blend, ensuring the formation of mechanically strong tablets. They help enhance particle adhesion during compression and improve the structural integrity of the tablet.

23. How do fillers contribute to tablet formulation?

Answer:

Fillers, also known as diluents, are added to increase the bulk of the tablet when the active pharmaceutical ingredient is present in low doses. They improve the flowability and compressibility of the formulation.

24. What is the function of disintegrants in tablet formulations?

Answer:

Disintegrants facilitate the breakup of tablets into smaller particles upon contact with gastrointestinal fluids, promoting rapid dissolution and absorption of the drug.

25. How do lubricants function in tablet formulation?

Answer:

Lubricants reduce friction between the tablet surface and the die wall during compression and ejection, preventing sticking and ensuring smooth manufacturing.

26. What is the role of glidants in tablet formulation?

Answer:

Glidants improve the flow properties of the powder blend, ensuring uniform filling of tablet dies during manufacturing and minimizing weight variation.

27. What is wet granulation, and why is it important in tablet manufacturing?

Answer:

Wet granulation involves adding a liquid binder to the powder blend to create granules. This method is important for improving flow properties, compressibility, and content uniformity, ensuring high-quality tablets.

28. What are the steps involved in wet granulation?

Answer:

The steps in wet granulation include mixing, wetting the powder blend with a liquid binder, granulation, drying the granules, and sieving the granules to achieve uniform particle size.

29. What is the difference between wet granulation and dry granulation?

Answer:

Wet granulation involves adding a liquid binder to form granules, while dry granulation involves compressing powders into larger aggregates without the use of solvents or heat. Wet granulation is typically used for drugs with poor flow properties, while dry granulation is ideal for moisture-sensitive APIs.

30. What is the role of direct compression in tablet manufacturing?

Answer:

Direct compression is a simpler and faster tablet manufacturing method where powders are directly compressed into tablets without any intermediate granulation steps. It is suitable for APIs with good flowability and compressibility.

31. What is tablet capping, and how can it be prevented?

Answer:

Capping occurs when the upper or lower surface of a tablet separates from the body. It can be prevented by adjusting compression force, optimizing binder concentration, and ensuring proper granule moisture content.

32. What is lamination in tablet manufacturing?

Answer:

Lamination refers to the horizontal splitting of a tablet into distinct layers. It can be prevented by adjusting granule size distribution, using appropriate binders, and avoiding excessive compression.

33. What is sticking in tablet manufacturing, and how can it be avoided?

Answer:
Sticking occurs when the tablet blend adheres to the surfaces of the punches. It can be avoided by increasing lubricant concentration, ensuring proper granule drying, and using anti-adherent coatings.

34. What is picking in tablet manufacturing?

Answer:
Picking is a localized form of sticking, where particles adhere to specific areas of the punch engraving. It can be prevented by ensuring uniform granule drying, increasing lubricant concentration, and modifying punch surfaces.

35. What is mottling in tablets?

Answer:
Mottling refers to uneven color distribution on the tablet surface, often caused by poor distribution of colorants. It can be prevented by premixing colorants and ensuring uniform particle sizes of components.

36. What are the main types of tablet coatings?

Answer:
The main types of tablet coatings are sugar coating, film coating, enteric coating, and controlled-release coating, each serving different purposes such as improving appearance, protecting the drug, and controlling the release of the active ingredient.

37. What is the primary advantage of film coating over sugar coating?

Answer:
Film coating provides better protection against environmental factors like

moisture, light, and oxygen, is faster to apply, and results in thinner layers compared to sugar coating.

38. What is enteric coating used for?

Answer:

Enteric coating is used to protect acid-sensitive drugs from degradation in the stomach and to ensure their release in the small intestine, where the drug can be absorbed effectively.

39. How does the choice of coating polymer affect tablet performance?

Answer:

The choice of polymer determines the dissolution profile, mechanical strength, and protection offered by the coating. For example, cellulose acetate phthalate is used for enteric coatings, while hydroxypropyl methylcellulose is used for immediate-release film coatings.

40. What is the purpose of using plasticizers in film coatings?

Answer:

Plasticizers are used to enhance the flexibility and elasticity of the film coating, reducing the risk of cracking and improving the durability of the coating.

41. What are some examples of enteric-coated drugs?

Answer:

Examples include omeprazole, aspirin (low-dose), mesalamine, and diclofenac, all of which benefit from enteric coating to protect the drug from gastric acid and improve therapeutic effectiveness.

42. What are the advantages of using enteric coatings in tablet formulations?

Answer:

Enteric coatings protect acid-sensitive APIs, reduce gastric irritation from drugs like aspirin, and allow for site-specific drug release, particularly for drugs intended for absorption in the intestines.

43. How do dissolution tests ensure the quality of tablet formulations?

Answer:

Dissolution tests ensure that the tablet releases its API at the correct rate and extent, providing predictive data for the drug's bioavailability and therapeutic effect.

44. What is the importance of disintegration time in tablet testing?

Answer:

Disintegration time is critical in determining how quickly a tablet breaks down in the gastrointestinal tract, influencing drug release and absorption, which directly affects bioavailability.

45. What is the typical limit for disintegration time for uncoated tablets?

Answer:

The USP specifies that uncoated tablets should disintegrate within 30 minutes in the dissolution medium.

46. What are some factors that affect disintegration time?

Answer:

Factors include tablet hardness, binder concentration, disintegrant type and concentration, and granule properties such as size and moisture content.

47. How is dissolution testing conducted for tablets?

Answer:

Dissolution testing is conducted using specialized equipment like the USP

Apparatus I (Basket Method) or Apparatus II (Paddle Method), where tablets are immersed in a dissolution medium, and the amount of drug released is measured over time.

48. What is the typical dissolution profile for immediate-release tablets?

Answer:

For immediate-release tablets, the dissolution profile typically specifies that at least 80% of the drug should dissolve within 30 minutes.

49. What is the purpose of using specific dissolution methods, such as the Basket or Paddle Method?

Answer:

These methods simulate the conditions of the gastrointestinal tract to predict the rate and extent of drug release, helping ensure that the drug will be absorbed efficiently and effectively in the body.

50. What are the advantages of controlled-release tablets?

Answer:

Controlled-release tablets maintain consistent plasma drug levels over an extended period, reducing the frequency of dosing, improving patient compliance, and providing prolonged therapeutic effects.

MCQs

1. *What is the primary advantage of tablets as a dosage form?*

a) Easy to administer
b) Expensive to produce
c) Requires refrigeration
d) Only suitable for oral administration
   Answer: a) Easy to administer

2. *Which of the following is NOT an ideal characteristic of tablets?*

a) Uniformity in weight
b) High hardness
c) Stability
d) Inconsistent disintegration
   Answer: d) Inconsistent disintegration

3. *What is the acceptable weight variation for tablets weighing less than 80 mg according to USP?*

a) ±1%
b) ±5%
c) ±10%
d) ±15%
   Answer: c) ±10%

4. *Which of the following is an example of a tablet that may fail weight uniformity due to inconsistent granulation?*

a) Paracetamol tablets
b) Aspirin tablets
c) Ibuprofen tablets
d) Cetirizine tablets

Answer: b) Aspirin tablets

5. What is the acceptable range of active drug content in tablets for content uniformity according to USP?

a) 80–120%
b) 85–115%
c) 90–110%
d) 100–120%
   Answer: b) 85–115%

6. What does mechanical strength of a tablet refer to?

a) Its ability to disintegrate rapidly
b) Its ability to resist physical stress during handling and transportation
c) Its resistance to moisture
d) Its dissolution rate
   Answer: b) Its ability to resist physical stress during handling and transportation

7. What is the typical hardness range for standard tablets?

a) 1–3 kp
b) 4–8 kp
c) 9–12 kp
d) 13–15 kp
   Answer: b) 4–8 kp

8. What is the acceptable friability limit for tablets according to pharmacopoeial standards?

a) ≤5%
b) ≤2%
c) ≤1%
d) ≤0.5%
   Answer: c) ≤1%

9. Which of the following is an example of a tablet that meets the friability requirements due to robust excipient binding?

a) Metformin tablets
b) Vitamin C tablets
c) Ibuprofen tablets
d) Aspirin tablets
   Answer: a) Metformin tablets

10. What should be the primary consideration for tablet size and shape in ensuring ease of swallowing?

a) Cost of production
b) Optimal size and shape for patient compliance
c) Increased tablet weight
d) Drug stability
   Answer: b) Optimal size and shape for patient compliance

11. Which type of coating is often used to improve the swallowing of tablets and mask unpleasant tastes?

a) Film coating
b) Sugar coating
c) Enteric coating
d) Controlled-release coating
   Answer: b) Sugar coating

12. What is the USP standard for disintegration time for uncoated tablets?

a) ≤10 minutes
b) ≤20 minutes
c) ≤30 minutes
d) ≤45 minutes
   Answer: c) ≤30 minutes

13. What is bioavailability in the context of tablet formulations?

a) The degree to which the drug reaches systemic circulation and exerts its effect
b) The drug's ability to be absorbed in the stomach
c) The time it takes for a tablet to disintegrate
d) The time it takes for a drug to be eliminated from the body
    Answer: a) The degree to which the drug reaches systemic circulation and exerts its effect

14. Which type of tablets is designed to release the drug rapidly upon ingestion for quick therapeutic action?

a) Immediate-release tablets
b) Controlled-release tablets
c) Sustained-release tablets
d) Delayed-release tablets
    Answer: a) Immediate-release tablets

15. Which type of tablet is formulated to release the drug at a predetermined rate for consistent plasma levels over time?

a) Immediate-release tablets
b) Controlled-release tablets
c) Effervescent tablets
d) Sublingual tablets
    Answer: b) Controlled-release tablets

16. What is the purpose of delayed-release tablets?

a) To release the drug immediately
b) To release the drug after a specified lag time
c) To release the drug over an extended period
d) To mask the taste of the drug
    Answer: b) To release the drug after a specified lag time

17. What is an effervescent tablet?

a) A tablet that dissolves rapidly upon contact with water
b) A tablet that releases gas upon contact with water
c) A tablet that has controlled-release properties
d) A tablet designed to be chewed before swallowing
    Answer: b) A tablet that releases gas upon contact with water

18. Which type of tablet is designed to dissolve rapidly in the mouth without the need for water?

a) Effervescent tablets
b) Chewable tablets
c) Orally disintegrating tablets (ODTs)
d) Film-coated tablets
    Answer: c) Orally disintegrating tablets (ODTs)

19. What is the primary function of a binder in tablet formulation?

a) To ensure the tablet disintegrates properly
b) To provide cohesiveness to the powder blend, ensuring tablet formation
c) To mask the taste of the active pharmaceutical ingredient
d) To reduce friction during compression
    Answer: b) To provide cohesiveness to the powder blend, ensuring tablet formation

20. What is the function of a filler in tablet formulations?

a) To aid in the disintegration of tablets
b) To add bulk when the API is in low doses
c) To improve the tablet's color
d) To enhance the dissolution rate
    Answer: b) To add bulk when the API is in low doses

21. What is the role of disintegrants in tablet formulations?

a) To provide cohesiveness
b) To enhance the flow properties of the powder blend
c) To facilitate the breakup of tablets in gastrointestinal fluids
d) To prevent the tablet from crumbling during packaging
   Answer: c) To facilitate the breakup of tablets in gastrointestinal fluids

22. What is the role of lubricants in tablet formulations?

a) To reduce friction during compression and ejection
b) To help the tablet disintegrate faster
c) To enhance the drug's solubility
d) To improve the appearance of the tablet
   Answer: a) To reduce friction during compression and ejection

23. What is the typical use of glidants in tablet formulations?

a) To reduce friction during compression
b) To improve the flow properties of the powder blend
c) To improve the tablet's dissolution rate
d) To enhance the tablet's mechanical strength
   Answer: b) To improve the flow properties of the powder blend

24. Which of the following excipients is often used as a lubricant in tablet formulations?

a) Magnesium stearate
b) Hydroxypropyl methylcellulose (HPMC)
c) Croscarmellose sodium
d) Microcrystalline cellulose
   Answer: a) Magnesium stearate

25. What is the primary advantage of wet granulation over dry granulation?

a) It requires no binders
b) It uses no heat
c) It improves the flow and compressibility of powders

d) It is faster
   Answer: c) It improves the flow and compressibility of powders

26. Which method of granulation does not involve the use of solvents or heat?

a) Wet granulation
b) Dry granulation
c) Roller compaction
d) Slugging
   Answer: b) Dry granulation

27. What is the main advantage of the roller compaction method in dry granulation?

a) Requires no special equipment
b) Suitable for large-scale production with reduced material loss
c) Involves the use of solvents
d) Requires significant heating
   Answer: b) Suitable for large-scale production with reduced material loss

28. What is the primary disadvantage of slugging in dry granulation?

a) High material loss during milling
b) Requires specialized equipment
c) Limited to small-scale production
d) Long processing time
   Answer: a) High material loss during milling

29. Which of the following is a typical example of a drug that benefits from wet granulation?

a) Paracetamol
b) Ibuprofen
c) Aspirin
d) Metformin

Answer: d) Metformin

30. What is a major disadvantage of sugar coating in tablet manufacturing?

a) High cost due to labor-intensive process
b) Faster processing compared to film coating
c) Minimal increase in tablet weight
d) No effect on tablet aesthetics
   Answer: a) High cost due to labor-intensive process

31. Which coating method is commonly used to mask unpleasant tastes or odors and provide aesthetic appeal?

a) Sugar coating
b) Film coating
c) Enteric coating
d) Controlled-release coating
   Answer: a) Sugar coating

32. Which of the following is the main advantage of film coating over sugar coating?

a) Provides better protection against environmental factors
b) Increases tablet weight by 30–50%
c) Takes more time to process
d) Requires more steps
   Answer: a) Provides better protection against environmental factors

33. What is the role of plasticizers in film coatings?

a) To increase the dissolution rate of the tablet
b) To enhance flexibility and elasticity of the coating
c) To improve tablet hardness
d) To increase the cost of production
   Answer: b) To enhance flexibility and elasticity of the coating

34. Which polymer is commonly used for enteric coatings that protect drugs from stomach acid?

a) Hydroxypropyl methylcellulose (HPMC)
b) Cellulose acetate phthalate (CAP)
c) Polyvinyl alcohol (PVA)
d) Ethylcellulose
Answer: b) Cellulose acetate phthalate (CAP)

35. Which of the following is a key advantage of enteric coating?

a) Protects drugs from gastric acid
b) Increases tablet size
c) Enhances the drug's taste
d) Provides immediate release of the drug
Answer: a) Protects drugs from gastric acid

36. Which polymer is commonly used for controlled-release coatings in tablet formulations?

a) Hydroxypropyl methylcellulose (HPMC)
b) Methacrylic acid copolymers
c) Polyvinyl alcohol (PVA)
d) Cellulose acetate phthalate (CAP)
Answer: b) Methacrylic acid copolymers

37. What is the typical thickness of a film coating applied to a tablet?

a) 50–150 microns
b) 100–300 microns
c) 20–100 microns
d) 150–500 microns
Answer: c) 20–100 microns

38. Which of the following is an example of a drug that benefits from enteric coating?

a) Paracetamol
b) Omeprazole
c) Metformin
d) Vitamin C
   Answer: b) Omeprazole

39. What is the purpose of using titanium dioxide in film coatings?

a) To enhance the color of the tablet
b) To provide opacity and protect light-sensitive drugs
c) To increase the tablet weight
d) To improve the dissolution rate
   Answer: b) To provide opacity and protect light-sensitive drugs

40. What is the primary challenge when using sugar coating in tablet manufacturing?

a) It may lead to a decrease in tablet bioavailability
b) It is labor-intensive and time-consuming
c) It increases the tablet dissolution rate too much
d) It leads to less aesthetic appeal
   Answer: b) It is labor-intensive and time-consuming

41. What is the main role of binders in tablet formulations?

a) To improve the flowability of the powder
b) To increase the stability of the active pharmaceutical ingredient (API)
c) To ensure cohesiveness and mechanical strength during compression
d) To facilitate the dissolution of the drug
   Answer: c) To ensure cohesiveness and mechanical strength during compression

42. Which excipient is commonly used as a disintegrant in tablet formulations?

a) Magnesium stearate
b) Croscarmellose sodium
c) Hydroxypropyl methylcellulose
d) Microcrystalline cellulose
   Answer: b) Croscarmellose sodium

43. Which type of tablet is designed to release the active ingredient in a specific region of the gastrointestinal tract?

a) Immediate-release tablets
b) Enteric-coated tablets
c) Sustained-release tablets
d) Effervescent tablets
   Answer: b) Enteric-coated tablets

44. What is the role of lubricants in tablet manufacturing?

a) To increase tablet weight
b) To reduce friction between the tablet surface and the die wall
c) To enhance the dissolution rate of the drug
d) To improve the taste of the tablet
   Answer: b) To reduce friction between the tablet surface and the die wall

45. What is a common method used to improve the compressibility of powders in tablet formulations?

a) Use of disintegrants
b) Use of lubricants
c) Addition of glidants
d) Use of binders
   Answer: d) Use of binders

46. What is the function of a glidant in tablet formulation?

a) To improve the compressibility of powders
b) To enhance powder flow during tablet production
c) To prevent the tablet from disintegrating
d) To increase tablet hardness
  Answer: b) To enhance powder flow during tablet production

47. Which method of granulation involves adding a liquid binder to the powder blend to create granules?

a) Wet granulation
b) Dry granulation
c) Slugging
d) Direct compression
  Answer: a) Wet granulation

48. What is the main benefit of dry granulation compared to wet granulation?

a) It is more time-consuming
b) It is suitable for moisture-sensitive drugs
c) It enhances the drug's bioavailability
d) It is used to produce smaller tablets
  Answer: b) It is suitable for moisture-sensitive drugs

49. What is the advantage of using roller compaction in dry granulation?

a) It does not require high compression forces
b) It produces uniform granules with minimal wastage
c) It is the most time-consuming method
d) It is ideal for drugs with low compressibility
  Answer: b) It produces uniform granules with minimal wastage

50. What is the role of compression in tablet manufacturing?

a) To liquefy the drug for easier absorption
b) To compact the powder blend into a solid tablet form
c) To dissolve the drug at a controlled rate

d) To reduce the weight of the tablet

Answer: b) To compact the powder blend into a solid tablet form

CHAPTER THREE

Liquid Orals

3.1 Formulation and Manufacturing

3.1.1 Solutions

Pharmaceutical solutions are homogeneous liquid preparations where one or more active pharmaceutical ingredients (APIs) are completely dissolved in a suitable solvent or solvent mixture. These formulations are essential for delivering drugs in liquid form, particularly for pediatric and geriatric patients who may have difficulty swallowing solid dosage forms. The importance of solutions lies in their rapid onset of action, as drugs in solution form are readily absorbed, leading to faster therapeutic effects. They also offer flexible dosing, allowing precise dose adjustments, and ease of administration, making them ideal for patients with swallowing difficulties or requiring nasogastric administration.

Overview of Solutions

Pharmaceutical solutions are classified into different types based on their composition and use. Syrups are concentrated aqueous solutions containing sugar or sugar substitutes, such as cough syrups with APIs like dextromethorphan or guaifenesin. Elixirs are clear, sweetened hydroalcoholic solutions containing ethanol (typically 5–40% v/v), such as chlorpheniramine maleate elixir used as an antihistamine. Mouthwashes are designed for local action in the oral cavity and often contain antiseptics or astringents, such as chlorhexidine mouthwash for oral hygiene. Topical solutions are applied to the skin or mucous membranes for local effects, such as hydrogen peroxide solution used as an antiseptic.

The components of pharmaceutical solutions include solvents, solutes, and stabilizers. Solvents dissolve the API and excipients to form a homogeneous mixture, with water being the most common solvent due to its safety and availability. Other solvents include ethanol, often used in elixirs to aid in the solubilization of poorly water-soluble APIs (concentration typically 5–40% v/v), and glycerin, which acts as a co-solvent while imparting viscosity and sweetness. Solutes include active ingredients such as paracetamol in syrups, sweeteners like sucrose or artificial sweeteners to improve palatability, and preservatives such as methylparaben or sodium benzoate to prevent microbial growth. Stabilizers protect the solution from degradation due to oxidation, light, or pH changes, with ascorbic acid commonly used as an antioxidant to prevent oxidation of APIs.

The manufacturing process of pharmaceutical solutions involves several key steps, beginning with solubilization, where the API and other solutes are dissolved in the solvent, often using co-solvents or solubilizing agents for poorly soluble drugs. This is followed by mixing, where a high-speed mixer or stirrer ensures uniform distribution of all components, reducing particle aggregation and enhancing dissolution. Filtration is then performed to remove undissolved particles or impurities, often using 0.2-micron membrane filters for sterile solutions. The final step, deaeration, involves the removal of dissolved gases like oxygen to prevent oxidation and foaming, achieved through vacuum application or nitrogen purging.

For example, the manufacturing of paracetamol syrup involves specific composition and processing steps. The composition includes an API concentration of 120 mg/5 mL of paracetamol, purified water as a solvent up to 1000 mL, 700 g of sucrose as a sweetener, 0.1% sodium benzoate as a preservative, and 0.05% citric acid as a stabilizer. The process involves dissolving paracetamol in warm purified water with gentle stirring, followed by the sequential addition of sodium benzoate, citric acid, and sucrose, ensuring complete dissolution. The solution is then filtered and deaerated before being packaged for distribution, ensuring product quality and stability.

3.1.2 Suspensions

Suspensions are biphasic liquid dosage forms in which fine particles of an insoluble active pharmaceutical ingredient (API) are uniformly dispersed throughout a liquid medium. Unlike solutions, the API remains suspended rather than dissolving, requiring stabilization to prevent aggregation and sedimentation. These formulations are particularly useful for administering poorly soluble drugs, making them ideal for medications like antacids (e.g., aluminum hydroxide and magnesium hydroxide). They are also preferred for pediatric and geriatric patients who may struggle with swallowing solid dosage forms, as seen in paracetamol suspensions. Additionally, suspensions serve topical applications, such as calamine lotion for skin irritation.

Basics of Suspensions

The key components of suspensions include the dispersed phase, dispersion medium, stabilizers, and preservatives. The dispersed phase consists of API particles, typically 1–50 microns in size, ensuring therapeutic action without dissolution, as seen in ibuprofen suspensions. The dispersion medium, often water, serves as the liquid phase, though oils like mineral oil are used in specialized formulations such as depot injections. Stabilizers, including suspending agents like xanthan gum (0.2–1% w/w) and wetting agents like polysorbates (e.g., Tween 80), maintain suspension uniformity by preventing particle aggregation. Preservatives, such as methylparaben (0.1% w/w) and sorbic acid (0.1–0.2%), inhibit microbial growth, ensuring product stability, as seen in sodium benzoate-preserved multivitamin suspensions.

The manufacturing process of suspensions involves several critical steps: preparation of the dispersed phase, where API particles are milled or micronized for uniformity; preparation of the dispersion medium, where stabilizers, wetting agents, and preservatives are dissolved; mixing, where the dispersed phase is added under continuous agitation to ensure even distribution; and homogenization, which applies high shear forces to improve stability and prevent particle aggregation. Quality control assessments include testing for particle size, sedimentation rate, and redispersibility.

Key processes in suspension manufacturing include wetting, dispersion, and homogenization, each crucial for ensuring product stability and uniformity. Wetting displaces air from hydrophobic API particles to enhance dispersion in the liquid phase, aided by wetting agents like Tween 80, as used in paracetamol suspensions. Dispersion involves breaking up particle clumps using agitation, commonly achieved through high-shear mixers, ensuring even particle distribution and preventing aggregation or caking. Homogenization further refines particle size and distribution, often using high-pressure homogenizers or colloid mills, ensuring stable suspensions, as seen in ibuprofen formulations.

Critical parameters for suspension stability include particle size and sedimentation volume (F). Ideal suspensions maintain a particle size of 1–50 µm, balancing sedimentation rate and redispersibility. Large particles settle quickly, causing dosing inconsistencies, while excessively fine particles may lead to caking, making redispersion difficult. Sedimentation volume (F) measures stability by comparing sediment to total suspension volume, with F=1 indicating stability, F<1 indicating significant sedimentation, and F>1 suggesting fluffy, easily redispersed sediment.

Examples of marketed suspensions highlight their versatility. Pediatric paracetamol suspension (120 mg/5 mL) is widely used for fever and pain relief, stabilized with xanthan gum and preserved with sodium benzoate. Ibuprofen suspension (100 mg/5 mL) functions as an anti-inflammatory and antipyretic, using Tween 80 as a wetting agent and methylparaben as a preservative. Antacid suspensions containing aluminum hydroxide and magnesium hydroxide neutralize stomach acid, with methylcellulose acting as a suspending agent and sorbitol as a sweetener. These formulations demonstrate the critical role of suspensions in ensuring effective and stable drug delivery.

3.1.3 Emulsions

Emulsions are biphasic liquid dosage forms composed of two immiscible liquids, where one liquid is dispersed as small droplets (dispersed phase) within another (continuous phase), stabilized by emulsifying agents to prevent separation. They are classified into oil-in-water (O/W) emulsions, where the oil phase is dispersed in the water phase, commonly used for oral and topical applications like milk and castor oil emulsions, and water-in-oil (W/O) emulsions, where water droplets are dispersed in the oil phase, often used in creams and ointments such as cold cream.

Emulsifying agents play a crucial role in stabilizing emulsions by reducing interfacial tension, forming protective films, and enhancing viscosity. Natural emulsifiers like acacia (gum Arabic) are commonly used for O/W emulsions, forming a colloidal protective layer around oil droplets, while tragacanth serves as an additional stabilizer. Synthetic emulsifiers include polysorbates (e.g., Tween 80), which are hydrophilic and suitable for O/W emulsions, and sorbitan esters (e.g., Span 60), which are lipophilic and used in W/O emulsions. These agents stabilize emulsions by reducing interfacial tension, forming mechanical barriers, imparting electrostatic repulsion, and increasing viscosity to reduce droplet movement.

Emulsions have diverse pharmaceutical applications, including oral emulsions that enhance the bioavailability of lipid-soluble drugs, such as cod liver oil emulsions; topical emulsions like moisturizing creams and sunscreens that hydrate and protect the skin; and parenteral emulsions used for intravenous administration of lipid-based nutrients, such as Intralipid®, a fat emulsion for parenteral nutrition.

The manufacturing of emulsions involves several critical steps, beginning with phase separation, where the oil and water phases are prepared separately. The oil phase consists of lipophilic active ingredients, oils, and emulsifiers, while the water phase contains hydrophilic ingredients, emulsifiers, preservatives, and stabilizers. Both phases are heated to a similar temperature (50–70°C) before mixing. Homogenization follows, involving high-shear mixing or homogenizers to break down large droplets into a fine dispersion (1–10 microns), ensuring stability. During emulsification, emulsifying agents stabilize the mixture, preventing droplet coalescence. The final formulation is gradually cooled, filtered, and packaged under aseptic conditions to ensure quality and stability.

Examples of pharmaceutical emulsions include vitamin D emulsions, which improve bioavailability by dissolving the vitamin in the oil phase and stabilizing it with emulsifiers like polysorbates; cod liver oil emulsions, stabilized with acacia or tragacanth; and topical sunscreen emulsions, formulated as W/O emulsions for water resistance and skin hydration.

The filling and packaging of liquid oral formulations, including emulsions, suspensions, and syrups, are critical to ensuring product safety, stability, and dosing accuracy. The filling process employs specialized equipment such as volumetric fillers and peristaltic pumps. Volumetric fillers operate by drawing a predetermined volume of liquid into a calibrated cylinder and dispensing it into containers, offering high precision (±1% variation) and suitability for high-volume production, such as paracetamol syrups. Peristaltic pumps, on the other hand, use a wave-like motion to propel liquid through flexible tubing, making them ideal for sterile formulations like oral vaccines due to their minimal contamination risk and accurate dosing.

After filling, the packaging process involves selecting suitable containers, such as amber glass or plastic bottles for light-sensitive products. Containers are sealed with tamper-evident or child-resistant caps to ensure safety. Labeling follows, providing essential information like dosage instructions, batch numbers, and expiration dates. The final step includes secondary packaging, where filled containers are packed into cartons with informational inserts.

Key considerations in filling and packaging include ensuring accurate dosing through calibrated equipment, maintaining sterility for sensitive formulations, selecting appropriate packaging materials to protect against environmental factors like light and moisture, and adhering to pharmacopoeial and regulatory standards for quality assurance and patient safety.

Overview of Emulsions

Types of Packaging for Liquid Oral Formulations

The packaging of liquid oral formulations plays a critical role in maintaining product stability, ensuring safety, and meeting regulatory requirements. The types of packaging include bottles, closures, and labels, each chosen based on the formulation's characteristics, intended use, and regulatory standards.

Bottles

Bottles are the most common primary packaging for liquid oral formulations. They are available in two main materials, glass and plastic, each with distinct advantages and compatibility considerations.

Glass bottles offer superior inertness and are less likely to interact chemically with the formulation. They are ideal for sensitive products, such as acidic or alkaline solutions, as they provide excellent protection against environmental factors like light and oxygen. Amber glass bottles are particularly useful for light-sensitive formulations, such as certain vitamins and APIs. However, glass bottles are heavier, more fragile, and less suitable for large-scale transportation or products intended for pediatric use.

Plastic bottles are lightweight, durable, and shatter-resistant, making them a preferred choice for pediatric formulations or products that require convenient handling. Plastics like polyethylene terephthalate (PET) and high-density polyethylene (HDPE) are commonly used due to their chemical resistance and stability. However, plastics may allow slight permeability to gases like oxygen or moisture, which can affect certain sensitive formulations. The selection of plastic materials should consider compatibility with the product, ensuring that no leaching or degradation occurs.

Closures

Closures are critical to maintaining the integrity and safety of the packaged product. Child-resistant caps are widely used for liquid oral formulations, especially for pediatric medications, to prevent accidental ingestion. These closures often feature a push-and-turn mechanism that makes them difficult for children to open but convenient for adults. In addition to safety, closures must provide an airtight seal to protect the formulation from contamination, evaporation, or degradation. Tamper-evident closures are another important feature, offering visual assurance to the consumer that the product has not been opened or altered.

Labels

Labels serve as an essential communication tool, providing critical information about the product's usage, storage, and regulatory compliance. Regulatory requirements for labeling include the name of the product, the active ingredient(s), concentration, batch number, manufacturing date, and expiry date. Additionally, labels must display dosage instructions, warnings, and any special storage conditions, such as "Store below 25°C" or "Protect from light." Labels should also include instructions for proper handling and precautions to ensure safe and effective use.

For liquid oral formulations, it is essential that labels are designed to remain intact and legible under various conditions, including exposure to moisture or chemicals. Labels for pediatric products may also include specific dosing instructions using calibrated measuring devices like syringes or cups.

Importance of Protection from Light, Moisture, and Air in Liquid Oral Packaging

Protecting liquid oral formulations from environmental factors such as light, moisture, and air is critical to maintaining their stability, efficacy, and safety. These factors can significantly affect the physical and chemical properties of the active pharmaceutical ingredient (API) and excipients, leading to degradation or reduced therapeutic effectiveness.

Light Protection

Many pharmaceutical compounds are sensitive to light, particularly ultraviolet (UV) radiation, which can catalyze degradation reactions such as oxidation or photolysis. Light-sensitive APIs, such as vitamins, antibiotics, and some hormones, require UV-protective packaging to prevent these adverse reactions. Amber-colored glass bottles are commonly used for their excellent UV-blocking properties while maintaining visibility of the liquid for quality checks. For plastic packaging, UV-stabilized materials like polyethylene terephthalate (PET) or high-density polyethylene (HDPE) may be employed, with added pigments or coatings to enhance light resistance. For example, riboflavin (vitamin B2) syrups are typically packaged in amber glass or UV-protective PET bottles to ensure stability during storage and use.

Moisture Protection

Moisture ingress can lead to dilution, precipitation, or microbial growth in aqueous liquid formulations. For hygroscopic APIs, exposure to moisture can cause caking or changes in solubility. Packaging materials must be carefully chosen to provide an effective barrier against moisture. Glass bottles inherently offer excellent moisture resistance, while plastic bottles may require special coatings or multilayer constructions to enhance their barrier properties. Closures with airtight seals, such as tamper-evident or child-resistant caps, further reduce the risk of moisture entry. For example, antacid suspensions containing aluminum hydroxide or magnesium hydroxide are packaged in moisture-resistant plastic bottles to maintain their effectiveness.

Air Protection

Exposure to air, particularly oxygen, can accelerate oxidation of APIs and excipients, leading to loss of potency or the development of unwanted degradation products. Antioxidants like ascorbic acid or sodium metabisulfite are often added to formulations to mitigate this risk, but appropriate packaging remains a primary defense. Packaging should minimize headspace in bottles and use materials with low oxygen permeability. For highly sensitive formulations, nitrogen flushing is employed during filling to replace oxygen in the headspace. For example, iron supplements in liquid form are packaged in glass or plastic bottles with minimal headspace to prevent oxidation of ferrous ions.

Examples of Packaging for Various Liquid Oral Dosage Forms

Syrups (e.g., Paracetamol Syrup):

Paracetamol syrups are typically packaged in amber PET bottles to protect the formulation from light and ensure child safety with child-resistant caps. Labels include precise dosage instructions for pediatric use, often accompanied by a calibrated measuring device like a dosing cup.

Suspensions (e.g., Ibuprofen Suspension):
Ibuprofen suspensions are packaged in opaque HDPE bottles to prevent light exposure. Moisture-resistant closures are used to maintain stability, and the packaging is designed to facilitate easy pouring or dosing for pediatric administration.

Elixirs (e.g., Chlorpheniramine Maleate Elixir):
Elixirs, being hydroalcoholic solutions, are packaged in glass bottles to avoid interactions with plastic and ensure alcohol retention. Clear or amber bottles may be used depending on the light sensitivity of the formulation.

Mouthwashes (e.g., Chlorhexidine Mouthwash):
Chlorhexidine mouthwash is often packaged in transparent or semi-transparent PET bottles to allow visibility while maintaining UV protection. Screw-top or flip-top caps are used for user convenience.

Vitamin Emulsions (e.g., Vitamin D Emulsion):
Vitamin D emulsions are highly sensitive to light and oxidation. They are typically packaged in amber glass bottles with airtight droppers or caps to provide precise dosing while maintaining stability.

3.3 Quality Control

3.3.1 Evaluation of Solutions

The quality control evaluation of pharmaceutical solutions involves several critical parameters to ensure that the product is safe, effective, and meets regulatory standards. Solutions, being homogeneous liquid preparations, must maintain specific characteristics such as clarity, pH compatibility, and precise active ingredient concentration.

Parameters for Solution Evaluation

Clarity and Visual Inspection
The clarity of pharmaceutical solutions is a key indicator of their quality and acceptability. Solutions must be free of visible particles, fibers, or other contaminants that could affect safety or indicate instability.

Procedure:
The solution is inspected under suitable lighting conditions against a white and black background. Any turbidity or particulate matter is noted.

Significance:
Visual inspection ensures that the solution meets aesthetic and safety

standards, particularly for products like syrups and oral solutions.

Example:

A pediatric paracetamol syrup should appear clear and free of sediment or cloudiness. Any presence of undissolved material could indicate poor formulation or degradation.

pH Measurement

The pH of a pharmaceutical solution plays a crucial role in its stability, solubility, and compatibility with the gastrointestinal (GI) tract. Most oral solutions have a pH range between 3 and 9 to ensure patient safety and therapeutic efficacy.

Procedure:

The pH is measured using a calibrated pH meter at room temperature. The sample is prepared by drawing a small aliquot of the solution directly into the electrode.

Significance:

Maintaining the pH within the desired range prevents irritation of the GI tract and ensures the stability of the active pharmaceutical ingredient.

Example:

A vitamin C solution typically has a pH around 4 to 5. Deviations from this range may indicate degradation, particularly oxidative changes that could affect potency.

Assay of Active Ingredients

The concentration of the active pharmaceutical ingredient (API) in the solution must be evaluated to ensure compliance with the labeled claim. This ensures dosing accuracy and therapeutic efficacy.

Methods:

High-Performance Liquid Chromatography (HPLC): Provides precise and accurate quantification of APIs, particularly in complex mixtures.

UV-Visible Spectrophotometry: Suitable for APIs with distinct absorbance characteristics, offering a rapid and cost-effective method for routine analysis.

Acceptance Limits:

Regulatory standards typically require the API content to be within **90–110% of the label claim** to account for analytical and manufacturing variations.

Example:

In a paracetamol oral solution labeled to contain 120 mg/5 mL, an HPLC assay might yield 118 mg/5 mL. This result (98.3%) falls within the acceptable range, confirming product compliance.

3.3.2 Evaluation of Suspensions

The quality control evaluation of suspensions is essential to ensure their stability, uniformity, and therapeutic efficacy. Suspensions, being biphasic systems, are prone to physical changes such as sedimentation or particle aggregation. Key tests for assessing the quality of suspensions include redispersibility, sedimentation volume, particle size distribution, and viscosity.

Tests for Suspension Quality

1. Redispersibility

Redispersibility assesses the ability of a suspension to regain its uniformity after settling. Since sedimentation is natural in suspensions, it is crucial that the sediment can be easily and completely redispersed upon shaking.

Test Method:

The suspension is allowed to stand undisturbed for a specified period to allow settling. Afterward, the container is shaken gently to redistribute the particles uniformly. The time and effort required for redispersion are recorded.

Significance:

Redispersibility ensures dose uniformity, as non-uniform suspensions can lead to inaccurate dosing.

Example:

A pediatric **paracetamol suspension** (120 mg/5 mL) should fully redisperse within 30 seconds of gentle shaking, ensuring even particle distribution.

2. Sedimentation Volume (F)

Sedimentation volume evaluates the stability of a suspension by measuring the volume of sediment formed relative to the total volume of the suspension.

Interpretation:

$F=1$: Stable suspension with no significant sedimentation.

$F<1$: Indicates sedimentation has occurred, which may still be acceptable if the sediment is easily redispersible.

$F>1$: Fluffy sediment occupies a larger volume than the original suspension, which may indicate excessive flocculation.

Example:

A **multivitamin suspension** has Vu=40 mL and Vo=100 mL

F=0.4

This indicates partial sedimentation but acceptable redispersibility.

3. Particle Size Distribution

Particle size distribution is a critical parameter that affects the stability, appearance, and bioavailability of suspensions.

Method:

Laser diffraction is commonly used to measure particle size and distribution. The suspension is analyzed to determine the range and uniformity of particle sizes, typically expressed as a mean diameter (e.g., $D50D\_\{50\}D50$, the diameter at which 50% of the particles are smaller).

Typical Range:

Pharmaceutical suspensions typically have particle sizes in the range of **1–50 microns.**

Example:

For an **ibuprofen suspension**, the mean particle size is measured as 10 microns, ensuring good stability and uniformity.

4. Viscosity

Viscosity measures the flow properties of a suspension, which influence its stability, ease of pouring, and patient compliance.

Method:

A Brookfield viscometer is used to measure viscosity at different shear rates. Viscosity is expressed in centipoise (cps).

Typical Range:

The viscosity of pharmaceutical suspensions typically falls between **500–5000 cps**, depending on the formulation and intended use.

Significance:

Higher viscosity reduces sedimentation but should not impede redispersibility or administration.

Example:

A pediatric **paracetamol suspension** may have a viscosity of 2000 cps, ensuring a balance between stability and ease of use.

Examples of Marketed Suspensions and Evaluation Results

Paracetamol Suspension (120 mg/5 mL):

Redispersibility: Uniform within 20 seconds of gentle shaking.

Sedimentation volume: $F=0.5F = 0.5F=0.5$, indicating acceptable stability.

Particle size: Mean diameter of 15 microns.

Viscosity: 1800 cps, ensuring good stability and easy pouring.

Ibuprofen Suspension (100 mg/5 mL):

Redispersibility: Fully uniform within 30 seconds.

Sedimentation volume: F=0.6F = 0.6F=0.6, with easily redispersible sediment.

Particle size: 10 microns, ensuring smooth consistency.

Viscosity: 2200 cps for stability and ease of dosing.

Antacid Suspension (Aluminum Hydroxide and Magnesium Hydroxide):

Redispersibility: Uniform within 15 seconds of shaking.

Sedimentation volume: F=0.8F = 0.8F=0.8, indicating good stability.

Particle size: Mean diameter of 20 microns.

Viscosity: 4000 cps, ensuring suspension remains stable during storage.

3.3.3 Evaluation of Emulsions

The quality control evaluation of emulsions ensures their stability, homogeneity, and therapeutic efficacy. Emulsions are biphasic systems that require careful monitoring of their physical and chemical properties to prevent separation or degradation over time. Key evaluation parameters include phase separation, globule size distribution, zeta potential, and viscosity, each providing insights into the emulsion's stability and functionality.

Evaluation Parameters for Emulsions

1. Phase Separation

Phase separation refers to the separation of the dispersed and continuous phases in an emulsion, indicating instability. The centrifugation test is commonly used to assess the likelihood of phase separation under accelerated conditions.

Test Method:

The emulsion is subjected to centrifugation at a specified speed (e.g., **3000 rpm for 15–30 minutes**) to simulate gravitational forces. Any signs of creaming, sedimentation, or coalescence are noted.

Significance:

Phase separation indicates instability and poor emulsifier performance. A stable emulsion remains homogenous, with no visible separation during the test.

Example:

A vitamin D oil-in-water (O/W) emulsion shows no phase separation after centrifugation, confirming its stability.

2. Globule Size Distribution

The size of dispersed globules is a critical factor influencing the stability, appearance, and bioavailability of emulsions. Uniform and small globule sizes reduce the likelihood of coalescence and creaming.

Measurement Methods:

Optical Microscopy: Used for direct visualization of globules, often with staining to enhance contrast.

Dynamic Light Scattering (DLS): Provides precise size distribution data for globules within the range of **0.1–10 microns.**

Significance:

Smaller globules (1–5 microns for pharmaceutical emulsions) enhance physical stability by reducing gravitational separation.

Example:

A topical sunscreen emulsion has a mean globule size of **2 microns,** ensuring uniform application and prolonged stability.

3. Zeta Potential

Zeta potential measures the surface charge of emulsion globules, which determines their electrostatic stability. A high absolute value of zeta potential prevents globule coalescence by creating electrostatic repulsion between droplets.

Typical Range:

Stable emulsions generally have zeta potential values of **±30 mV or greater.**

Positive or negative values indicate strong repulsive forces, ensuring stability.

Measurement:

Zeta potential is measured using techniques like electrophoretic mobility analysis.

Significance:

Low zeta potential values (<±20 mV) may result in instability, requiring adjustments in the emulsifier concentration or type.

Example:

A soybean oil emulsion for parenteral nutrition exhibits a zeta potential of **-35 mV,** indicating excellent stability.

4. Viscosity

Viscosity plays a crucial role in the physical stability of emulsions by reducing the rate of phase separation. High viscosity slows down creaming and sedimentation, enhancing the shelf life of the emulsion.

Measurement:
A Brookfield viscometer is commonly used to assess viscosity, expressed in centipoise (cps).

Typical Range:
The viscosity of emulsions varies widely depending on their type and application. For example, oral emulsions typically have viscosities between **500–5000 cps**, while topical emulsions may exhibit higher viscosities for enhanced application properties.

Example:
A cod liver oil emulsion exhibits a viscosity of **1500 cps**, ensuring adequate pourability and stability during storage.

Examples of Defects and Remedies

Creaming

Description: The dispersed phase rises to the top or settles at the bottom, forming a layer.

Cause: Large globule size or low viscosity of the continuous phase.

Remedy: Reduce globule size through homogenization or increase viscosity using thickeners like xanthan gum.

Coalescence

Description: Globules merge to form larger droplets, leading to complete phase separation.

Cause: Inadequate emulsifier concentration or low zeta potential.

Remedy: Optimize emulsifier type and concentration; adjust zeta potential by using ionic stabilizers.

Flocculation

Description: Globules aggregate without merging, forming clumps.

Cause: Insufficient repulsion between droplets.

Remedy: Improve electrostatic stability by modifying emulsifier properties or using charge-enhancing agents.

Breaking

Description: Irreversible phase separation, rendering the emulsion unusable.

Cause: High temperature or mechanical stress during storage.

Remedy: Enhance formulation stability with heat-resistant emulsifiers and proper storage conditions.

Review Questions

1. What are pharmaceutical solutions, and why are they important?

Answer:
Pharmaceutical solutions are homogeneous liquid preparations in which one or more active pharmaceutical ingredients (APIs) are completely dissolved in a solvent or solvent mixture. They are important for providing drugs in liquid form, offering rapid absorption, precise dosing, and ease of administration, particularly for patients who have difficulty swallowing tablets.

2. What types of pharmaceutical solutions are commonly used?

Answer:
Common types of pharmaceutical solutions include syrups, elixirs, mouthwashes, and topical solutions. Syrups are concentrated aqueous solutions containing sugar, elixirs are sweetened hydroalcoholic solutions, mouthwashes are for local oral action, and topical solutions are applied to the skin or mucous membranes.

3. What is the role of solvents in pharmaceutical solutions?

Answer:
Solvents are used to dissolve the active pharmaceutical ingredients (APIs) and excipients, forming a homogeneous mixture. Water is the most commonly used solvent due to its safety and availability, but other solvents like ethanol and glycerin are also used, depending on the solubility requirements of the API.

4. How do stabilizers contribute to pharmaceutical solutions?

Answer:

Stabilizers protect the solution from degradation due to factors like oxidation, light, or changes in pH. Ascorbic acid is an example of an antioxidant used to prevent the oxidation of APIs in solutions.

5. Describe the general manufacturing process of pharmaceutical solutions.

Answer:

The manufacturing process involves solubilizing the API and excipients in a suitable solvent, followed by mixing to ensure uniform distribution. Filtration is done to remove undissolved particles, and deaeration is performed to remove dissolved gases to prevent oxidation and foaming.

6. What are the key components of pharmaceutical suspensions?

Answer:

Pharmaceutical suspensions consist of the dispersed phase (fine particles of API), dispersion medium (usually water), stabilizers (like suspending agents), and preservatives to prevent microbial growth.

7. Why are suspensions used for poorly soluble drugs?

Answer:

Suspensions are ideal for poorly soluble drugs because they allow the active ingredient to remain suspended in the liquid form rather than dissolved, ensuring effective delivery of the drug.

8. What is the role of stabilizers in suspensions?

Answer:

Stabilizers, such as xanthan gum or polysorbates, prevent the aggregation and sedimentation of particles, ensuring uniform dispersion and stability in the suspension.

9. How are suspensions manufactured?

Answer:

The manufacturing process includes the preparation of the dispersed phase (by milling or micronizing the API), preparation of the dispersion medium (dissolving stabilizers and preservatives), mixing, and homogenization to improve stability and prevent particle aggregation.

10. What is sedimentation volume (F) in suspension quality control?

Answer:

Sedimentation volume (F) measures the volume of sediment relative to the total suspension volume. A value of F=1 indicates stability, F<1 indicates sedimentation, and F>1 suggests a fluffy sediment that can be easily redispersed.

11. How does particle size influence the stability of suspensions?

Answer:

Smaller particle sizes (1–50 microns) enhance the stability of suspensions by reducing the rate of sedimentation. Large particles settle quickly, leading to dosing inconsistencies, while excessively fine particles may lead to caking.

12. What is the importance of redispersibility in suspensions?

Answer:

Redispersibility ensures uniformity in dosing. It measures how easily a suspension can be re-homogenized after settling. Poor redispersibility can lead to inaccurate dosing and therapeutic inefficacy.

13. How is viscosity related to the stability of suspensions?

Answer:

Viscosity affects the flow properties of the suspension, with higher viscosity reducing sedimentation and improving stability. However, excessive viscosity can make the suspension difficult to pour and administer.

14. What is the function of emulsions in pharmaceutical formulations?

Answer:

Emulsions are biphasic systems where one liquid (dispersed phase) is finely dispersed within another immiscible liquid (continuous phase). They are used to deliver both lipophilic and hydrophilic drugs, improving the bioavailability of poorly water-soluble drugs and enhancing topical formulations.

15. What are the two main types of emulsions, and how do they differ?

Answer:

The two main types of emulsions are oil-in-water (O/W) and water-in-oil (W/O). In O/W emulsions, the oil phase is dispersed in water, commonly used for oral and topical applications. In W/O emulsions, water droplets are dispersed in oil, often used in creams and ointments for skin protection and hydration.

16. What is the role of emulsifying agents in emulsions?

Answer:

Emulsifying agents reduce the interfacial tension between the two immiscible liquids, stabilizing the emulsion by forming protective layers around the droplets and preventing phase separation.

17. What are natural and synthetic emulsifiers, and how do they differ?

Answer:

Natural emulsifiers include substances like acacia and tragacanth, which are used in O/W emulsions. Synthetic emulsifiers include polysorbates (e.g., Tween 80) for O/W emulsions and sorbitan esters (e.g., Span 60) for W/O emulsions. Natural emulsifiers tend to be biodegradable, while synthetic emulsifiers may offer more consistent performance.

18. How do emulsions improve drug bioavailability?

Answer:
Emulsions enhance the solubility of lipophilic drugs by dispersing them in a suitable medium, increasing the surface area available for absorption, thus improving bioavailability.

19. What is the manufacturing process of emulsions?

Answer:
The manufacturing process involves preparing the oil and water phases separately, heating them to a similar temperature, followed by homogenization to break down large droplets into smaller ones, enhancing stability. The final emulsion is cooled, filtered, and packaged under sterile conditions.

20. What is the significance of globule size in emulsions?

Answer:
The globule size affects the stability and appearance of emulsions. Smaller globules (1–5 microns) improve stability by reducing the likelihood of coalescence and creaming, and they also enhance the emulsion's therapeutic effects.

21. What is the role of zeta potential in emulsions?

Answer:
Zeta potential measures the surface charge of emulsion globules, which determines their electrostatic stability. High zeta potential values prevent coalescence of droplets by creating repulsive forces, ensuring stability.

22. How does viscosity affect the stability of emulsions?

Answer:
Higher viscosity slows down creaming and sedimentation in emulsions, helping to maintain homogeneity and stability over time. However, excessive viscosity can reduce pourability and ease of application.

23. What are some common defects in emulsions, and how can they be remedied?

Answer:

Common defects include creaming, coalescence, flocculation, and breaking. Remedies include reducing globule size, adjusting emulsifier concentration, and optimizing storage conditions to prevent phase separation and enhance stability.

24. How does phase separation indicate instability in emulsions?

Answer:

Phase separation occurs when the dispersed phase separates from the continuous phase, indicating that the emulsion is unstable. This can be due to insufficient emulsifier concentration or improper formulation conditions.

25. What is homogenization in emulsion manufacturing?

Answer:

Homogenization is the process of applying high-shear forces to reduce the size of emulsion droplets, ensuring uniformity and improving the emulsion's stability.

26. What is the role of preservatives in pharmaceutical solutions and emulsions?

Answer:

Preservatives inhibit microbial growth in pharmaceutical formulations, ensuring product safety and extending shelf life. Examples include methylparaben in suspensions and sodium benzoate in solutions.

27. How are quality control tests for solutions conducted?

Answer:

Quality control for solutions includes testing for clarity (visual inspection), pH measurement, and assay of the active ingredient concentration using methods like HPLC or UV-visible spectrophotometry.

28. What is the importance of clarity in pharmaceutical solutions?

Answer:

Clarity ensures that the solution is free of visible particles, fibers, or contaminants, which could affect safety or indicate degradation, particularly for products like syrups and oral solutions.

29. What is the role of pH in the stability of pharmaceutical solutions?

Answer:

The pH of a solution affects the solubility, stability, and compatibility of the active ingredient with the gastrointestinal tract. Solutions are usually maintained in a pH range of 3–9 to ensure efficacy and minimize irritation.

30. How is the assay of active ingredients performed in solutions?

Answer:

Active ingredient concentration in solutions is typically measured using HPLC or UV-visible spectrophotometry, with regulatory standards requiring the API content to be within 90–110% of the labeled claim.

31. What tests are performed to evaluate suspensions?

Answer:

Tests for suspensions include redispersibility, sedimentation volume, particle size distribution, and viscosity, ensuring stability, uniformity, and proper therapeutic delivery.

32. How does redispersibility affect the quality of suspensions?

Answer:

Redispersibility ensures that the suspension can be easily restored to uniformity after settling. It is important for accurate dosing and maintaining therapeutic efficacy.

33. What is the significance of sedimentation volume in suspensions?

Answer:

Sedimentation volume indicates the stability of a suspension. An ideal suspension maintains a sedimentation volume (F) close to 1, indicating good stability without excessive sedimentation.

34. What is the role of homogenization in suspension manufacturing?

Answer:

Homogenization in suspensions helps reduce particle size, improving stability and preventing aggregation. It ensures even distribution of particles within the suspension.

35. How do emulsions differ from suspensions in their formulation and stability?

Answer:

Emulsions are biphasic systems where one liquid is dispersed in another, while suspensions contain solid particles dispersed in a liquid. Emulsions require emulsifiers to stabilize the mixture, whereas suspensions require stabilizers to prevent particle aggregation.

36. What is the role of particle size in suspension quality?

Answer:

Particle size affects the rate of sedimentation and redispersibility in suspensions. Smaller particles tend to settle slower and ensure better uniformity and stability.

37. How is phase separation evaluated in emulsions?

Answer:

Phase separation in emulsions is evaluated by centrifugation, where the emulsion is subjected to centrifugal forces, and any signs of creaming, sedimentation, or coalescence are noted.

38. What are the advantages of using emulsions for oral drug delivery?

Answer:

Emulsions improve the bioavailability of lipid-soluble drugs by enhancing their solubility and absorption in the gastrointestinal tract. They also offer better stability for certain drugs that are poorly water-soluble.

39. How do preservatives help maintain the quality of suspensions?

Answer:

Preservatives prevent microbial growth, ensuring the safety and longevity of suspensions. They are particularly important in aqueous formulations where microbial contamination can lead to spoilage.

40. What is the significance of using child-resistant closures for oral formulations?

Answer:

Child-resistant closures prevent accidental ingestion of medications by children, enhancing safety, especially for products containing active ingredients that may be harmful if ingested in large amounts.

41. What are the different types of packaging used for liquid oral formulations?

Answer:

Liquid oral formulations are commonly packaged in glass or plastic bottles, with child-resistant closures, tamper-evident seals, and labels providing essential information. The packaging is designed to protect the formulation from light, moisture, and air.

42. Why are amber glass bottles used for light-sensitive formulations?

Answer:

Amber glass bottles provide UV protection, preventing the degradation of light-sensitive APIs and maintaining the stability of the formulation.

43. How does packaging protect liquid oral formulations from moisture?

Answer:

Packaging materials such as glass or moisture-resistant plastic bottles with airtight seals prevent the ingress of moisture, which could lead to degradation or microbial growth in aqueous formulations.

44. What is the role of nitrogen flushing in the packaging process?

Answer:

Nitrogen flushing is used to replace oxygen in the headspace of packaging, preventing oxidation of sensitive APIs and improving the stability of the formulation.

45. Why is viscosity important in liquid oral formulations?

Answer:

Viscosity affects the ease of pouring and dosing of liquid oral formulations. For suspensions and emulsions, the appropriate viscosity ensures proper stability and patient compliance.

46. What is the role of stabilizers in the formulation of emulsions?

Answer:

Stabilizers in emulsions, such as emulsifiers, prevent phase separation by reducing interfacial tension and ensuring the formation of a stable, homogenous mixture.

47. What is the function of wetting agents in suspension formulations?

Answer:

Wetting agents, such as polysorbates, help improve the dispersion of hydrophobic API particles by reducing surface tension, allowing for better particle distribution in the liquid phase.

48. What is the primary challenge in formulating pharmaceutical suspensions?

Answer:

The primary challenge in formulating suspensions is preventing particle aggregation and ensuring that the particles remain uniformly dispersed in the liquid phase throughout the shelf life of the product.

49. How do preservatives contribute to the shelf life of emulsions?

Answer:

Preservatives inhibit microbial growth in emulsions, maintaining the formulation's safety and stability over time by preventing contamination.

50. What is the importance of packaging materials in maintaining the stability of liquid formulations?

Answer:

Packaging materials play a crucial role in protecting liquid formulations from environmental factors like light, moisture, and air, which can degrade the formulation. The right packaging ensures product stability, safety, and effectiveness throughout its shelf life.

MCQS

1. What is the primary solvent used in most pharmaceutical solutions?

a) Ethanol
b) Water
c) Glycerin
d) Propylene glycol
   Answer: b) Water

2. Which of the following is a characteristic of syrups?

a) They are hydroalcoholic solutions.
b) They contain sugar or sugar substitutes.
c) They are applied to the skin.
d) They are used for intravenous administration.
   Answer: b) They contain sugar or sugar substitutes.

3. What is the role of stabilizers in pharmaceutical solutions?

a) To increase the solubility of the active ingredient
b) To protect the solution from degradation
c) To increase the viscosity of the solution
d) To make the solution opaque
   Answer: b) To protect the solution from degradation

4. Which of the following is an example of a commonly used co-solvent in pharmaceutical solutions?

a) Ethanol
b) Water
c) Acetone
d) Methanol
   Answer: a) Ethanol

5. What is the purpose of deaeration in the manufacturing of pharmaceutical solutions?

a) To increase the temperature of the solution
b) To remove dissolved gases
c) To increase the concentration of the API
d) To add preservatives
   Answer: b) To remove dissolved gases

6. What is the typical concentration range of ethanol in pharmaceutical elixirs?

a) 1-5%
b) 5-40%
c) 50-70%
d) 75-90%
   Answer: b) 5-40%

7. What type of drug delivery system is a suspension?

a) Homogeneous
b) Biphasic
c) Lipophilic
d) Gel-based
   Answer: b) Biphasic

8. Which of the following is an example of a common suspending agent?

a) Xanthan gum
b) Sucrose
c) Sodium chloride
d) Hydroxypropyl methylcellulose (HPMC)
   Answer: a) Xanthan gum

9. What is the primary function of preservatives in suspensions?

a) To increase particle size
b) To prevent microbial growth
c) To enhance the viscosity
d) To improve the redispersibility
    Answer: b) To prevent microbial growth

10. What does the term "redispersibility" refer to in the context of suspensions?

a) The ability to dissolve the API
b) The ability to achieve uniformity after shaking
c) The ability to absorb moisture
d) The ability to resist temperature changes
    Answer: b) The ability to achieve uniformity after shaking

11. What is the ideal particle size range for pharmaceutical suspensions?

a) 1–10 microns
b) 10–50 microns
c) 50–100 microns
d) 100–200 microns
    Answer: b) 10–50 microns

12. What is the purpose of homogenization in suspension manufacturing?

a) To enhance the solubility of the API
b) To reduce particle size and improve stability
c) To increase the viscosity
d) To remove preservatives
    Answer: b) To reduce particle size and improve stability

13. What is the significance of sedimentation volume (F) in suspension quality control?

a) It measures the viscosity of the suspension.
b) It indicates the uniformity of the particle size.

c) It measures the stability of the suspension.
d) It measures the clarity of the suspension.
   Answer: c) It measures the stability of the suspension.

14. How does the viscosity of a suspension affect its stability?

a) Higher viscosity reduces particle aggregation
b) Higher viscosity increases sedimentation
c) Higher viscosity decreases shelf life
d) Higher viscosity enhances particle size
   Answer: a) Higher viscosity reduces particle aggregation

15. What type of emulsion is used for topical applications such as creams?

a) Oil-in-water (O/W)
b) Water-in-oil (W/O)
c) Solid-in-liquid
d) Liquid-in-liquid
   Answer: b) Water-in-oil (W/O)

16. Which of the following is a commonly used emulsifying agent?

a) Acacia
b) Sodium chloride
c) Glycerin
d) Potassium bromide
   Answer: a) Acacia

17. What is the primary function of emulsifiers in emulsions?

a) To increase particle size
b) To stabilize the emulsion by reducing interfacial tension
c) To improve the solubility of the API
d) To increase the viscosity

Answer: b) To stabilize the emulsion by reducing interfacial tension

18. What is the ideal particle size range for globules in emulsions?

a) 1–5 microns
b) 10–20 microns
c) 20–50 microns
d) 50–100 microns
    Answer: a) 1–5 microns

19. What is the purpose of phase separation testing in emulsions?

a) To evaluate the viscosity of the emulsion
b) To measure the globule size
c) To detect instability and prevent phase separation
d) To check the pH of the emulsion
    Answer: c) To detect instability and prevent phase separation

20. What technique is commonly used to measure the globule size in emulsions?

a) Optical Microscopy
b) UV-Vis Spectrophotometry
c) High-Performance Liquid Chromatography (HPLC)
d) Thin-layer chromatography (TLC)
    Answer: a) Optical Microscopy

21. What does the zeta potential in emulsions indicate?

a) The surface charge of globules and their stability
b) The viscosity of the emulsion
c) The amount of active ingredient present
d) The solubility of the emulsion
    Answer: a) The surface charge of globules and their stability

22. What is the typical range of zeta potential for stable emulsions?

a) ±5 mV
b) ±10 mV
c) ±30 mV
d) ±50 mV
   Answer: c) ±30 mV

23. How is viscosity measured in pharmaceutical emulsions?

a) By using a UV-Vis spectrophotometer
b) By using a Brookfield viscometer
c) By using a high-pressure homogenizer
d) By using a laser diffraction instrument
   Answer: b) By using a Brookfield viscometer

24. What is the typical viscosity range for pharmaceutical emulsions?

a) 50–500 cps
b) 500–5000 cps
c) 5000–10000 cps
d) 10000–20000 cps
   Answer: b) 500–5000 cps

25. What is the typical viscosity of topical emulsions?

a) 100–500 cps
b) 500–2000 cps
c) 2000–5000 cps
d) 5000–10000 cps
   Answer: b) 500–2000 cps

26. What is the role of preservatives in emulsions?

a) To prevent microbial growth
b) To increase the viscosity of the emulsion

c) To enhance the solubility of the active ingredient

d) To stabilize the emulsion against light

Answer: a) To prevent microbial growth

27. What type of closure is commonly used for pediatric oral formulations?

a) Child-resistant caps

b) Regular screw caps

c) Flip-top caps

d) Cork closures

Answer: a) Child-resistant caps

28. Which of the following packaging materials is commonly used for light-sensitive pharmaceutical formulations?

a) Clear plastic

b) Amber glass

c) Metal cans

d) Transparent PET bottles

Answer: b) Amber glass

29. What is the primary function of packaging in liquid oral formulations?

a) To enhance the API's bioavailability

b) To protect the formulation from environmental factors like light, moisture, and air

c) To increase the formulation's viscosity

d) To reduce the need for preservatives

Answer: b) To protect the formulation from environmental factors like light, moisture, and air

30. Which type of bottle is commonly used for pediatric medications due to its shatter-resistant nature?

a) Glass bottles

b) Aluminum cans

c) Plastic bottles
d) Ceramic bottles
   Answer: c) Plastic bottles

31. What is the typical use of tamper-evident closures?

a) To increase the shelf life of the formulation
b) To ensure safety by providing evidence of product tampering
c) To enhance the aesthetics of the packaging
d) To reduce the weight of the packaging
   Answer: b) To ensure safety by providing evidence of product tampering

32. Why is nitrogen flushing used in packaging of sensitive pharmaceutical products?

a) To reduce packaging costs
b) To replace oxygen in the packaging to prevent oxidation
c) To enhance the color of the product
d) To improve the solubility of the API
   Answer: b) To replace oxygen in the packaging to prevent oxidation

33. What is the main purpose of packaging material selection for oral liquid formulations?

a) To ensure accurate dosing
b) To provide optimal light protection
c) To allow for easy application
d) To prevent interaction between the packaging and the formulation
   Answer: d) To prevent interaction between the packaging and the formulation

34. What does a clarity test for pharmaceutical solutions assess?

a) The presence of particulates or cloudiness
b) The pH of the solution
c) The concentration of the active ingredient

d) The solubility of the API

Answer: a) The presence of particulates or cloudiness

35. What is the typical pH range for most oral pharmaceutical solutions?

a) 1–3
b) 3–9
c) 9–12
d) 12–14

Answer: b) 3–9

36. What is the acceptable range for active ingredient content in pharmaceutical solutions according to regulatory standards?

a) 80–90% of labeled claim
b) 90–110% of labeled claim
c) 110–120% of labeled claim
d) 70–80% of labeled claim

Answer: b) 90–110% of labeled claim

37. What method is commonly used to assay the concentration of active ingredients in pharmaceutical solutions?

a) Thin-layer chromatography
b) High-performance liquid chromatography (HPLC)
c) Gas chromatography
d) Infrared spectroscopy

Answer: b) High-performance liquid chromatography (HPLC)

38. Which of the following is a key quality control test for suspensions?

a) Particle size distribution
b) Viscosity of the solvent
c) Clarity

d) pH of the suspension
   Answer: a) Particle size distribution

39. What is the significance of viscosity measurement in suspensions?

a) It helps determine the correct dosage of the API
b) It influences the ease of pouring and dosing
c) It ensures the clarity of the suspension
d) It measures the sedimentation rate
   Answer: b) It influences the ease of pouring and dosing

40. What is the impact of particle size on suspension stability?

a) Larger particles settle faster, leading to instability
b) Smaller particles settle faster, leading to instability
c) Larger particles improve the suspension's bioavailability
d) Smaller particles enhance the suspension's viscosity
   Answer: a) Larger particles settle faster, leading to instability

41. What method is used to measure the globule size in emulsions?

a) High-pressure homogenization
b) Laser diffraction
c) HPLC
d) Atomic absorption spectroscopy
   Answer: b) Laser diffraction

42. What is the primary reason for using emulsifying agents in the manufacturing of emulsions?

a) To decrease the viscosity
b) To stabilize the emulsion and prevent phase separation
c) To enhance the solubility of the active ingredient
d) To increase the particle size
   Answer: b) To stabilize the emulsion and prevent phase separation

43. What is the role of preservatives in emulsions?

a) To reduce the particle size
b) To prevent microbial contamination
c) To enhance the emulsifier's performance
d) To increase the viscosity
   Answer: b) To prevent microbial contamination

44. What does phase separation in emulsions indicate?

a) The formulation is stable
b) The emulsion is homogeneous
c) The formulation is unstable
d) The emulsion is free from preservatives
   Answer: c) The formulation is unstable

45. What method is commonly used to assess the stability of emulsions?

a) Centrifugation test
b) HPLC
c) UV-Vis spectroscopy
d) High-pressure liquid chromatography
   Answer: a) Centrifugation test

46. Which of the following is a characteristic of a stable emulsion?

a) Separation of the oil and water phases
b) Uniform distribution of droplets with no creaming
c) High viscosity and poor pourability
d) Large globules of dispersed phase
   Answer: b) Uniform distribution of droplets with no creaming

47. What is the typical range for particle size in emulsions?

a) 1–5 microns
b) 5–10 microns
c) 10–50 microns
d) 50–100 microns
   Answer: a) 1–5 microns

48. *How does zeta potential affect the stability of emulsions?*

a) High zeta potential indicates instability
b) Low zeta potential enhances the stability of emulsions
c) High zeta potential ensures stability by preventing coalescence
d) Zeta potential has no effect on emulsion stability
   Answer: c) High zeta potential ensures stability by preventing coalescence

49. *What is the significance of zeta potential measurement in emulsions?*

a) It determines the viscosity of the emulsion
b) It measures the globule size
c) It assesses the electrostatic stability of the droplets
d) It measures the pH of the emulsion
   Answer: c) It assesses the electrostatic stability of the droplets

50. *What is a common defect in emulsions that occurs when droplets merge to form larger ones?*

a) Flocculation
b) Breaking
c) Coalescence
d) Creaming
   Answer: c) Coalescence

CHAPTER FOUR

Capsules

4.1 Hard Gelatin Capsules

4.1.1 Gelatin Extraction and Capsule Shell Production

Definition and Sources of Gelatin

Gelatin is a natural polymer derived from the partial hydrolysis of collagen, a structural protein found in animal connective tissues such as skin, bones, and tendons. Gelatin is widely used in the pharmaceutical industry due to its biocompatibility, safety, and ability to form flexible, strong films that dissolve readily in gastrointestinal fluids.

The primary sources of gelatin for pharmaceutical applications include:

Bovine-derived gelatin: Extracted from the skin and bones of cattle.

Porcine-derived gelatin: Sourced from pigskin.

Fish-derived gelatin: An alternative for products catering to specific dietary or religious requirements.

Gelatin Extraction Process

The extraction of gelatin involves the hydrolysis of collagen using controlled acid or alkali treatments to break down the protein into smaller polypeptides. The method used determines the properties of the resulting gelatin, categorized into **Type A** and **Type B**.

Acid-Treated Gelatin (Type A):

- Collagen is treated with dilute acid to hydrolyze the peptide bonds.
- This method produces gelatin with an isoelectric point (pH 7–9), making it slightly cationic in nature.
- Type A gelatin is commonly sourced from pigskin.

Alkali-Treated Gelatin (Type B):

Collagen undergoes prolonged treatment with an alkali solution (e.g., lime) to remove non-collagenous proteins and hydrolyze the collagen.

The isoelectric point of Type B gelatin is lower (pH 4.7–5), giving it an anionic character.

This type is primarily derived from bovine hides and bones.

The choice between Type A and Type B gelatin depends on the specific requirements of the application, such as pH compatibility and desired mechanical properties.

Pharmaceutical-Grade Gelatin Properties

To ensure its suitability for capsule shell production, gelatin must meet specific physical and chemical quality parameters, including bloom strength and viscosity.

Bloom Strength:

Bloom strength is a measure of the gel's firmness and elasticity, determined by the force required to depress the surface of a gelatin gel by a specified amount.

Pharmaceutical-grade gelatin typically has a bloom strength of **150–250 grams**, ensuring strong and flexible capsule shells.

Viscosity:

The viscosity of gelatin solutions, measured in millipoise (mP), affects its ability to form smooth, uniform films.

Pharmaceutical-grade gelatin solutions typically have a viscosity range of **30–60 mP**, depending on the concentration and temperature.

Capsule Shell Production

The production of hard gelatin capsule shells involves the formation of a uniform gelatin film and its subsequent molding into capsule halves.

Preparation of Gelatin Solution:

Gelatin granules are dissolved in deionized water at a controlled temperature (50–60°C) to produce a viscous solution.

Additional ingredients, such as plasticizers (e.g., glycerin or sorbitol), coloring agents, and preservatives, are incorporated to improve flexibility, appearance, and shelf life.

Dipping Process:

Stainless steel pins are dipped into the gelatin solution to form thin, uniform films on their surfaces.

The thickness of the gelatin film determines the strength and size of the capsule shell.

Drying:

The gelatin-coated pins are passed through a controlled drying chamber to remove excess moisture.

The drying process ensures the shells retain optimal mechanical strength and dimensional stability.

Trimming and Joining:

The dried gelatin films are cut to form the **capsule cap** and **body**, which are later joined to produce the complete capsule shell.

The capsules are polished to remove rough edges and enhance their appearance.

4.1.1 Gelatin Extraction and Capsule Shell Production

Production of Capsule Shells

The production of hard gelatin capsule shells is a precise and multistep process designed to create uniform, durable, and dissolvable capsules. This process involves dipping, spinning, drying, trimming, and joining, followed by the addition of essential additives for functionality and aesthetics.

1. Dipping Process

The dipping process forms the gelatin film that becomes the capsule shell.

Steps:

Stainless steel pins or molds are dipped into a heated gelatin solution maintained at **50–60°C**.

The gelatin coats the pins evenly to form a thin layer, which will become the capsule body and cap.

The depth of dipping and the viscosity of the gelatin solution determine the thickness of the capsule walls.

Significance:

The uniformity of the dipping process ensures that the capsules have consistent strength and size.

2. Spinning

After dipping, the coated pins are rotated slowly to ensure even distribution of the gelatin film and to prevent pooling at the bottom.

Objective:

Spinning ensures uniform wall thickness and avoids irregularities in the capsule shell.

3. Drying

The gelatin-coated pins are passed through controlled drying chambers to remove excess moisture from the film.

Conditions:

Temperature and humidity are carefully monitored to prevent cracking or over-drying.

The drying process typically takes **30–45 minutes**, depending on the shell thickness.

Moisture Content:

Dried capsule shells should have a residual moisture content of **12–16%**, ensuring flexibility and structural integrity.

4. Trimming

Once dried, the gelatin film is trimmed to form the **body** and **cap** of the capsule.

Process:

The film is cut to precise lengths using automated trimmers.

The trimmed parts are separated into capsule bodies (longer) and caps (shorter).

Precision:

Trimming ensures that the capsule parts fit perfectly during the assembly process.

5. Joining

In the final step, the capsule body and cap are joined to form the complete shell.

Process:

The cap and body are aligned and loosely joined to allow easy filling during the manufacturing process.

For pre-locked capsules, the two parts are fitted more securely to prevent accidental separation.

Dimensions and Sizes of Capsules

Hard gelatin capsules are available in various sizes to accommodate different doses of drugs. Capsule size is determined by the volume it can hold.

The choice of capsule size depends on the dose, density of the fill material, and intended use.

Additives in Capsule Shells

Several additives are incorporated into the gelatin solution during capsule shell production to improve performance, stability, and appearance.

1. Plasticizers

Plasticizers enhance the flexibility and elasticity of the gelatin shell, reducing brittleness.

Examples:

Glycerin and sorbitol are commonly used.

Typical concentration ranges between **10–30% w/w** of the gelatin.

2. Coloring Agents

Coloring agents are added to improve the aesthetic appeal and facilitate product differentiation.

Types:

Natural Colorants: Titanium dioxide for white capsules, iron oxides for shades of red, yellow, or brown.

Synthetic Dyes: FD&C colors approved by regulatory agencies.

Purpose:

Color coding helps identify specific drugs or doses and prevents medication errors.

3. Preservatives

Preservatives inhibit microbial growth during storage, ensuring the safety and shelf life of the capsules.

Examples:

Methylparaben and propylparaben are commonly used in low concentrations (0.1–0.2%).

4.1.2 Filling Techniques

4.1.2.1 Manual Filling

Manual capsule filling is a straightforward and cost-effective technique used for small-scale or customized production of hard gelatin capsules. This method employs simple tools such as capsule boards or filling trays, making it ideal for compounding pharmacies, research laboratories, or small-batch manufacturing.

Manual Filling Process

The manual filling process involves several steps to ensure uniformity and precision while filling capsules by hand. The steps are:

Preparation of Materials:

The required dose of the active pharmaceutical ingredient (API) and excipients are weighed and blended uniformly.

Excipients such as fillers, lubricants, and glidants are added to improve the flowability and packing properties of the powder mixture.

Separation of Capsule Parts:

Capsule boards or trays hold the capsules securely.

The caps and bodies are separated manually, with the bodies retained in the tray for filling.

Filling the Capsules:

The prepared powder mixture is evenly spread over the open capsule bodies using a scraper or spatula.

The powder is tamped down to ensure proper packing and achieve the required dose. This process may be repeated to fill the capsules completely.

Capping and Sealing:

The caps are placed back onto the filled bodies and pressed gently to secure them.

The capsules are inspected for uniformity and proper closure.

Role of Fillers, Lubricants, and Glidants

To achieve accurate dosing and uniform filling, excipients are incorporated into the powder mixture:

Fillers:

Fillers, such as lactose, microcrystalline cellulose (MCC), or starch, are used to bulk up the formulation when the API dose is small.

Example: MCC is widely used because it provides good compressibility and flow.

Lubricants:

Lubricants like magnesium stearate reduce friction between particles and the capsule walls, facilitating smooth filling.

Typical concentration: 0.25–2% w/w.

Glidants:

Glidants such as colloidal silicon dioxide improve the flow properties of the powder, ensuring even distribution and reducing clumping.

Typical concentration: 0.1–0.5% w/w.

These excipients enhance the efficiency of the manual filling process and ensure dose uniformity.

Filling Rates

Manual capsule filling is labor-intensive and slower compared to automated techniques.

Typical Rates:

Using capsule boards or trays, an operator can fill **50–100 capsules per hour**, depending on the complexity of the formulation and operator skill.

Capsule boards are available in configurations that hold between **50 and 300 capsules** at a time, with larger boards increasing efficiency slightly.

Applications

Manual filling is primarily used in:

1. **Compounding Pharmacies**: To prepare personalized medications for patients with specific needs.
2. **Research Laboratories**: For clinical trials or pilot studies requiring small batches of capsules.
3. **Specialty Products**: For rare or low-demand drugs where automation is not cost-effective.

4.1.2.2 Semi-Automatic Filling

Semi-automatic capsule filling is a hybrid process that combines manual intervention with mechanized systems to enhance efficiency and accuracy in capsule production. These machines are designed for small-to-medium scale manufacturing, offering a significant improvement over manual methods while being more cost-effective than fully automated systems.

Semi-Automatic Capsule Fillers

Semi-automatic capsule filling machines consist of distinct systems for powder feeding, tamping, and capsule closing, all operating in a coordinated manner.

1. Powder Feeding System

The powder feeding system delivers the prepared powder mixture into the open capsule bodies.

Process:

The powder is loaded into a hopper positioned above the capsule holding tray.

A dosing mechanism, often with rotating screws or plates, evenly distributes the powder into the capsule bodies.

Operators manually position the capsule tray and ensure proper alignment.

Advantages:

The system minimizes material wastage and ensures consistent dosing across multiple capsules.

2. Tamping System

The tamping system compresses the powder into the capsule body to achieve the desired fill weight and packing density.

Process:

Once powder is fed into the capsules, a series of tamping pins or punches compress the powder into a uniform plug.

This process can be repeated several times to fill the capsule to its optimal capacity.

Significance:

Tamping ensures that the powder is compacted evenly, improving dose uniformity.

It is particularly useful for formulations with poor flow properties or low bulk density.

3. Capsule Closing System

The capsule closing system joins the pre-filled bodies with their corresponding caps.

Process:

The filled capsule bodies are manually transferred to the closing station.

The machine aligns the caps and bodies, then securely locks them together.

The operator inspects the closed capsules for defects or misalignments.

Efficiency:

Capsule closing in semi-automatic systems is precise and faster than manual methods, reducing operator fatigue.

Production Rates

Semi-automatic capsule filling machines offer a significant increase in production capacity compared to manual filling.

Typical Production Rate:

Machines can fill **20,000 to 25,000 capsules per hour**, depending on the operator's skill and the formulation's characteristics.

The speed varies with capsule size, powder flow properties, and required fill weights.

Suitability for Small-to-Medium Scale Manufacturing

Semi-automatic capsule fillers are particularly suited for operations requiring flexibility and moderate production volumes.

Cost-Effectiveness:

These machines are less expensive than fully automated systems, making them ideal for small-to-medium-sized pharmaceutical companies or contract manufacturers.

Flexibility:

Semi-automatic machines can handle a wide range of capsule sizes (typically **000 to 5**) and are compatible with various formulations, including powders, granules, and pellets.

Operators can easily adjust the settings for different batch requirements.

Ease of Operation:

While requiring manual intervention, semi-automatic machines are straightforward to operate, with minimal training required.

They also have a smaller footprint, saving space in manufacturing facilities.

Applications:

Ideal for small-to-medium scale production in nutraceuticals, herbal supplements, and pharmaceutical formulations.

Useful for pilot-scale batches or niche products where fully automated systems may not be cost-effective.

4.1.2.3 Automatic Filling

Automatic capsule filling machines are advanced systems designed for high-speed, large-scale production of hard gelatin capsules. These machines perform all steps of capsule filling, from orientation to sealing, with minimal human intervention, ensuring precision, efficiency, and consistency.

Steps in Automatic Filling Machines

1. Capsule Orientation

Capsule orientation ensures that the capsules are correctly aligned for separation and filling.

Process:

Empty capsules are fed into the machine from a hopper.

A sorting mechanism orients the capsules such that the cap and body are positioned correctly for separation.

This step uses centrifugal force, gravity, or vacuum-assisted mechanisms.

Significance:

Proper orientation minimizes jamming and ensures smooth operation during subsequent steps.

2. Capsule Separation

Capsule separation involves the precise detachment of the cap from the body to prepare the capsules for filling.

Process:

Vacuum suction gently separates the cap from the body while keeping both parts securely in place.

The body is held in a lower chamber for filling, while the cap is transferred to an upper chamber for later rejoining.

3. Dosing

The dosing system measures and dispenses the appropriate amount of material into the capsule body. Depending on the formulation, the dosing mechanism may vary:

Powders: Tamping pins or dosing discs compress and transfer the powder into the capsule.

Granules and Pellets: Volumetric or weight-based systems ensure precise dosing.

Liquids: Special attachments inject liquids into the capsules, often requiring sealing.

4. Filling

The filling process introduces the measured dose into the capsule body with high accuracy and efficiency.

Process:

The pre-measured dose is transferred into the open capsule body using a dosing tube, plate, or piston system.

The machine ensures uniform distribution of material to maintain consistent dosage.

5. Sealing

Once filled, the capsule body and cap are rejoined and sealed to ensure integrity and prevent leakage.

Process:

Mechanical or vacuum pressure securely locks the cap onto the body.

For liquid-filled capsules, additional sealing methods, such as banding with gelatin or polymer films, are applied.

Technical Specifications

1. **Production Speeds:**
   Automatic capsule filling machines are highly efficient, with production speeds ranging from **100,000 to 200,000 capsules per hour**, depending on the model and capsule size.

2. **Dosage Weight Variation:**
   These machines maintain strict weight uniformity, with dosage weight

variation typically within **±5%** of the target fill weight, meeting regulatory standards.

Capsule Sizes:

Most machines handle standard capsule sizes ranging from **000 to 5**, accommodating a variety of dosage forms.

Compatibility with Formulation Types

Automatic filling machines are versatile and compatible with a wide range of formulations, making them suitable for diverse pharmaceutical applications:

1. **Powders:**

   - Efficient handling of free-flowing and cohesive powders using tamping or vacuum-assisted systems.
   - Example: Antibiotics like amoxicillin are commonly filled as powders.

2. **Granules and Pellets:**

   - Volumetric filling ensures uniform dosing of granules or pellets.
   - Example: Sustained-release formulations of drugs like omeprazole are filled as pellets.

3. **Liquids:**

   - Specialized attachments allow precise liquid filling, often followed by sealing.
   - Example: Omega-3 fish oil capsules are often filled as liquids.

4. **Combination Forms:**

   - Some machines can fill capsules with multiple components, such as powder-pellet combinations or liquid-pellet blends.
   - Example: Fixed-dose combinations for treating multiple conditions.

Applications

Automatic capsule filling machines are used in large-scale manufacturing facilities to produce capsules for pharmaceuticals, nutraceuticals, and dietary supplements. They are particularly advantageous for:

- High-demand products requiring large volumes.
- Complex formulations needing precision dosing.
- Products with stringent regulatory requirements for uniformity and quality.

4.1.3 Finishing and Special Formulation Techniques

The production of hard gelatin capsules includes finishing steps to ensure a polished and defect-free product, along with advanced formulation techniques that enable the development of specialized drug delivery systems, such as sustained and delayed-release capsules.

Finishing Steps

1. Polishing

Polishing is a crucial step to enhance the appearance of capsules by removing excess powder and improving their surface quality.

Process:

Capsules are passed through polishing equipment, such as a cloth-lined rotating drum or a capsule polisher.

The process removes residual powder from the capsule surface, providing a smooth and glossy finish.

Significance:

Polished capsules improve patient acceptability due to their enhanced aesthetics.

Clean capsules reduce the risk of contamination and ensure compatibility with packaging systems.

2. Inspection

Inspection ensures that the final capsules meet quality standards and are free from defects such as cracks, dents, or incomplete sealing.

Manual Inspection:

Capsules are visually examined by operators under bright lighting to identify surface defects.

Automated Inspection:

Advanced machines equipped with cameras and sensors detect defects at high speeds.

Parameters checked include capsule size, weight, color uniformity, and seal integrity.

Significance:

Inspection guarantees uniformity and ensures compliance with regulatory requirements, preventing defective capsules from reaching the market.

Special Formulation Techniques

1. Pellet-Filled Capsules for Sustained Release

Pellet-filled capsules are designed to provide sustained or controlled drug release over an extended period. This approach ensures prolonged therapeutic effects and reduces dosing frequency.

- **Process:**

  - Drug pellets are produced through extrusion and spheronization, coated with polymers that control the release rate.
  - The coated pellets are then filled into hard gelatin capsules using semi-automatic or automatic filling machines.

- **Mechanism:**

  - The polymer coating regulates the release of the drug as the pellets pass through the gastrointestinal tract.

- **Example:**

  - **Diclofenac sodium sustained-release capsules** contain polymer-coated pellets that release the drug gradually over 12–24 hours.

2. Enteric-Coated Capsules for Delayed Release

Enteric-coated capsules are designed to resist dissolution in the acidic environment of the stomach and release the drug only in the intestine. This prevents drug degradation in gastric acid and minimizes gastric irritation.

- **Process:**

The active ingredient is formulated into pellets or granules and coated with an enteric polymer, such as cellulose acetate phthalate (CAP) or Eudragit.

The enteric-coated pellets are filled into hard gelatin capsules.

Mechanism:

The enteric coating dissolves at a higher pH (typically above 5.5), allowing the drug to be released in the intestine.

Example:

Omeprazole enteric-coated capsules contain acid-labile omeprazole in coated pellets that dissolve in the duodenum, ensuring optimal absorption and efficacy in treating gastric acid-related conditions.

Examples of Specialized Capsule Formulations

Sustained-Release Capsules:

Propranolol sustained-release capsules release the drug over 12 hours, maintaining consistent blood levels and improving patient compliance.

Enteric-Coated Capsules:

Esomeprazole enteric-coated capsules protect the drug from stomach acid, ensuring effective delivery to the intestine.

Combination Formulations:

Fixed-dose combinations like **aspirin and omeprazole capsules** use both sustained and enteric-coated pellets to deliver multiple drugs with distinct release profiles.

4.2 Soft Gelatin Capsules

4.2.1 Nature of Shell and Content

Soft gelatin capsules (softgels) are a specialized dosage form designed to encapsulate liquid or semi-solid materials. They consist of a single, seamless outer shell made of gelatin, plasticizers, and water, enclosing a variety of fill materials. Softgels are highly versatile and widely used for pharmaceutical and nutraceutical applications due to their ability to enhance bioavailability and improve patient compliance.

Definition of Soft Gelatin Capsules

Soft gelatin capsules are a **one-piece structure** made of a flexible gelatin shell filled with liquid, semi-solid, or oily substances. Unlike hard gelatin capsules, softgels are formed and sealed in a single process, making them ideal for containing liquids that are incompatible with conventional two-piece capsules.

Components of the Shell

The softgel shell is composed of several ingredients that provide flexibility, durability, and protection to the encapsulated material:

Gelatin:

The primary structural material, derived from collagen via acid (Type A) or alkali (Type B) treatment.

Gelatin forms a strong, flexible film when combined with water and plasticizers.

Plasticizers:

Plasticizers such as **glycerin** and **sorbitol** are added to impart flexibility to the shell, preventing brittleness.

The ratio of gelatin to plasticizers is carefully adjusted to achieve the desired shell properties.

Water:

Water acts as a solvent during shell formation and contributes to the shell's plasticity.

The moisture content in the final product is reduced to **6–10%** to maintain capsule stability.

Optional Additives:

Coloring agents and opacifiers, such as titanium dioxide, may be included to enhance appearance and provide light protection for sensitive contents.

Moisture Content in Softgel Capsules

The final moisture content of softgel capsules is maintained between **6–10%**. This moisture level ensures:

Sufficient flexibility to prevent cracking or brittleness.

Stability of the encapsulated material, reducing the risk of microbial growth or degradation.

To maintain this moisture balance, softgels are typically packaged in moisture-resistant containers with desiccants.

Typical Contents of Soft Gelatin Capsules

Softgel capsules are versatile and can accommodate a wide range of fill materials, including:

Solutions:

Aqueous or non-aqueous solutions, such as drugs dissolved in water or polyethylene glycol (PEG).

Example: **Docusate sodium solution** in stool softeners.

Suspensions:

Fine particles suspended in a suitable liquid medium.

Example: **Ibuprofen softgels** containing suspended drug particles in a liquid carrier.

Pastes:

Semi-solid materials, such as ointments or waxes, mixed with liquid components.

Example: **Coenzyme Q10 paste-filled capsules** for nutritional supplementation.

Oily Liquids:

Lipid-based formulations, including essential oils, vitamins, or fish oils.

Example: **Vitamin E softgels**, which contain tocopherol dissolved in vegetable oil.

Examples of Soft Gelatin Capsules

Vitamin E Softgels:

Contain tocopherol in an oily medium to protect against oxidative degradation and improve absorption.

Omega-3 Fish Oil Capsules:

Encapsulate fish oil to provide essential fatty acids while masking the unpleasant taste and odor.

Evening Primrose Oil Capsules:

Contain gamma-linolenic acid (GLA) for skin health and hormonal balance.

Antifungal Medications:

Softgels such as **terbinafine capsules** are used for systemic treatment of fungal infections.

4.2.2 Base Adsorption and Minimum/Gram Factor

Base Adsorption (BA)

Definition and Significance

Base adsorption (BA) is a critical parameter in the formulation of soft gelatin capsules. It quantifies the weight of the base material (e.g., oil, solvent, or excipient) that can be adsorbed per unit weight of the active pharmaceutical ingredient (API). This value is essential to ensure uniform distribution of the active ingredient within the base and maintain consistent drug content in each capsule.

The significance of base adsorption lies in:

- Ensuring proper mixing and homogeneity of the API with the base.
- Preventing precipitation or separation of the API during storage.
- Facilitating accurate dose delivery in each capsule.

Minimum/Gram Factor (MGF)
Definition and Role

The minimum/gram factor (MGF) represents the total weight of the capsule content required to incorporate 1 gram of the active ingredient. This parameter helps determine the capsule size necessary to accommodate the formulation.

The role of the MGF includes:

- Assisting in the selection of the appropriate capsule size for a given dose.
- Ensuring that the final capsule volume is sufficient to hold the API, base, and excipients without spillage or compromise in structural integrity.

Calculation of MGF

The MGF is derived using the formula:

MGF=BA+Weight of Other Excipients

For example, if the base adsorption (BA) for fish oil is 1.2 and the weight of other excipients added is 0.3 grams, the MGF is: MGF=1.2+0.3=1.5

This means that 1.5 grams of capsule fill material are required for every gram of API.

For instance, a formulation using fish oil with an API dose of 500 mg would require:

Total Fill Weight=0.5 g×MGF (0.9)=0.45 g

This value helps determine the capsule size required to accommodate the total fill weight.

4.2.3 Filling and Sealing Techniques

Rotary Die Process for Filling and Sealing Soft Gelatin Capsules

The rotary die process is the most widely used method for manufacturing soft gelatin capsules (softgels). This automated technique integrates the formation of the gelatin shell, the filling of the liquid or semi-solid content, and the sealing of the capsules into a single, continuous operation. This ensures efficiency, precision, and high production volumes.

1. Gelatin Ribbon Formation

The first step in the rotary die process is the formation of gelatin ribbons, which serve as the outer shell of the capsules.

Process:

Gelatin, plasticizers (e.g., glycerin or sorbitol), and water are mixed and heated to form a molten gelatin solution.

The solution is then spread into thin, uniform ribbons (typically **0.4–0.8 mm thick**) using heated drums or rollers.

These gelatin ribbons are cooled to a manageable temperature and transported to the encapsulation area.

Significance:

The ribbons must maintain precise thickness and flexibility to ensure uniform capsule strength and minimize defects during filling and sealing.

2. Liquid Filling and Sealing

The filling and sealing process occurs simultaneously as the gelatin ribbons are shaped into capsules and filled with the liquid formulation.

- **Process:**

The gelatin ribbons are fed into the rotary die machine, where rotating die rollers create capsule cavities by pressing the ribbons together.

The liquid or semi-solid fill material is injected into the capsules through precision nozzles as the ribbons are molded.

As the two ribbons come together, the capsule edges are sealed using pressure and heat, forming hermetically sealed softgels.

Machine Specifications:

Production speed: **150,000–200,000 capsules per hour**, depending on the machine model and capsule size.

Capsule sizes: Accommodates a wide range of sizes, typically holding **0.05 to 5 mL** of fill material.

3. Drying and Finishing

Once the capsules are formed, they undergo a drying and finishing process to achieve the desired mechanical properties and stability.

Drying:

Softgels are transferred to a tumble dryer to remove surface moisture.

The capsules are then dried further in temperature- and humidity-controlled drying tunnels for **24–48 hours** until the moisture content reaches the optimal range of **6–10%**.

Finishing:

Dried capsules are inspected for defects, polished to enhance their appearance, and sorted by size and weight.

○ The finished capsules are packaged in moisture-resistant containers to maintain stability.

Advantages of Hermetic Sealing in Softgels

Hermetic sealing is a key feature of soft gelatin capsules, offering several benefits:

Enhanced Stability:

The hermetic seal prevents leakage of the liquid content, ensuring the integrity and uniformity of the formulation.

It also protects the fill material from environmental factors such as oxygen, light, and moisture, which can degrade sensitive APIs.

Improved Bioavailability:

Softgels can encapsulate poorly soluble drugs in lipid-based formulations, enhancing solubility and absorption.

The hermetic seal ensures that these bioavailability-enhancing properties are preserved during storage and use.

Tamper Evidence:

The seamless structure of softgels provides tamper-evident packaging, ensuring consumer safety and product authenticity.

Patient Compliance:

Hermetically sealed softgels are easier to swallow, have no unpleasant taste or odor, and provide a smooth texture, improving patient adherence.

Versatility:

Hermetically sealed softgels can accommodate a wide range of formulations, including oils, suspensions, and even combinations of liquids and solids, making them suitable for diverse therapeutic and nutraceutical applications.

Examples of Products Made Using the Rotary Die Process

1. **Omega-3 Fish Oil Softgels:**
   Encapsulate fish oil in a hermetically sealed softgel, protecting it from oxidation and preserving its potency.
2. **Vitamin D3 Softgels:**
   Deliver lipid-soluble vitamin D3 in an easily absorbable and stable form.

3. **Coenzyme Q10 Softgels:**
Contain a lipid-based formulation that improves the bioavailability of this antioxidant.

4.3 Quality Control Tests

4.3.1 In-Process Tests

In-process quality control (IPQC) tests for capsules are critical to ensuring consistent product quality and compliance with regulatory standards. These tests focus on key parameters such as weight variation, moisture content, and fill uniformity, ensuring that capsules meet the required specifications during production.

Weight Variation

Weight variation evaluates whether the total weight of filled capsules falls within acceptable limits. This test is crucial for ensuring uniformity in dosing and compliance with pharmacopoeial standards. The procedure begins with randomly selecting a sample of capsules, which are then weighed individually. The mean weight is calculated by summing the individual weights and dividing by the total number of capsules. The percentage deviation of each capsule from the mean is determined using an appropriate formula to assess consistency.

The acceptance criteria for weight variation depend on the capsule weight. For capsules weighing ≤300 mg, the acceptable deviation is ±7.5%, whereas for capsules weighing >300 mg, the limit is ±5%. For example, if the mean weight of a batch of capsules is 250 mg and one capsule weighs 240 mg, the deviation is calculated accordingly. If the deviation falls within the specified limits, the capsule complies with the standard. Weight variation testing is an essential part of in-process control, helping manufacturers detect inconsistencies and maintain product quality before final release.

2. Moisture Content

Moisture content is a critical parameter for the stability and integrity of capsule shells, particularly soft gelatin capsules. Excess moisture can cause microbial growth, while insufficient moisture may lead to brittleness.

Determination Method:

Moisture content is measured using **Karl Fischer titration**, a highly sensitive technique for quantifying water content.

The sample is dissolved in a suitable solvent, and the water content is titrated with Karl Fischer reagent until an endpoint is reached.

Acceptable Range:

Soft gelatin capsules must maintain a moisture content between **6–10%** to ensure flexibility and prevent cracking or deformation.

Significance:

Maintaining the specified moisture content ensures the capsules' physical and chemical stability during storage and use.

3. Fill Uniformity

Fill uniformity ensures that the active pharmaceutical ingredient (API) content in each capsule is consistent with the labeled claim, providing accurate and reliable dosing. The procedure involves selecting a random sample of capsules, opening them, and analyzing the fill material for API content using techniques such as UV-Vis spectrophotometry or High-Performance Liquid Chromatography (HPLC). The API content of each capsule is then compared to the labeled claim to determine uniformity.

The acceptance criteria require that the API content in each capsule must fall within 85–115% of the labeled claim. For example, for capsules labeled to contain 500 mg of API, the acceptable range is 425 mg to 575 mg. Capsules falling within this range are considered compliant, ensuring that patients receive the intended therapeutic dose. Fill uniformity testing is a crucial aspect of in-process quality control, helping to maintain consistency and reliability in pharmaceutical formulations.

4.3.2 Finished Product Tests

Finished product quality control tests are essential for ensuring that capsules meet pharmacopoeial standards, ensuring efficacy, safety, and consistency. These tests evaluate parameters such as disintegration, dissolution, content uniformity, and microbial quality.

1. Disintegration Testing

Disintegration testing assesses whether capsules break down into smaller particles within a specified time to ensure proper drug release.

For Hard Gelatin Capsules

Procedure:

Capsules are placed in a basket-rack assembly, submerged in water or a simulated gastric fluid at **37°C ± 2°C**, and subjected to gentle agitation. The time taken for the capsules to completely disintegrate is recorded.

Acceptance Criteria:

Hard gelatin capsules must disintegrate within **30 minutes**, as per **USP standards.**

For Enteric-Coated Capsules

Procedure:

Enteric-coated capsules are tested for resistance to gastric fluid by immersing them in simulated gastric fluid (pH 1.2) for **≥2 hours** without rupture. Subsequently, the capsules are transferred to simulated intestinal fluid (pH 6.8), where disintegration must occur within **60 minutes.**

Significance:

Ensures enteric-coated capsules protect the drug from stomach acid and release the active ingredient in the intestine.

2. Dissolution Testing

Dissolution testing measures the rate and extent of drug release from capsules into a dissolution medium, simulating in vivo conditions.

Apparatus:

USP Apparatus 1 (Basket): Capsules are placed in a rotating basket submerged in the dissolution medium.

USP Apparatus 2 (Paddle): Capsules are placed directly in the dissolution medium with a rotating paddle maintaining uniform agitation.

Procedure:

Capsules are tested in a medium such as water, simulated gastric fluid (pH 1.2), or simulated intestinal fluid (pH 6.8).

Samples are withdrawn at predetermined intervals, and the concentration of the drug is measured using **UV-Vis spectrophotometry** or **HPLC.**

Dissolution profiles are generated by plotting the percentage of drug dissolved versus time.

Example:

For a marketed **ibuprofen capsule**, dissolution testing may show 80% drug release within 30 minutes, confirming rapid release properties.

3. Content Uniformity

Content uniformity ensures that the active pharmaceutical ingredient (API) content in individual capsules lies within an acceptable range of the label claim.

Procedure:

A random sample of capsules is analyzed for API content using techniques such as **HPLC** or **UV-Vis spectrophotometry**.

The API content of each capsule is compared to the labeled claim.

Acceptance Criteria:

The API content in each capsule must fall within **85–115% of the labeled claim**, as per pharmacopoeial standards.

Significance:

Ensures consistent dosing and therapeutic efficacy across the batch.

4. Microbial Testing

Microbial testing ensures the microbial quality of capsules by evaluating the presence of total aerobic microbes and specific pathogens.

Tests:

Total Aerobic Microbial Count (TAMC): The total number of viable aerobic microorganisms present in a sample.

Specific Pathogens: Tests for the absence of harmful pathogens such as E. coli, **Salmonella, Staphylococcus aureus**, and **Pseudomonas aeruginosa**.

Acceptance Criteria:

TAMC must not exceed 10^3 **CFU/g**.

Pathogens such as **E. coli** and **Salmonella** must be absent in the tested sample.

Significance:

Ensures the safety of the product by preventing microbial contamination, which can pose risks to patient health.

Review Questions

1. What are hard gelatin capsules?

Hard gelatin capsules are solid dosage forms made from gelatin, primarily used for filling solid drugs or granules.

2. Which material is used to prepare hard capsule shells?

Hard capsule shells are made from gelatin derived from animal collagen.

3. What is the main difference between hard and soft gelatin capsules?

Hard gelatin capsules are used for dry solid formulations, while soft gelatin capsules are used for liquids or semi-solids.

4. What is the typical moisture content of hard gelatin capsules?

The moisture content is typically between 13% and 16%.

5. Name one method used for filling hard gelatin capsules.

Manual filling is one common method, especially in small-scale operations.

6. What is capsule locking?

Capsule locking is a technique used to prevent the cap and body of the capsule from separating after filling.

7. What are the two main parts of a hard gelatin capsule?

The two parts are the body (longer part) and the cap (shorter part).

8. What is used as a plasticizer in soft gelatin capsules?

Glycerin or sorbitol is used to make the gelatin flexible.

9. What are opacifying agents?

Opacifying agents like titanium dioxide are added to make the capsule opaque and protect light-sensitive drugs.

10. Why are soft gelatin capsules hermetically sealed?

They are sealed to prevent leakage of their liquid contents and ensure product stability.

11. What is the base adsorption value?

Base adsorption refers to the amount of liquid that a powder can retain per gram without becoming sticky.

12. What is the significance of the minimum/gram factor?

It helps calculate how much vehicle is needed to fill a soft gelatin capsule with a solid-liquid mix.

13. How are soft gelatin capsules filled?

They are filled during manufacturing using a rotary die process, which fills and seals the capsule simultaneously.

14. What are some typical contents of soft gelatin capsules?

They can contain oils, solutions, suspensions, or pastes.

15. What is band sealing in capsules?

Band sealing is a security feature where a gelatin band is applied at the joint between the cap and body.

16. Why are capsules colored?

They are colored for product identification and to make them more visually appealing.

17. What is a telescoping defect?

Telescoping occurs when the body and cap of a hard capsule are not properly aligned or separate prematurely.

18. Which test checks the disintegration of capsules?

The disintegration test ensures capsules break down within the prescribed time in a liquid medium.

19. What is the ideal disintegration time for capsules?

It should not exceed 30 minutes in simulated gastric fluid.

20. What is capsule polishing?

It is a post-filling process that removes powder residues from the outer surface of capsules.

21. How are filled capsules dried?

They are dried using tray drying under controlled temperature and humidity conditions.

22. What is the function of lubricants in capsule filling?

Lubricants reduce friction and prevent the formulation from sticking to the equipment.

23. Name a common lubricant used in capsules.

Magnesium stearate is widely used as a lubricant.

24. What is the importance of particle size in capsule filling?

Uniform particle size ensures accurate dosing and prevents segregation during filling.

25. What is meant by softgel encapsulation?

It is the process of producing soft gelatin capsules by filling and sealing in a single step.

26. What is gelatin bloom strength?

It measures the firmness or gel strength of gelatin; higher bloom value indicates stronger gelatin.

27. What is capsule finishing?

Finishing includes cleaning, inspecting, and sorting capsules after filling.

28. Why is moisture content critical in capsules?

Too much moisture can soften the shell, while too little can make it brittle.

29. What is the role of preservatives in capsules?

Preservatives prevent microbial contamination, especially in soft gelatin capsules.

30. What causes capsule shell brittleness?

Loss of moisture or exposure to low-humidity conditions leads to brittleness.

31. How are capsules stored?

They are stored in airtight containers at controlled temperature and humidity.

32. What is encapsulation?

Encapsulation is the process of enclosing a drug within a capsule shell.

33. What is gelatin derived from?

Gelatin is obtained by hydrolysis of collagen from animal bones or skin.

34. What are enteric capsules?

They are capsules coated to resist stomach acid and dissolve only in the intestine.

35. Name one use of hard gelatin capsules.

They are used to encapsulate powders, pellets, or granules.

36. How is capsule shell thickness measured?

It is measured using specialized instruments like micrometers.

37. What is meant by hygroscopic substances in capsules?

These substances absorb moisture from the air and can affect capsule stability.

38. What is tamper-evident sealing?

It is a technique used to indicate unauthorized opening or tampering of the capsule.

39. What are capsule sizes?

Capsule sizes range from 000 (largest) to 5 (smallest).

40. What is the use of colorants in capsules?

Colorants help in brand identification and prevent confusion among medications.

41. Why are some capsules opaque?

To protect light-sensitive drugs from degradation caused by exposure to light.

42. What is a capsule-filling machine?

It is equipment used to fill powder or granules into empty capsules efficiently.

43. What is the role of diluents in capsule formulation?

Diluents add bulk to ensure the capsule is properly filled when drug dose is small.

44. What does a semi-automatic capsule filler do?

It automates some parts of the filling process while requiring manual intervention for others.

45. What is gelatin plasticization?

It is the process of softening gelatin using plasticizers to make it moldable.

46. Why is uniformity of fill important?

It ensures each capsule contains the same amount of drug, which is essential for efficacy and safety.

47. What is meant by capsule shell cross-linking?

It refers to the chemical reaction in gelatin shells that can reduce solubility over time.

48. How are capsule defects detected?

Defects are identified through visual inspection or automated detection systems.

49. What is spray drying in capsule formulation?

Spray drying is a method used to prepare dry powders with controlled particle size for encapsulation.

50. What is the effect of temperature on capsule stability?

High temperatures can cause capsule shells to deform, melt, or stick together, affecting drug integrity.

MCQs

1. The primary material used to make hard gelatin capsules is
A. Starch
B. Cellulose
C. Chitosan
D. Gelatin
Answer: D

2. Soft gelatin capsules are most suitable for
A. Granules
B. Powders
C. Liquids
D. Tablets
Answer: C

3. A common plasticizer in soft gelatin capsules is
A. Glycerin
B. Magnesium stearate
C. Talc
D. Sucrose
Answer: A

4. Hard gelatin capsules are composed of two parts called
A. Top and bottom
B. Body and cap
C. Shell and seal
D. Cap and base
Answer: B

5. The typical moisture content of hard gelatin capsules is
A. 17–20%
B. 13–16%
C. 5–7%
D. 10–12%
Answer: B

6. Gelatin is obtained from
A. Animal collagen
B. Yeast
C. Cellulose
D. Starch

Answer: A

7. Soft gelatin capsules are sealed using

A. Capsule locking

B. Gelatin banding

C. Heat sealing

D. Glue

Answer: B

8. The strength of gelatin is expressed as

A. Viscosity

B. Elasticity

C. Bloom strength

D. Hardness

Answer: C

9. Capsule size 000 represents

A. Smallest size

B. Irregular size

C. Largest size

D. Average size

Answer: C

10. Enteric capsules dissolve in

A. Mouth

B. Blood

C. Intestine

D. Stomach

Answer: C

11. Capsules are colored to

A. Improve solubility

B. Enhance taste

C. Aid identification

D. Increase weight

Answer: C

12. A lubricant commonly used in capsule filling is

A. Glycerin

B. Sucrose

C. Magnesium stearate

D. Silica

Answer: C

13. Capsule locking prevents

A. Overfilling
B. Breakage
C. Leakage
D. Separation of parts
Answer: D

14. Disintegration test checks

A. Weight
B. Hardness
C. Time to dissolve
D. Color
Answer: C

15. The component that helps in keeping liquid in soft gelatin capsules is

A. Binder
B. Plasticizer
C. Preservative
D. Coating
Answer: B

16. Which is suitable for hygroscopic drugs?

A. Hard capsules
B. Soft capsules
C. Coated tablets
D. Pellets
Answer: B

17. Manual filling is suitable for

A. Large-scale
B. Sterile filling
C. Small-scale
D. Liquid filling
Answer: C

18. Soft gelatin capsules are prepared using

A. Rotary die process
B. Tablet press
C. Roller compaction
D. Dry mixing
Answer: A

19. Base adsorption is used to determine

A. Hardness

B. Lubricant need

C. Liquid retention

D. Weight

Answer: C

20. The capsule polishing step is used for

A. Sealing

B. Lubrication

C. Cleaning

D. Drying

Answer: C

21. Capsule brittleness is due to

A. High moisture

B. Low temperature

C. Low humidity

D. Colorants

Answer: C

22. Tamper-evident sealing ensures

A. Flavor masking

B. Authenticity

C. Dissolution

D. Compression

Answer: B

23. The process of enclosing drug in capsule shell is

A. Enrobing

B. Encapsulation

C. Tableting

D. Coating

Answer: B

24. Preservatives in capsules prevent

A. Color change

B. Leakage

C. Microbial growth

D. Odor

Answer: C

25. Capsules should be stored in

A. Open trays

B. Refrigerators

C. Dry containers

D. Freezers

Answer: C

26. Cross-linking in capsule shells reduces

A. Weight

B. Disintegration

C. Strength

D. Color

Answer: B

27. A defect where cap and body separate is called

A. Splitting

B. Telescoping

C. Capping

D. Chipping

Answer: B

28. Enteric capsules protect drugs from

A. Heat

B. Light

C. Acidic environment

D. Moisture

Answer: C

29. Size 5 capsule is used for

A. High dose

B. Liquid fill

C. Small dose

D. Double dose

Answer: C

30. Soft capsules are ideal for

A. Hydrophobic liquids

B. Water

C. Dusts

D. Foams

Answer: A

41. Aqueous liquids are not suitable for

A. Tablets

B. Hard capsules

C. Soft capsules

D. Syrups

Answer: C

42. A shell made from fish gelatin is preferred in

A. Tropical areas

B. Cold storage

C. Halal products

D. Pet products

Answer: C

43. The color of capsule may indicate

A. Taste

B. Strength

C. Manufacturer

D. Size

Answer: C

44. Filled capsules are dried to prevent

A. Leakage

B. Bulging

C. Stickiness

D. Weight gain

Answer: C

45. Gelatin concentration affects

A. Taste

B. Disintegration

C. Hardness

D. Shelf life

Answer: C

46. Base adsorption relates to

A. Capsule size

B. Liquid capacity

C. Moisture uptake

D. Weight loss

Answer: B

47. Drying tunnels are used in

A. Granulation

B. Capsule storage

C. Softgel production

D. Tablet coating

Answer: C

48. Capsule polishing machines remove

A. Microbes

B. Stains

C. Powder residues

D. Water

Answer: C

49. Enteric capsules are designed to

A. Dissolve immediately

B. Withstand stomach acid

C. Mask bad taste

D. Increase capsule size

Answer: B

50. Hard gelatin capsules are not suitable for

A. Solid drugs

B. Granules

C. Aqueous liquids

D. Pellets

Answer: C

CHAPTER FIVE

Pellets

5.1 Introduction to Pellets

Pellets are a specialized dosage form widely used in pharmaceutical applications due to their unique properties and ability to deliver drugs in a controlled, predictable manner. These small, spherical or semi-spherical, free-flowing particles offer significant advantages over conventional dosage forms such as tablets or powders, enhancing drug performance and patient compliance.

5.1.1 Advantages of Pellets

Definition and Characteristics

Pellets are defined as **small, discrete, spherical, or semi-spherical particles** typically ranging in size from **0.5 to 2 mm in diameter**. They are produced through techniques such as extrusion-spheronization, layering, or spray drying. Pellets are known for their uniform size, high mechanical strength, and excellent flow properties, making them ideal for further processing into capsules or compressed into tablets.

Advantages Over Conventional Dosage Forms

Pellets offer several advantages that make them superior to conventional dosage forms like powders or tablets:

Uniform Distribution in the Gastrointestinal (GI) Tract for Controlled Drug Release

Pellets exhibit uniform size and density, enabling their even distribution throughout the GI tract.

This uniform distribution minimizes variability in drug absorption, ensuring consistent plasma drug levels and reducing the risk of dose dumping.

For example, **pantoprazole pellets** coated for delayed release ensure uniform delivery in the small intestine, enhancing therapeutic outcomes.

Minimized Local Irritation and Improved Patient Compliance

Drugs with a high potential for local irritation, such as **nonsteroidal anti-inflammatory drugs (NSAIDs)**, benefit from pellet formulations that distribute the active ingredient uniformly, reducing localized side effects.

Pellets encapsulated in capsules or compressed into tablets provide a smooth surface, making them easier to swallow, enhancing patient compliance.

Versatility in Coating for Modified Release Profiles

Pellets can be coated with polymers to achieve **delayed release**, **sustained release**, or **targeted drug delivery**.

Multiple layers can be applied to create complex release profiles, such as biphasic or pulsatile drug release.

Example: **Omeprazole enteric-coated pellets** resist stomach acid and release the drug in the intestine, protecting the drug from degradation and ensuring effective absorption.

Enhanced Processability in Capsule Filling or Tablet Compression

The spherical shape and excellent flow properties of pellets improve their processability, making them ideal for encapsulation or direct compression into tablets.

Uniform size and density ensure consistent fill weights and drug content in capsules.

Example: **Pellet-filled capsules of metoprolol** ensure accurate dosing and controlled release over 24 hours.

Improved Bioavailability and Therapeutic Outcomes

Pellet formulations have been shown to improve drug bioavailability and therapeutic efficacy due to their controlled release and uniform distribution:

Case Study: Lansoprazole Pellets

Lansoprazole, a proton pump inhibitor (PPI), formulated as enteric-coated pellets, demonstrated enhanced bioavailability compared to conventional tablets.

The enteric coating protected the drug from stomach acid, ensuring its delivery to the small intestine, where it is absorbed effectively.

Result: Patients experienced improved symptom relief from acid reflux and better long-term management of gastric ulcers.

Data Example: Theophylline Sustained-Release Pellets

Theophylline, used for asthma management, was formulated into sustained-release pellets.

Pharmacokinetic studies showed that the pellets provided consistent plasma drug levels over 12 hours, reducing the frequency of dosing and improving patient adherence.

Compared to immediate-release tablets, the sustained-release pellets reduced adverse effects like nausea and headaches associated with peak plasma concentrations.

5.1.2 Requirements for Formulation

The successful formulation of pellets relies on meeting specific physical and chemical requirements to ensure their performance during manufacturing, storage, and drug delivery. Proper selection of excipients and adherence to formulation parameters contribute to achieving these desired characteristics.

Essential Properties of Pellets

1. Narrow Size Distribution

Definition:

Pellets should have a uniform size distribution, typically within the range of **500–1500 μm.**

This ensures consistent flow properties during manufacturing and uniform coating during processing.

Significance:

Narrow size distribution minimizes segregation during blending and improves dosing accuracy.

It also ensures even release profiles when pellets are coated with polymers for modified release.

2. High Mechanical Strength and Low Friability

Definition:

Pellets should exhibit **high mechanical strength** to withstand handling, transportation, and compression, with friability (weight loss during handling) not exceeding **0.5%.**

Significance:

High strength ensures pellets do not break or generate dust during processing, which could lead to inconsistent dosing.

Low friability enhances their suitability for processes such as capsule filling or tablet compression.

Example:

Pellets for **ibuprofen sustained-release capsules** exhibit a friability of less than 0.2%, ensuring durability during encapsulation.

3. Uniform Drug Content and Smooth Surface

Definition:

Pellets should have a uniform distribution of the active pharmaceutical ingredient (API) to ensure consistent dosing. A **smooth surface** is essential for efficient and uniform coating with polymers or other materials.

Significance:

Uniform drug content ensures therapeutic efficacy by minimizing dose variability.

A smooth surface facilitates even application of coating materials, critical for achieving desired release profiles.

Example:

Enteric-coated **omeprazole pellets** demonstrate uniform drug loading and smooth surfaces for efficient acid-resistant coating.

Key Formulation Components

The formulation of pellets involves the use of specific excipients that provide structural integrity, ensure drug stability, and enhance manufacturability. These include binders, fillers, and plasticizers.

1. Binders

Purpose:

Binders provide cohesiveness to the formulation, aiding in pellet formation during processes like extrusion-spheronization.

Examples:

Povidone (PVP): Used in concentrations of **2–5% w/w** for strong binding without affecting drug release.

Hydroxypropyl Methylcellulose (HPMC): Provides both binding and film-forming properties.

Application:

Propranolol sustained-release pellets use PVP as a binder for uniform drug dispersion and robust structure.

2. Fillers

Purpose:

Fillers provide bulk to the pellet formulation, ensuring suitable size and mechanical strength.

Examples:

Lactose: Used for its excellent compressibility and solubility properties.

Microcrystalline Cellulose (MCC): Used in concentrations of **40–60% w/w**, offering superior binding properties and uniform particle size.

Application:

Theophylline sustained-release pellets utilize MCC for structural integrity and smooth pellet formation.

3. Plasticizers

Purpose:

Plasticizers are added to enhance the flexibility and reduce brittleness of the pellets, especially when they are coated with polymers.

Examples:

Polyethylene Glycol (PEG): Improves coating flexibility, preventing cracks during handling.

Triethyl Citrate: Enhances mechanical stability during storage.

Application:

Enteric-coated **pantoprazole pellets** incorporate triethyl citrate to ensure coating durability under variable conditions.

Examples of Excipients and Pellet Formulations

Omeprazole Enteric-Coated Pellets:

Binder: PVP (3% w/w).

Filler: MCC (50% w/w).

Plasticizer: Triethyl citrate for enteric coating flexibility.

Outcome: Efficient acid-resistant delivery in the intestine.

Theophylline Sustained-Release Pellets:

Binder: HPMC (5% w/w).

Filler: Lactose (40% w/w).

Plasticizer: PEG for extended release coating.

Outcome: Smooth and robust pellets with prolonged drug release over 12 hours.

Ibuprofen Pellets for Controlled Release:

Binder: PVP (4% w/w).

Filler: MCC (45% w/w).

Plasticizer: Triacetin for coating flexibility.

Outcome: Uniformly coated pellets with minimized dose dumping.

5.2 Pelletization Process

5.2.1 Extrusion-Spheronization

Extrusion-spheronization is a widely used pelletization technique in pharmaceutical manufacturing. It enables the production of uniform, spherical pellets with excellent mechanical strength and consistent drug content. The process involves several sequential steps, including wet massing, extrusion, spheronization, and drying.

Step-by-Step Process

1. Wet Massing

Wet massing is the initial step, where the dry powder blend is mixed with a liquid binder to form a cohesive, pliable mass suitable for extrusion.

Critical Factors:

The concentration of the binder solution (e.g., water or hydro-alcoholic mixture) must be optimized.

Typical binder content is **5–15% w/w** of the total powder blend, depending on the nature of the active ingredient and excipients.

Over-wetting can cause stickiness, while under-wetting leads to poor pellet formation.

Significance:

A uniformly wetted mass ensures smooth extrusion and consistent pellet size.

Example:

A formulation containing microcrystalline cellulose (MCC, 50% w/w) and lactose (40% w/w) may require 8% w/w of water to achieve optimal wet mass consistency.

2. Extrusion

Extrusion transforms the wet mass into cylindrical extrudates by forcing it through a die under controlled pressure.

Types of Extruders:

Axial Extruders: The material is pushed along the axis of the die using screws or pistons.

Radial Extruders: The material exits radially through perforations in the die plate.

Operating Parameters:

Extrusion Force: Typically ranges between **1–5 MPa**, depending on the formulation properties.

Die Diameter: Influences the initial size of the extrudates, which impacts the final pellet size (e.g., 0.5–1.2 mm diameter).

Mathematical Relationship:

The extrudate diameter (D) is influenced by the die diameter (d) and moisture content (M):

$$D \propto d \cdot M$$

Significance:

Cylindrical extrudates with consistent diameter are essential for forming uniform pellets during spheronization.

3. Spheronization

Spheronization converts cylindrical extrudates into spherical pellets by subjecting them to rotational forces within a spheronizer.

Equipment:

The spheronizer consists of a rotating friction plate and stationary walls. The extrudates are broken into smaller lengths and rounded by friction and centrifugal forces.

Operating Parameters:

Plate Speed: Typically set between **1000–1500 rpm**.

Residence Time: Ranges from **5–10 minutes**, depending on the desired pellet size and shape.

Mechanism:

The speed of the friction plate influences the rounding process:

The formula to express the relationship between the **plate speed, residence time**, and the **spheronization process** is:

$$S \propto \text{Plate Speed} \times \text{Residence Time}$$

S (Sphericity or Roundness of Pellets): The efficiency of the spheronization process depends on how well the particles are rounded.

Plate Speed: Higher speeds increase the frictional forces, improving the rounding effect.

Residence Time: The longer the material stays on the friction plate, the greater the chance for uniform rounding.

Implication:

Increasing **plate speed** or **residence time** improves **sphericity**.

However, **excessive plate speed** can lead to pellet breakage or deformation.

4. Drying

Drying stabilizes the pellets by removing excess moisture while preserving their spherical shape and mechanical integrity.

Drying Techniques:

Tray Drying: Pellets are spread in thin layers on trays and dried using heated air.

Fluidized Bed Drying: Hot air circulates through a fluidized bed, offering rapid and uniform drying.

Optimal Moisture Content:
The final moisture content is typically reduced to **2–5% w/w**, ensuring pellet stability and preventing microbial growth.

Significance:
Proper drying prevents pellet shrinkage or cracking, maintaining their size and mechanical properties.

5.2.2 Layering Techniques

Layering techniques are widely used in pelletization to build up layers of active pharmaceutical ingredients (APIs) and excipients onto an inert core, such as sugar spheres or microcrystalline cellulose pellets. This process produces uniformly coated pellets with desirable properties for sustained or controlled drug release.

Powder Layering

Process Description

Powder layering involves the sequential application of dry powder and a liquid binder onto an inert core. The liquid binder acts as an adhesive, allowing the powder to stick to the core and build up uniform layers.

Steps:
The inert cores are placed in a fluidized bed or a rotating drum.

A liquid binder (e.g., hydroxypropyl methylcellulose solution) is sprayed onto the cores.

Powdered API or excipient is introduced, adhering to the wet cores.

The process is repeated to achieve the desired pellet size and drug content.

Applications:
Powder layering is used for APIs with poor solubility or stability in liquid form.

Example: **Theophylline sustained-release pellets** are prepared by layering theophylline powder onto sugar spheres using a binder solution.

Solution/Suspension Layering

Process Description

Solution or suspension layering involves the application of a drug solution or suspension directly onto an inert core, forming a uniform layer of the API.

Steps:

The inert cores are fluidized or tumbled in a rotating drum.

A solution or suspension of the API is sprayed onto the cores.

The solvent evaporates, leaving behind a uniform drug layer.

Multiple layers can be applied for desired drug loading or release profiles.

Applications:

Suitable for APIs that are stable in liquid form.

Example: **Omeprazole delayed-release pellets** are prepared by layering an API suspension onto sugar spheres, followed by enteric coating.

Equipment and Process Parameters

Fluidized Bed Processors

Fluidized bed processors (FBPs) are commonly used for both powder and solution layering due to their precise control over process parameters. These machines fluidize the inert cores using an upward flow of air, ensuring even coating during the layering process.

Key Process Parameters:

Spray Rate:

The liquid binder or solution is sprayed at a controlled rate, typically **2–10 g/min**, to avoid overwetting or undercoating.

Airflow Velocity:

Maintained at **~1.5 m/s** to keep the cores fluidized without excessive turbulence that could disrupt layering.

Inlet Air Temperature:

Controlled at **40–60°C** to evaporate the liquid binder or solvent efficiently without degrading the API.

Advantages of Fluidized Bed Processors

Ensures uniform coating and minimizes agglomeration.

Suitable for batch or continuous production.

Examples of Layering for Sustained or Controlled Release

Sustained-Release Pellets:

Example: Metoprolol succinate sustained-release pellets are prepared using powder layering. The active drug layer is applied onto inert cores, followed by a polymer coating to control release over 12–24 hours.

Controlled-Release Pellets:

Example: Propranolol hydrochloride controlled-release pellets use solution layering to apply the drug, followed by a combination of rate-controlling and protective coatings.

Delayed-Release Pellets:

Example: Omeprazole enteric-coated pellets are produced by solution layering of the API, followed by enteric coating to ensure release in the intestine.

5.2.3 Fluidized Bed Coating

Fluidized bed coating is a versatile and efficient technique widely used in the pharmaceutical industry to coat pellets, granules, and other small particles. This method involves suspending particles in an upward air stream while spraying a coating material onto their surfaces, resulting in a uniform and smooth layer.

Principle of Fluidization

The principle of fluidization is based on suspending solid particles in a controlled upward flow of air, creating a fluid-like state.

Mechanism:

Particles are introduced into the fluidized bed processor, where air flows upward through a perforated plate or distributor.

The airflow velocity is adjusted to balance the gravitational forces acting on the particles, suspending them in the air stream.

The particles remain in constant motion, ensuring even exposure to the sprayed coating material.

Advantages:

Uniform coating due to consistent particle movement.

Improved drying efficiency as the air stream facilitates solvent evaporation during the coating process.

Process Parameters

To achieve optimal coating quality, several process parameters must be carefully controlled:

1. Airflow Velocity

Range: Typically maintained at **1–3 m/s.**

Significance:

Low airflow velocity may cause particles to settle, leading to uneven coating.

Excessively high velocity can result in particle attrition or loss from the system.

2. Spray Atomization Pressure

Range: 1–2 bar.

Significance:

Proper atomization ensures the coating solution is broken into fine droplets, promoting uniform distribution.

Insufficient pressure can lead to large droplets, causing uneven coating or agglomeration.

3. Coating Solution Viscosity

Range: ≤200 cps.

Significance:

Low-viscosity solutions spread easily over the particle surface, creating a smooth, defect-free coating.

High-viscosity solutions may cause clogging of the spray nozzle or uneven coating.

Applications in Pellet Coating

Fluidized bed coating is used for a variety of pharmaceutical applications, including:

1. Taste Masking

Objective: To mask the unpleasant taste of APIs in oral formulations, improving patient compliance.

Process:

A layer of taste-masking polymer, such as **Eudragit E**, is applied to the pellets.

Example: **Paracetamol pellets** are coated to mask their bitter taste in pediatric formulations.

2. Sustained Release

Objective: To control the release of the API over an extended period, reducing dosing frequency.

Process:

A rate-controlling polymer, such as **ethyl cellulose** or **HPMC**, is sprayed onto the pellets.

The thickness of the coating determines the release rate.

Example: **Theophylline sustained-release pellets** provide consistent plasma levels over 12–24 hours.

3. Enteric Protection

Objective: To protect acid-labile drugs from stomach acid or to prevent drug release until the pellets reach the intestine.

Process:

Enteric polymers, such as **cellulose acetate phthalate (CAP)** or **Eudragit L**, are used for coating.

The polymer dissolves at a pH above 5.5, ensuring release in the small intestine.

Example: **Omeprazole enteric-coated pellets** protect the drug from gastric degradation and ensure intestinal absorption.

5.3 Equipment for Pellet Manufacture

5.3.1 Working Principle of Fluidized Bed Coater (FBC)

The fluidized bed coater (FBC) is a versatile piece of equipment widely used for coating and drying pellets, granules, and powders in the pharmaceutical industry. It combines fluidization, spraying, and drying in a single process, ensuring efficient and uniform coating.

Working Principle

1. Fluidization of Particles Using Air

Particles are introduced into the fluidization chamber of the FBC.

An upward flow of air suspends and circulates the particles, creating a fluidized state where the particles behave like a liquid.

Fluidization ensures uniform exposure of the particles, preventing aggregation and ensuring even coating.

2. Uniform Coating Through Spray Nozzles

A coating solution or suspension is atomized and sprayed onto the fluidized particles through strategically positioned nozzles.

The spray forms fine droplets that uniformly coat the surface of the moving particles.

3. Drying with Heated Air

Heated air is introduced into the chamber to evaporate the solvent or water from the coating solution, leaving behind a dry and uniform coating layer on each particle.

The process ensures simultaneous coating and drying, preventing clumping or uneven coating.

Key Components

1. Fluidization Chamber

The chamber holds the particles and facilitates their fluidization using a controlled air stream.

It ensures consistent particle movement and prevents aggregation during the coating process.

2. Spray System

The spray system atomizes the coating solution and directs it onto the fluidized particles.

There are three main configurations:

Top-Spray: The spray nozzle is positioned above the fluidized bed, commonly used for layering or granulation.

Bottom-Spray (Wurster Process): The nozzle is located below the fluidized bed, ideal for precise coating applications, such as enteric or sustained-release coatings.

Tangential Spray: The nozzle is positioned at an angle, allowing for complex layering or coating processes.

3. Temperature Control System

The system regulates the temperature of the inlet air and product bed to optimize drying and prevent thermal degradation of the coating material or active ingredient.

Operating Parameters

1. Air Temperature

The inlet air temperature is typically maintained between **40–80°C** to facilitate rapid solvent evaporation without damaging the API or coating material.

2. Spray Rate

The spray rate is controlled within the range of **10–30 mL/min** to ensure a steady application of the coating solution while preventing overwetting or clogging.

3. Product Bed Temperature

The product bed temperature is maintained between **35–50°C** to ensure the coating dries evenly without compromising the integrity of the pellets.

Applications

1. Enteric-Coated Pellets

    Example: Omeprazole Pellets

Coating: A suspension of enteric polymers like **cellulose acetate phthalate (CAP)** or **Eudragit L** is applied using a bottom-spray system.

Purpose: Protect the drug from gastric acid and release it in the intestine, ensuring effective absorption.

    2. Sustained-Release Pellets

    Example: Theophylline Pellets

Coating: A solution of **ethyl cellulose** or **HPMC** is applied using a tangential spray system.

Purpose: Regulate drug release over 12–24 hours, ensuring consistent plasma levels and reducing dosing frequency.

Review Questions

1. What are pharmaceutical pellets?
Pellets are small, free-flowing, spherical or semi-spherical solid units typically made from powder or granules.

2. Which dosage form commonly uses pellets?
Modified-release oral dosage forms often utilize pellets.

3. What is one key advantage of pellets?
Pellets offer controlled and sustained drug release.

4. Why are pellets preferred for coating?
Pellets provide a uniform surface for functional coating.

5. How do pellets improve patient compliance?
They allow for flexible dosing and reduced side effects.

6. What is extrusion-spheronization?
It is a multi-step process used to form uniform, spherical pellets from wet mass.

7. Which unit operation follows extrusion in pellet formation?
Spheronization follows extrusion.

8. What is the role of binders in pellet formulation?
Binders improve the cohesiveness of the formulation.

9. Why is particle size control important in pellets?
It ensures uniformity in drug release and coating.

10. What is a key requirement for pellet formulation?
Formulation must have suitable plasticity for extrusion.

11. What is the function of the spheronizer?
It shapes extrudates into spherical pellets.

12. Which polymer is commonly used in coating of pellets?
Eudragit is frequently used.

13. What is layering in pelletization?
Layering is the application of drug or excipients onto inert cores.

14. What are non-pareil seeds?
These are inert spherical cores used in drug layering.

15. What type of spray gun is used in fluid bed coating?
A bottom spray gun is commonly used.

16. What does a fluidized bed do?
It suspends particles in air to allow uniform coating.

17. What is the function of a fluid bed coater?

It applies coatings to particles or pellets using fluidized air.

18. What is Wurster coating?

A bottom spray technique used in fluidized bed systems.

19. What are pellets used for in multiparticulate systems?

They provide better distribution and reduced risk of dose dumping.

20. What are the mechanical properties required in pellets?

Pellets must be strong enough to withstand compression.

21. What does high sphericity in pellets indicate?

It ensures better flow and uniform coating.

22. Which method is used for rapid layering?

Tangential spray in fluid bed coating.

23. How does pellet coating influence drug release?

The coating controls the site and rate of drug release.

24. What is the ideal size range of pharmaceutical pellets?

Typically between 0.5 mm and 1.5 mm.

25. What kind of excipients are used in extrusion-spheronization?

Microcrystalline cellulose is commonly used.

26. What causes friability in pellets?

Low binder content or poor mechanical strength.

27. What does spheronization time affect?

It affects the roundness and size of pellets.

28. How are pellets dried after coating?

Using hot air in a fluid bed dryer.

29. What is the advantage of multiparticulate dosage forms?

They reduce local irritation and provide uniform absorption.

30. What is the minimum requirement for layering material?

It must adhere uniformly to the core.

31. What is the difference between top spray and bottom spray?

Top spray coats irregularly, bottom spray provides uniform layering.

32. What is agglomeration in pelletization?

Undesired clumping of pellets.

33. Why is process optimization important in pellet production?

To ensure consistency in quality and performance.

34. Which parameters are controlled in FBC?

Temperature, air velocity, and spray rate.

35. What happens if spray rate is too high in FBC?

It may cause agglomeration or poor coating.

36. What is the main function of MCC in pellets?
It provides plasticity and binding during extrusion.

37. What type of pellets are used in capsule filling?
Free-flowing spherical pellets.

38. What equipment is used to dry pellets after spheronization?
Tray dryer or fluid bed dryer.

39. What is the purpose of screening pellets?
To separate pellets of desired size.

40. What is the moisture content range for extrusion?
Usually 16–22% w/w.

41. What affects the hardness of pellets?
Binder content, drying rate, and formulation.

42. What shape do extrudates have before spheronization?
Cylindrical segments.

43. How is uniform layering achieved?
By controlling spray rate and drying air in fluid bed.

44. What is the outcome of poor spheronization?
Irregular shaped pellets with poor flow.

45. Why are pellets preferred in pediatric formulations?
They offer flexibility in dose titration.

46. What is the impact of pellet size on dissolution?
Smaller pellets dissolve faster due to higher surface area.

47. What is one common issue in fluid bed coating?
Agglomeration due to high moisture or spray rate.

48. What does FBC stand for?
Fluidized Bed Coater.

49. What is the principle of fluidization?
Suspending solid particles in an upward air stream.

50. Why is air velocity critical in FBC?
Too low causes poor fluidization, too high causes loss of product.

MCQS

1. Pellets are commonly used in
A. Injectables
B. Transdermals
C. Eye drops
D. Oral modified-release

Answer: D

2. Spherical pellets are mainly produced by

A. Extrusion-spheronization

B. Lyophilization

C. Compression

D. Granulation

Answer: A

3. The core used in layering is called

A. Tablet core

B. Non-pareil seed

C. Shell pellet

D. Microbead

Answer: B

4. One key advantage of pellets is

A. Taste masking

B. Uniform coating

C. Cheaper production

D. Dose reduction

Answer: B

5. The function of a spheronizer is to

A. Mix granules

B. Compress powder

C. Round extrudates

D. Dry pellets

Answer: C

6. Layering is applied by

A. Tablet press

B. Fluid bed

C. Manual scoop

D. Roller compactor

Answer: B

7. Microcrystalline cellulose acts as a

A. Diluent

B. Disintegrant

C. Plasticizer

D. Binding agent

Answer: D

8. In fluidized bed coating, bottom spray provides

A. Uneven coating

B. Thin coating

C. Uniform coating

D. Fast coating

Answer: C

9. A typical pellet size is

A. 0.2–0.4 mm

B. 0.5–1.5 mm

C. 2–3 mm

D. 3–5 mm

Answer: B

10. Agglomeration in coating is due to

A. Low moisture

B. Fast air flow

C. High spray rate

D. Short drying

Answer: C

11. Fluidized bed coaters work on

A. Heat convection

B. Mechanical vibration

C. Air suspension

D. Centrifugal force

Answer: C

12. Wurster process uses

A. Top spray

B. Tangential spray

C. Side spray

D. Bottom spray

Answer: D

13. Extrudates before spheronization are

A. Granules

B. Powders

C. Cylindrical

D. Flat discs

Answer: C

14. Drying of coated pellets is done in

A. Tray dryer

B. Fluid bed

C. Rotary kiln

D. Hot plate

Answer: B

15. A key benefit of multiparticulate pellets is

A. Smaller packaging

B. Reduced side effects

C. Improved taste

D. Lower cost

Answer: B

16. The mechanical strength of pellets ensures

A. Shining

B. Color

C. Compression resistance

D. Elasticity

Answer: C

17. One process variable in pellet coating is

A. Granule size

B. Capsule fill

C. Spray rate

D. Tableting force

Answer: C

18. Binder concentration influences

A. Pellet color

B. Pellet hardness

C. Pellet size

D. Pellet shape

Answer: B

19. Spheronization time affects

A. Moisture

B. Sphericity

C. Viscosity

D. Weight

Answer: B

20. Pellets are used in capsules for

A. Aesthetic value

B. Dose division

C. Coating needs

D. Cost saving

Answer: B

21. Fluid bed coating ensures

A. Drug solubility

B. Flowability

C. Disintegration

D. Uniform layering

Answer: D

22. Pellets are commonly dried using

A. Microwave

B. Sunlight

C. Fluid bed

D. Water bath

Answer: C

23. Friability in pellets refers to

A. Cracking

B. Stickiness

C. Hardness

D. Loss of weight

Answer: D

24. Uniformity of pellet size affects

A. Release rate

B. Taste

C. Weight

D. Odor

Answer: A

25. One disadvantage of high moisture content is

A. Powdering

B. Color fading

C. Capping

D. Deformation

Answer: D

26. Pellets are used in combination therapy to

A. Reduce cost

B. Improve color

C. Add flavors

D. Separate drugs

Answer: D

27. Layering is done using

A. Tablet punch

B. Milling

C. Rotating drum

D. Spray nozzles

Answer: D

28. The principle of fluidization involves

A. Steam flow

B. Air lift

C. Mechanical shaking

D. Air suspension

Answer: D

29. Pellet hardness is affected by

A. Color

B. Binder

C. Lubricant

D. Coating thickness

Answer: B

30. A common process problem is

A. Underdosing

B. Foaming

C. Agglomeration

D. Segregation

Answer: C

31. Process validation ensures

A. Drug taste

B. Batch consistency

C. Coating color

D. Shelf life

Answer: B

32. Granules for extrusion must be

A. Plastic

B. Lubricated

C. Dry

D. Wet but brittle

Answer: A

33. Wurster coating is preferred for

A. Small pellets

B. Large tablets

C. Ointments

D. Liquids

Answer: A

34. The spheronizer plate has

A. Grooves

B. Pins

C. Pores

D. Holes

Answer: A

35. Coating thickness impacts

A. Taste

B. Release profile

C. Capsule fit

D. Color

Answer: B

36. The spray rate in coating must be

A. Balanced

B. Constant

C. High

D. Random

Answer: A

37. The key reason for screening pellets is

A. Drying

B. Density control

C. Color sorting

D. Size separation

Answer: D

38. High sphericity improves

A. Flow

B. Aroma

C. Hardness

D. Taste

Answer: A

39. Pellets are ideal for

A. Ointments

B. Compressed tablets

C. Oral liquids

D. Multiparticulate systems

Answer: D

40. Poor drying causes

A. Weight gain

B. Shell rupture

C. High friability

D. Coating cracks

Answer: D

41. Pellets can carry

A. Only dyes

B. Only excipients

C. Multiple drugs

D. Single excipient

Answer: C

42. Excess spray in coating causes

A. Crusting

B. Swelling

C. Drying

D. Sticking

Answer: D

43. Fluid bed coater uses

A. Heated air

B. Vacuum

C. Radiation

D. Cool air

Answer: A

44. The formulation must exhibit

A. Elasticity

B. Plasticity

C. Hardness

D. Viscosity

Answer: B

45. Loss on drying controls

A. Disintegration

B. Shell thickness

C. Tablet punch

D. Moisture content

Answer: D

46. Coating time depends on

A. Drying time

B. Drug type

C. Nozzle size

D. Air velocity

Answer: D

47. Uniform layering prevents

A. Weight variation

B. Dose dumping

C. Foaming

D. Powdering

Answer: B

48. Moisture content during extrusion affects

A. Strength

B. Color

C. Taste

D. Extrudability

Answer: D

49. The minimum function of MCC is to

A. Act as surfactant

B. Improve binding

C. Enhance color

D. Act as plasticizer

Answer: B

50. Drying of wet mass before extrusion leads to

A. Flowable mix

B. Cracks

C. Hard pellets

D. Failure

Answer: D

CHAPTER SIX

Parenteral Products

6.1.1 Definition and Types

Definition of Parenteral Products

Parenteral products are **sterile pharmaceutical preparations** administered directly into the body via injection or infusion, bypassing the gastrointestinal (GI) tract. This route ensures rapid onset of action, precise drug delivery, and high bioavailability, making parenteral formulations indispensable in critical and controlled drug therapy.

Key Features:

Parenterals must be free from microbial contamination, pyrogens, and particulate matter.

They are required to maintain sterility, isotonicity, and stability to ensure safety and efficacy.

Classification of Parenteral adminstration

Parenteral drug administration can be classified based on the route of administration and the dosage form used. Intravenous (IV) administration involves delivering medication directly into a vein, ensuring rapid systemic circulation. This method is commonly used in emergency situations, fluid replenishment, and drug infusion. Examples include antibiotics such as ceftriaxone and vancomycin, electrolyte solutions like sodium chloride 0.9% and Ringer's lactate, and chemotherapy drugs such as doxorubicin and cisplatin.

Intramuscular (IM) injections are administered into muscle tissue, providing sustained absorption over hours or days. This route is ideal for depot preparations and moderate volume injections. Some common IM-administered drugs include vaccines like the hepatitis B vaccine and tetanus toxoid, hormones such as progesterone and testosterone injections, and pain relievers like ketorolac and diclofenac.

Subcutaneous (SC) administration involves injecting medication into the subcutaneous tissue beneath the skin, allowing for slow and steady absorption. This method is commonly used for biologics and anticoagulants. Examples include insulin preparations such as regular insulin and insulin glargine, biologics like adalimumab and etanercept, and anticoagulants including enoxaparin and heparin.

Intradermal (ID) injections are administered into the dermal layer of the skin for localized effects or diagnostic purposes. This route is primarily used for sensitivity testing and small-volume vaccines. The Mantoux test for tuberculosis screening is a well-known intradermal application. Additionally, certain vaccines like the rabies vaccine can be administered via the intradermal route, and allergen testing for diagnostic purposes also utilizes this method.Parenteral drugs can also be classified based on dosage forms. Solutions are clear, sterile liquids in which the active pharmaceutical ingredients (APIs) are completely dissolved. Examples include intravenous solutions like dextrose 5% and normal saline, as well as subcutaneous formulations such as insulin aspart solution. Suspensions, on the other hand, consist of sterile preparations where insoluble APIs are dispersed in a liquid medium. Procaine penicillin G suspension is commonly used for intramuscular injections, while triamcinolone acetonide suspension is administered subcutaneously.Emulsions are sterile mixtures of two immiscible liquids stabilized by emulsifying agents, commonly used for parenteral nutrition and lipid-based drugs. Lipid emulsions for total parenteral nutrition (TPN) are often administered intravenously, while intramuscular emulsions include vitamin A injection emulsions. Lyophilized powders are freeze-dried sterile powders that require reconstitution before administration. These are commonly used in intravenous and intramuscular applications, such as cefazolin sodium powder for IV reconstitution and erythropoietin lyophilized powder for IM injection. Each of these dosage forms and administration routes is carefully selected based on the therapeutic requirements, ensuring optimal drug efficacy and patient safety.

6.1.2 Advantages and Limitations

Parenteral products play a pivotal role in modern medicine, offering unique benefits for the delivery of drugs that cannot be effectively administered through oral or other non-invasive routes. However, the use of parenterals is also associated with specific challenges that necessitate careful handling, preparation, and administration.

Advantages of Parenteral Products

1. Immediate Drug Action

- **Rapid Onset of Effect**: Parenterals deliver drugs directly into the systemic circulation or target tissues, bypassing absorption barriers such as the gastrointestinal (GI) tract. This ensures rapid therapeutic action, making parenterals essential in emergencies like cardiac arrest, anaphylaxis, or severe infections.
- **Example**: Intravenous (IV) administration of **epinephrine** in anaphylactic shock produces effects within seconds.

2. Suitable for Poorly Absorbed or Degraded Drugs

- **Overcoming Absorption Issues**: Drugs with poor bioavailability due to low solubility, instability in gastric acid, or first-pass metabolism can be effectively delivered via parenterals.
- **Example**: **Insulin**, degraded by digestive enzymes, is administered subcutaneously to ensure therapeutic efficacy.
- **Biologics**: Parenterals are the primary route for protein-based drugs, including monoclonal antibodies like **adalimumab** (for rheumatoid arthritis).

3. Precise Dosage Control

- **Accuracy and Adjustability**: Parenterals allow precise control over drug dosing and concentration, enabling titration to the desired therapeutic effect. This is particularly useful for potent drugs with a narrow therapeutic index.
- **Example**: IV infusion of **heparin** for anticoagulation is closely monitored to maintain therapeutic levels without causing bleeding.

Limitations of Parenteral Products

1. Requires Aseptic Preparation and Administration

- **Sterility Concerns**: Parenteral formulations must be manufactured and administered under stringent aseptic conditions to prevent microbial contamination and pyrogenic reactions. This increases the complexity and cost of production.
- **Data**: Studies show that aseptic preparation accounts for **15–25%** of the total cost of parenteral manufacturing.

2. Risk of Pain, Infection, and Incompatibilities

- **Pain and Discomfort**: The invasive nature of parenterals can cause pain and anxiety in patients, particularly with frequent or high-volume injections.
- **Infection Risk**: Poor technique or unsterilized equipment can lead to local or systemic infections such as cellulitis or sepsis.

  - **Data**: The risk of catheter-related bloodstream infections (CRBSIs) in IV therapy is estimated at **0.5–1 per 1000 catheter days** globally.

- **Incompatibilities**: Mixing drugs in the same syringe or IV line can cause chemical or physical interactions, leading to reduced efficacy or precipitation.

  - Example: **Calcium and phosphate** in IV nutrition can precipitate if not carefully balanced.

3. Higher Cost and Specialized Handling

Parenterals require specialized facilities, trained personnel, and expensive equipment for preparation and administration, limiting their accessibility in resource-constrained settings.

Global Market Trends and Usage Statistics

Market Growth:

The global parenteral drug market is projected to grow from **USD 81 billion in 2020** to **USD 140 billion by 2028**, driven by the increasing prevalence of chronic diseases, rising demand for biologics, and advancements in delivery technologies.

Biologics and biosimilars represent a significant portion, with **monoclonal antibodies accounting for ~25%** of the total parenteral market.

Regional Usage:

North America and Europe dominate the market due to high healthcare spending and advanced infrastructure, accounting for ~**60%** of global parenteral consumption.

Emerging markets like India and China are witnessing rapid growth, driven by improving healthcare systems and increasing demand for injectable therapies.

Therapeutic Applications:

Parenterals are extensively used in oncology, diabetes, autoimmune disorders, and infectious diseases. For example, oncology drugs like **trastuzumab** (Herceptin) and **nivolumab** (Opdivo) dominate the IV biologics segment.

6.2 Preformulation Considerations

6.2.1 Vehicles and Additives

The preformulation stage for parenteral products involves careful selection of vehicles and additives to ensure the stability, safety, and efficacy of the formulation. Vehicles serve as the primary medium for dissolving or suspending the active pharmaceutical ingredient (API), while additives improve the product's stability, isotonicity, and sterility.

Vehicles

1. Aqueous Vehicles

Aqueous vehicles are the most commonly used solvents in parenteral formulations due to their compatibility with the human body and ease of administration.

Water for Injection (WFI):

Highly purified water free from pyrogens and contaminants.

Used as the primary vehicle in solutions, emulsions, and reconstituted lyophilized products.

Example: **Ceftriaxone** is reconstituted with WFI before IV administration.

Ringer's Solution:

A sterile isotonic solution containing sodium chloride, potassium chloride, and calcium chloride.

Used as a vehicle and electrolyte replenisher.

Example: **Ringer's lactate** is commonly administered to restore hydration and electrolyte balance.

2. Non-Aqueous Vehicles

Non-aqueous vehicles are used for drugs that are unstable or poorly soluble in water. These include oils and synthetic solvents.

Fixed Oils:

Natural oils such as **sesame oil, peanut oil,** or **cottonseed oil.**

Used for oily solutions or depot injections to provide sustained drug release.

Example: **Progesterone injection** uses sesame oil as a vehicle.

Polyethylene Glycol (PEG):

A synthetic solvent with varying molecular weights. PEG is commonly used to dissolve hydrophobic drugs.

Example: **Diazepam injection** employs PEG as a solvent for its non-aqueous formulation.

Additives

Additives play essential roles in maintaining the physicochemical and microbiological stability of parenteral products. Each additive has a specific function, and its concentration must be carefully controlled to ensure safety and efficacy.

1. Buffers

Purpose: Buffers maintain the pH of the formulation within a physiologically acceptable range (pH 3–8) to enhance drug stability and prevent irritation.

Examples and Concentrations:

Phosphate Buffers: Used to stabilize acidic or basic drugs (concentration range: **0.01–0.1 M**).

Citrate Buffers: Commonly used in acidic formulations.

Example: **Doxorubicin injection** employs a phosphate buffer to maintain pH stability.

2. Preservatives

Purpose: Preservatives inhibit microbial growth in multidose vials and ensure sterility during use.

Examples and Concentrations:

Benzyl Alcohol: Widely used at a concentration of **0.9% w/v**.

Phenol and Methylparaben: Alternative preservatives for multidose formulations.

Example: **Lidocaine injection** contains benzyl alcohol as a preservative.

3. Antioxidants

Purpose: Antioxidants prevent oxidation of APIs, which can lead to degradation and loss of efficacy.

Examples and Concentrations:

Ascorbic Acid: A common antioxidant used at **0.1–0.2%**.

Sodium Metabisulfite: Effective for preventing oxidative degradation in injectable formulations.

Example: **Epinephrine injection** includes ascorbic acid to prevent oxidation.

4. Chelating Agents

Purpose: Chelating agents bind to metal ions, which can catalyze oxidation or hydrolysis reactions, thereby stabilizing the formulation.

Examples and Concentrations:

EDTA (Ethylenediaminetetraacetic Acid): Commonly used at **0.01–0.05%** to stabilize formulations sensitive to trace metal ions.

Example: **Amphotericin B injection** contains EDTA to maintain its stability in solution.

6.3 Production and Quality Control

6.3.1 Sterilization Methods

Sterilization is a critical step in the production of parenteral products, ensuring that the formulations are free from viable microorganisms and pyrogens. Heat sterilization, one of the most effective and widely used methods, employs high temperatures to achieve sterility through microbial destruction.

6.3.1.1 Heat Sterilization

Methods of Heat Sterilization

1. Moist Heat Sterilization (Autoclaving)

Process:

Uses saturated steam under pressure to sterilize equipment, containers, and solutions.

Standard conditions involve **121°C** at **15 psi pressure** for **15–20 minutes**. Higher temperatures (e.g., **134°C**) can be used for shorter durations (e.g., **3–5 minutes**) for faster sterilization.

Mechanism:

Microbial destruction occurs through **denaturation of proteins** and disruption of cellular membranes.

Steam penetrates microbial cells, causing coagulation of intracellular proteins, which is lethal to microorganisms.

Applications:

Suitable for heat-stable aqueous solutions, surgical instruments, and glassware.

Example: Sterilization of **dextrose saline solutions** and **Ringer's solution**.

2. Dry Heat Sterilization (Oven Sterilization)

Process:

Involves the use of hot air in a dry heat sterilizer or oven.

Standard conditions are **160–170°C** for **2 hours**. For depyrogenation, temperatures of **250°C for 30 minutes** are used to destroy pyrogens like endotoxins.

Mechanism:

Microbial destruction occurs through **oxidation of cellular components**, including proteins, nucleic acids, and lipids.

The absence of water makes this method suitable for materials that are sensitive to moisture.

Applications:

Used for sterilizing non-aqueous formulations, glass containers, and metal instruments.

Example: **Ampoules, vials**, and **syringes** are often sterilized using dry heat.

The effectiveness of heat sterilization depends on the type of microorganism, temperature, and duration. Moist heat is generally more effective than dry heat due to the greater energy transfer of steam.

6.3.1.2 Filtration

Filtration is a widely used sterilization method in pharmaceutical manufacturing, particularly for heat-sensitive drugs. It employs physical barriers, such as membrane filters, to remove microorganisms and particulate matter without compromising the integrity of the formulation.

Membrane Filters for Sterilization

Membrane filters are thin, porous membranes made from materials such as **polyethersulfone (PES), polyvinylidene fluoride (PVDF)**, or **nylon**. These filters act as a physical barrier to microorganisms and particles.

Pore Size:

Filters with a pore size of **0.22 µm** are considered standard for sterilization, effectively removing bacteria, fungi, and some viruses.

Filters with larger pore sizes (e.g., **0.45 µm**) are used for clarification rather than sterilization.

Significance:

Membrane filters provide a sterile product without the need for heat or chemicals, making them ideal for temperature-sensitive formulations.

They maintain the sterility of the product by trapping contaminants while allowing the sterile liquid to pass through.

Filtration Mechanism

The filtration process operates primarily on the principle of **size exclusion**:

Size Exclusion:

Microorganisms and particles larger than the filter's pore size are physically blocked from passing through the membrane.

Smaller molecules, such as the drug substance and solvents, freely pass through the pores, ensuring the drug's integrity.

Additional Mechanisms:

Some filters also use **adsorption**, where contaminants adhere to the filter material, enhancing the filtration efficiency.

Depth Filtration: In multi-layered filters, particles are trapped within the filter matrix.

Effectiveness:

A **0.22 µm membrane filter** can remove most vegetative bacteria (e.g., **E. coli**) and bacterial spores (e.g., **Bacillus subtilis**) but may not remove certain smaller viruses.

Applications for Heat-Sensitive Drugs

Filtration is the preferred sterilization method for drugs that are unstable at high temperatures, such as protein-based biologics, vaccines, and monoclonal antibodies.

Protein-Based Biologics:

Filtration prevents denaturation or aggregation of proteins, ensuring their therapeutic efficacy.

Example: **Insulin formulations** are sterilized using membrane filters to maintain their stability and activity.

Monoclonal Antibodies:

High temperatures can denature these complex molecules; filtration ensures sterility without compromising their structure.

Example: **Adalimumab (Humira)**, used for autoimmune disorders, relies on filtration for sterilization.

Vaccines:

Heat-sensitive vaccines, such as **mRNA vaccines (e.g., COVID-19 vaccines)**, are sterilized using filtration to preserve their delicate nucleic acid structures.

Parenteral Nutrition Solutions:

Lipid emulsions and amino acid solutions used in total parenteral nutrition (TPN) are sterilized via filtration to avoid heat-induced degradation.

Advantages of Filtration Sterilization

Non-Thermal Process:

Ideal for heat-sensitive drugs, ensuring product stability and efficacy.

Fast and Efficient:

Filtration is a rapid process that can handle large volumes in a continuous flow system.

Flexibility:

Can be integrated into aseptic manufacturing setups for sterile product production.

6.3.1.3 Irradiation

Irradiation sterilization is a non-thermal method that uses high-energy radiation, such as gamma rays or electron beams, to eliminate microorganisms and ensure sterility. This method is particularly useful for sterilizing packaging materials, medical devices, and certain heat-sensitive pharmaceutical products.

Sterilization Using Gamma Rays and Electron Beams

Gamma Ray Sterilization

Source:

Gamma rays are emitted from **Cobalt-60 (Co-60)** or **Cesium-137** isotopes.

These rays penetrate deeply into materials, ensuring uniform sterilization.

Mechanism:

Gamma rays generate free radicals by interacting with water molecules in microbial cells, leading to DNA damage and cell death.

Applications:

Sterilization of prefilled syringes, vials, and pharmaceutical packaging materials.

Example: Gamma rays are used to sterilize disposable medical products like syringes and catheters.

Electron Beam (E-Beam) Sterilization

Source:

Electron beams are produced by high-energy electron accelerators.

Unlike gamma rays, electron beams have a shallower penetration depth, making them suitable for thin or surface-level sterilization.

Mechanism:

The high-energy electrons disrupt microbial DNA, leading to cell death.

Applications:

Sterilization of shallow-packaged materials and thin films.

Example: E-beams are used to sterilize blister packs and lightweight pharmaceutical packaging.

Applications in Packaging Materials and Heat-Sensitive Drugs

Packaging Materials

Utility:

Both gamma rays and E-beams are ideal for sterilizing packaging materials like blister packs, ampoules, and medical-grade polymers.

These methods ensure sterility without compromising the physical integrity of heat-sensitive packaging.

Heat-Sensitive Drugs

Gamma Rays:

Gamma radiation is often used for sterilizing drugs that degrade at high temperatures.

Example: **Hormone preparations, monoclonal antibodies,** and **vaccines** benefit from gamma sterilization.

Electron Beams:

E-beams are used for surface sterilization of drugs with minimal penetration requirements, such as pre-filled syringes containing sensitive biologics.

Safety and Limitations

Safety

Controlled Process:

The process is conducted in specialized facilities with strict radiation shielding and safety protocols to protect workers and the environment.

No Residual Radiation:

After sterilization, the treated products do not become radioactive, making them safe for use.

Limitations

Radiolytic Degradation:

High-energy radiation can cause radiolytic reactions, leading to the formation of free radicals that degrade sensitive drugs or materials.

Example: Gamma radiation may degrade APIs like vitamins or biological molecules, altering their potency.

Material Compatibility:

Some materials, like plastics, may undergo structural changes, discoloration, or brittleness after exposure to radiation.

Cost and Infrastructure:

The requirement for specialized equipment and facilities makes irradiation sterilization more expensive compared to other methods.

6.3.2 Stability Testing

Stability testing is a critical aspect of parenteral product development and quality control. It involves the systematic evaluation of a product's **chemical, physical, and microbiological stability** under specified conditions to ensure safety, efficacy, and compliance throughout its shelf life. Parenterals, being sterile preparations, require rigorous testing to maintain their integrity and functionality during storage and use.

Definition and Importance of Stability Testing

Stability testing refers to the evaluation of a pharmaceutical product's ability to maintain its intended properties over time when subjected to varying environmental conditions. For parenterals, this includes assessments of the **chemical stability** (API potency and degradation products), **physical stability** (appearance, pH, and particulate matter), and **microbiological stability** (sterility and preservative efficacy).

The primary objectives of stability testing are to:

1. **Establish Shelf Life**: Determine the period during which the product remains stable under recommended storage conditions.
2. **Define Storage Conditions**: Recommend suitable conditions such as temperature, humidity, and light exposure to preserve the product's quality.
3. **Ensure Safety and Efficacy**: Detect any changes that might compromise the sterility, potency, or safety of the product.

For parenterals, stability testing is particularly important due to their sterile nature and the potential for adverse effects from even minor quality changes. For example, a slight degradation in **insulin potency** due to improper storage can lead to subtherapeutic dosing and inadequate glucose control.

Stress Conditions for Stability Testing

Stability testing involves exposing the product to accelerated and real-time conditions to predict its behavior over its shelf life. The **International Council for Harmonisation (ICH)** guidelines provide specific recommendations for stability studies.

1. Temperature and Humidity

Temperature and humidity are critical factors that influence the chemical and physical stability of parenterals. Real-time and accelerated stability testing conditions are employed to simulate storage environments.

Standard Testing Conditions:

Long-Term Testing: 25°C ± 2°C/60% RH ± 5% RH (room temperature).

Accelerated Testing: 40°C ± 2°C/75% RH ± 5% RH.

Impact:

Elevated temperatures can accelerate chemical degradation, such as hydrolysis or oxidation.

High humidity can affect the integrity of primary packaging, such as rubber stoppers or plastic ampoules, leading to moisture ingress.

Example:

In a stability study of **dextrose injection**, chemical analysis revealed that prolonged exposure to 40°C led to caramelization and discoloration due to the Maillard reaction.

2. Light Exposure

Photostability testing assesses the impact of light, particularly UV radiation, on the product's stability. Certain APIs and excipients are prone to photodegradation, leading to potency loss or formation of harmful degradation products.

Testing Conditions:

Exposure to **UV light (200–400 nm)** and visible light for specified durations.

The product is tested in both primary packaging and exposed conditions to evaluate the protective effect of packaging materials.

Impact:

Photodegradation may result in discoloration, turbidity, or loss of potency.

Example: **Riboflavin injection** exposed to UV light showed significant potency loss due to its photosensitive nature.

Control Measures:

Packaging in amber-colored glass vials reduces UV light penetration and minimizes photodegradation.

Evaluation Parameters

1. Chemical Stability

Chemical stability involves measuring the potency of the active ingredient and identifying degradation products.

Testing Methods:

HPLC and **UV-Vis Spectrophotometry** are commonly used to quantify API concentration and detect impurities.

For example, in stability testing of **amoxicillin injection**, degradation products like penicilloic acid are monitored to ensure compliance with ICH limits.

Acceptance Criteria:

The API content must remain within **90–110% of the labeled claim.**

2. Physical Stability

Physical stability tests assess changes in appearance, pH, and particulate matter.

Appearance:

Visual inspection ensures the solution remains clear and free from turbidity or precipitates.

Example: **Calcium gluconate injection** forms visible precipitates when stored at high temperatures, indicating physical instability.

pH:

Changes in pH can indicate hydrolysis or chemical degradation.

Example: The pH of **insulin solutions** is monitored to prevent loss of potency due to pH shifts outside the range of **7.0–7.8**.

Particulate Matter:

USP guidelines specify limits for particulate matter in parenterals.

Example: ≤**10 particles/mL** for particles ≥10 µm and ≤**3 particles/mL** for particles ≥25 µm in large-volume parenterals.

3. Microbiological Stability

Microbiological stability ensures sterility and preservative efficacy throughout the product's shelf life.

Sterility Testing:

Conducted as per USP <71> to confirm the absence of microbial contamination.

Example: **Ceftriaxone injection** retained sterility after 12 months under long-term storage conditions.

Preservative Efficacy Testing (PET):

Multidose parenterals are tested to ensure the preservative system remains effective in preventing microbial growth.

Example: **Benzyl alcohol (0.9%)** in lidocaine injection was found effective for 18 months under room temperature conditions.

Real-World Data on Stability Studies

Study 1: Stability of Dextrose Injection

Conditions: 25°C/60% RH (long-term) and 40°C/75% RH (accelerated).

Results:

No significant changes in chemical composition after 12 months at room temperature.

At 40°C, caramelization and discoloration occurred after 3 months.

Study 2: Insulin Stability

Conditions: 2–8°C (recommended) vs. room temperature.

Results:

Insulin retained >**95% potency** after 12 months at 2–8°C.

At room temperature, potency dropped to **85%** after 6 months.

6.3.3 Evaluation of Parenterals

The evaluation of parenteral products is a critical step in ensuring their safety, efficacy, and compliance with pharmacopoeial standards. Parenterals, being sterile formulations administered directly into the body, must pass rigorous tests to guarantee their sterility, pyrogen-free nature, and absence of particulate matter. These tests are conducted under strict laboratory conditions as specified by global pharmacopoeias such as the **United States Pharmacopeia (USP), European Pharmacopoeia (EP)**, and **Indian Pharmacopoeia (IP)**.

Pharmacopoeial Tests for Parenterals

1. Sterility Testing

Sterility testing is a mandatory test for parenteral products to confirm the absence of viable microorganisms. It is conducted under aseptic conditions using validated procedures.

Test Conditions:

The product is incubated in two different growth media:

Fluid Thioglycollate Medium (FTM): For detecting bacteria, incubation is carried out at **30–35°C** for **14 days**.

Soybean Casein Digest Medium (SCDM): For detecting fungi and aerobic bacteria, incubation is conducted at **20–25°C** for **14 days**.

A minimum sample volume, typically **10 mL for solutions in containers** >100 mL, is tested.

Procedure:

Direct Inoculation Method: The product is directly inoculated into the media under aseptic conditions.

Membrane Filtration Method: The product is filtered through a **0.45 μm or 0.22 μm membrane filter**, and the filter is transferred to the growth media for incubation.

Acceptance Criteria:

No microbial growth should be observed after the incubation period.

Example:

A batch of **dextrose 5% injection** must demonstrate sterility in both bacterial and fungal media during the testing period.

2. Pyrogen Testing

Pyrogen testing ensures that parenteral products are free from pyrogens, which are fever-inducing substances, often caused by bacterial endotoxins.

Methods:

Rabbit Test:

1. A sample of the product is injected into the marginal ear vein of healthy rabbits.
2. The rabbits' rectal temperatures are monitored at regular intervals over a period of **3 hours.**
3. The product passes the test if the temperature increase does not exceed **0.6°C** in any rabbit or a cumulative total of **1.4°C** for three rabbits.

Limulus Amoebocyte Lysate (LAL) Test:

1. A quantitative test based on the reaction between bacterial endotoxins and lysate extracted from the blood of the **horseshoe crab (Limulus polyphemus).**
2. The presence of endotoxins forms a gel or turbidity, which can be measured to determine endotoxin concentration.
3. Sensitivity: LAL can detect endotoxins as low as **0.125 EU/mL.**

Acceptance Criteria:
As per the USP, the endotoxin limit for large-volume parenterals (LVPs) is typically **0.25 EU/mL,** and for small-volume parenterals (SVPs), it is **5.0 EU/kg of body weight.**
Example:
A batch of **ceftriaxone injection** must meet the endotoxin limit to be safe for intravenous administration.

3. Particulate Matter Testing
Particulate matter testing evaluates the presence of visible and sub-visible particles in parenteral solutions to ensure the product is free from contaminants that could harm patients.
Methods:
Visual Inspection:

1. Each container is inspected manually under a black and white background with suitable illumination (2000–3750 lux).
2. Visible particles should not be detected in any container.

Microscopic and Automated Methods:

Microscopic Count: Using calibrated microscopes to count particles in a measured sample volume.

Light Obscuration Particle Count Test: Measures the shadow or light blockage caused by particles passing through a detection zone.

USP Limits for Particulate Matter:

1. For **Large-Volume Parenterals (LVPs)** (>100 mL):
2. **Particles ≥10 µm: ≤ 25 particles/mL.**
3. **Particles ≥25 µm: ≤ 3 particles/mL.**
4. For **Small-Volume Parenterals (SVPs)** (<100 mL):
5. **Particles ≥10 µm: ≤ 6000 particles/container.**
6. **Particles ≥25 µm: ≤ 600 particles/container.**

Example:

During the testing of **amino acid solutions for parenteral nutrition**, no visible particles should be observed, and the sub-visible particle counts must fall within USP limits.

6.4 Ophthalmic Preparations

Ophthalmic preparations are sterile pharmaceutical products designed specifically for administration to the eye. They are formulated to meet stringent requirements for sterility, isotonicity, and pH compatibility to ensure safety and efficacy. Among the most common forms of ophthalmic preparations are **eye drops**, which are extensively used to treat a variety of ocular conditions.

6.4.1 Eye Drops

Definition of Eye Drops

Eye drops are sterile, isotonic solutions or suspensions intended for administration to the eye. They are formulated to deliver active pharmaceutical ingredients (APIs) directly to the conjunctival sac or cornea, ensuring localized therapeutic effects with minimal systemic absorption.

Key Characteristics:

Must be free from microbial contamination.

Should be isotonic with tears (equivalent to **0.9% sodium chloride solution**).

pH adjusted to physiological compatibility, typically in the range of **6–8**, to minimize irritation.

Requires specific viscosity to enhance retention time on the ocular surface.

Formulation Components

Eye drop formulations are composed of several essential components that ensure their safety, efficacy, and patient comfort.

1. Vehicles

Purpose: Vehicles act as the medium for dissolving or suspending APIs, ensuring uniform delivery to the eye.

Examples:

Water for Injection (WFI): Commonly used as a primary vehicle in aqueous formulations due to its purity and compatibility with ocular tissues.

Mineral Oil: Used in oil-based suspensions for APIs that are poorly soluble in water.

Application:

Aqueous Eye Drops: Most commonly used, as in **timolol eye drops for glaucoma**.

Oil-Based Suspensions: Used for lipophilic drugs like **cyclosporine** in the treatment of dry eye syndrome.

2. Buffers

Purpose: Buffers help maintain the pH of the formulation within a range compatible with the eye's natural pH (~7.4).

Examples:

Phosphate Buffers: Widely used to stabilize pH between **6–8**.

Citrate Buffers: Used for acidic APIs to prevent precipitation.

Significance: Maintaining a stable pH is crucial for ensuring drug stability and minimizing irritation.

Example: **Tropicamide eye drops** use phosphate buffers to maintain pH and improve patient comfort during diagnostic procedures.

3. Preservatives

Purpose: Preservatives inhibit microbial growth in multidose containers, ensuring sterility throughout the product's shelf life.

Examples:

Benzalkonium Chloride (BAC): A widely used preservative, typically at a concentration of **0.01% w/v**.

Chlorobutanol: An alternative preservative, effective against a broad spectrum of microorganisms.

Significance:

Preservatives ensure the safety of multidose formulations but may cause irritation in sensitive individuals. Preservative-free formulations are available for such cases.

Example: **Latanoprost eye drops** for glaucoma often contain BAC to maintain sterility in multidose containers.

Therapeutic Applications

Eye drops are formulated for a variety of therapeutic purposes, depending on the API and the ocular condition being treated.

Examples of Therapeutic Applications:

Glaucoma:

Timolol (0.25–0.5% solution) reduces intraocular pressure by decreasing aqueous humor production.

Dry Eye Syndrome:

Artificial Tears contain polymers like carboxymethylcellulose to lubricate and hydrate the ocular surface.

Infections:

Tobramycin (antibiotic) is used to treat bacterial conjunctivitis.

Inflammation:

Ketorolac Tromethamine (NSAID) reduces inflammation after cataract surgery.

6.4.2 Eye Ointments

Definition of Eye Ointments

Eye ointments are **semi-solid sterile preparations** designed for application to the eye. These formulations provide prolonged contact time with the ocular surface, allowing for sustained drug release and enhanced therapeutic efficacy. Due to their semi-solid nature, eye ointments adhere to the conjunctival sac and cornea, making them ideal for nighttime use or for conditions requiring extended drug exposure.

Key Characteristics:

Must be sterile to prevent ocular infections.

Typically non-irritating and free from particulate matter to ensure patient comfort.

Often used for delivering antibiotics, anti-inflammatory agents, or lubricants.

Formulation Considerations

The development of eye ointments involves careful selection of base materials and adherence to stringent sterilization methods to ensure safety, stability, and efficacy.

1. Base Materials

The base is the primary vehicle for dispersing or dissolving the active pharmaceutical ingredient (API). It plays a critical role in drug stability, release, and compatibility with ocular tissues.

Petrolatum:

A widely used base due to its excellent occlusive properties and chemical inertness.

Provides prolonged adherence to the ocular surface, ensuring sustained drug release.

Lanolin:

Sometimes used as a base or co-base for its emollient and hydrophilic properties.

Allows for better incorporation of water-soluble APIs.

Significance of Base Selection:

The base must be non-irritating, stable, and able to retain sterility.

Example: **Erythromycin ointment** uses petrolatum as the base to treat bacterial conjunctivitis.

2. Sterilization Methods

Due to their semi-solid nature, sterilization of eye ointments requires specialized techniques to maintain sterility without compromising the formulation's stability.

Gamma Irradiation:

High-energy gamma rays are used to sterilize the ointment in its final packaging.

Suitable for heat-sensitive APIs or bases that degrade under thermal sterilization.

Aseptic Preparation:

Ingredients are sterilized individually, and the ointment is prepared and filled under aseptic conditions.

Commonly used for formulations that cannot withstand irradiation.

Challenges:

Ensuring uniform sterility in semi-solid formulations.

Maintaining the chemical and physical integrity of the base materials during sterilization.

Examples of Ophthalmic Ointments

Eye ointments are formulated for various therapeutic applications, primarily to treat infections, inflammation, and dry eye syndrome.

Antibiotic Ointments:

Erythromycin Ointment:

Used for treating bacterial conjunctivitis and preventing neonatal eye infections.

Formulated with petrolatum as the base to ensure prolonged contact time.

Lubricating Ointments:

Artificial Tear Ointments:

Contain mineral oil or petrolatum to treat dry eye syndrome by providing long-lasting hydration and lubrication.

Anti-Inflammatory Ointments:

Hydrocortisone Ointment:

Reduces inflammation and swelling in ocular conditions like uveitis or postoperative recovery.

6.4.3 Eye Lotions

Definition of Eye Lotions

Eye lotions are **sterile aqueous solutions** specifically formulated for **washing, irrigating, or cleansing the eye.** They are used to remove debris, foreign particles, or chemicals from the ocular surface, offering relief and preventing further irritation or damage. These products are designed to be non-irritating and safe for direct contact with sensitive ocular tissues.

Key Characteristics:

Must be sterile to avoid introducing infections.

Typically isotonic with tears to ensure comfort during use.

Free from preservatives or other components that may irritate the eye.

Formulation Criteria

The formulation of eye lotions requires strict adherence to criteria that ensure patient safety, comfort, and efficacy.

1. Isotonicity and pH Adjustment

Isotonicity:

Eye lotions must be isotonic to match the osmotic pressure of natural tears, equivalent to a **0.9% sodium chloride solution.**

Maintaining isotonicity prevents discomfort such as stinging or irritation during application.

Example: **Saline eyewash** is formulated to be isotonic for use in ocular irrigation.

pH Adjustment:

The pH of eye lotions is adjusted to **7.0–7.4**, closely matching the natural pH of tears.

Buffer systems, such as **phosphate buffers**, are commonly used to maintain pH stability.

A stable pH prevents irritation and preserves the integrity of the formulation.

2. Packaging in Single-Use Containers

Single-Use Containers:

Eye lotions are packaged in single-use, pre-sterilized containers to eliminate the risk of contamination during multiple uses.

This packaging ensures sterility and safety, especially for products used in emergency or sensitive situations, such as chemical exposure.

Benefits:

Prevents microbial contamination that could occur with multi-dose packaging.

Eliminates the need for preservatives, making the product suitable for sensitive individuals.

Example:

Sterile saline eyewash bottles, available in 10 mL to 500 mL sizes, are commonly used in healthcare settings and emergency kits.

Examples of Marketed Eye Lotions

Eye lotions are readily available for various ocular applications, primarily for cleansing and irrigation.

Saline Eyewash:

A sterile isotonic saline solution used to wash away dust, allergens, or irritants from the eye.

Example: **Bausch & Lomb Advanced Eye Relief Saline Eyewash.**

Buffered Eyewash:

Contains phosphate buffers for pH adjustment, suitable for rinsing chemicals or harmful substances from the eyes.

Example: **Physiological saline eye rinse** used in laboratories and industrial safety kits.

Antimicrobial Eye Irrigation Solutions:

Sterile solutions containing mild antiseptics for use after minor ocular surgeries or injuries.

Example: **Chlorhexidine eye wash** for post-surgical cleaning.

Review questions

1. What are parenteral products?
Parenteral products are sterile preparations intended for administration by injection through the skin or mucous membranes.

2. Name three common routes for parenteral administration.
Intravenous, intramuscular, and subcutaneous.

3. What is a key requirement for parenteral products?
They must be sterile and pyrogen-free.

4. What are pyrogens?
Pyrogens are fever-causing substances, usually bacterial endotoxins.

5. Why is isotonicity important in parenterals?
To prevent irritation, hemolysis, or tissue damage at the site of injection.

6. What is the ideal pH range for parenteral preparations?
Generally between pH 3 and pH 9.

7. Which water is used in parenteral preparation?
Water for injection (WFI).

8. What is the role of buffers in parenterals?
Buffers maintain pH stability of the formulation.

9. What is a vehicle in parenteral formulation?
A vehicle is the medium used to dissolve or suspend the drug.

10. What are co-solvents?
Co-solvents are water-miscible solvents used to improve solubility of poorly soluble drugs.

11. What is the function of antioxidants in parenterals?
They prevent oxidation of active ingredients.

12. Why are preservatives added to parenteral products?
To inhibit microbial growth in multi-dose containers.

13. Name one commonly used antioxidant in parenteral formulations.
Sodium metabisulfite.

14. Which sterilization method is preferred for heat-stable drugs?
Moist heat sterilization.

15. What is autoclaving?
Autoclaving is steam sterilization at 121°C under pressure.

16. Which method is suitable for thermolabile drugs?
Sterile filtration.

17. What is aseptic processing?

A process where sterile ingredients are compounded in a sterile environment.

18. What is terminal sterilization?

Sterilization of the final filled and sealed product.

19. Why is particulate matter control important?

To prevent embolism or vascular blockage upon injection.

20. What is a LAL test?

Limulus Amebocyte Lysate test, used to detect endotoxins.

21. What are large volume parenterals?

Sterile solutions usually more than 100 mL, used for infusion.

22. What are small volume parenterals?

Sterile products less than 100 mL used for injection.

23. What are single-dose containers?

Containers meant for one-time use without preservatives.

24. What are multi-dose containers?

Containers with preservatives to allow multiple withdrawals.

25. What is an ampoule?

A sealed glass container holding a single dose of a parenteral product.

26. What is a vial?

A small container made of glass or plastic used for multiple or single doses.

27. Why are rubber closures used in vials?

To allow penetration by needle while maintaining sterility.

28. What are lyophilized parenterals?

Freeze-dried powders for reconstitution before injection.

29. What is a prefilled syringe?

A single-use syringe prefilled with a fixed dose of drug.

30. What are ophthalmic preparations?

Sterile products intended for instillation into the eyes.

31. Give an example of an ophthalmic dosage form.

Eye drops.

32. What is the requirement for eye preparations?

They must be sterile and non-irritating.

33. What is isotonicity equivalent to in sodium chloride?

0.9% w/v sodium chloride solution.

34. What is an intramuscular injection site?

Typically the gluteus maximus or deltoid muscle.

35. What is the maximum volume for intramuscular injection?
Usually up to 5 mL.

36. Why are parenterals packed in glass containers?
Glass is inert and impermeable to gases.

37. What are plastic ampoules used for?
Single-dose units that are easier to open.

38. What is dry heat sterilization used for?
For glassware and oily preparations.

39. What temperature is used in dry heat sterilization?
Generally 160–180°C for 1–2 hours.

40. What is flash sterilization?
A rapid sterilization method used in emergencies.

41. What does depyrogenation mean?
Removal of pyrogens from containers or products.

42. Why is visual inspection performed?
To detect particulate matter and container integrity.

43. What is stability testing in parenterals?
Testing to ensure the product remains safe and effective over time.

44. Name a test for sterility.
Membrane filtration test.

45. Why is pH adjustment necessary in some parenterals?
To improve drug solubility and minimize irritation.

46. What is a TPN solution?
Total Parenteral Nutrition, providing all nutrients intravenously.

47. What are emulsions used for in parenterals?
To deliver fat-soluble drugs or nutrients.

48. What does SRP stand for?
Sterile Ready-to-Use Products.

49. What is an infusion pump?
A device used to deliver fluids at a controlled rate.

50. Why is packaging critical in parenterals?
To maintain sterility, protect from light and contamination.

MCQS

1. Parenteral products are administered via
A. Sublingual

B. Oral

C. Topical

D. Injection

Answer: D

   2. Which water is used for parenteral preparations?

A. Purified water

B. WFI

C. Distilled water

D. Tap water

Answer: B

   3. Which of the following must be pyrogen-free?

A. Capsules

B. Tablets

C. Syrups

D. Parenterals

Answer: D

   4. Which is a method of sterilizing heat-sensitive drugs?

A. Filtration

B. Irradiation

C. Autoclaving

D. Dry heat

Answer: A

   5. Ideal pH range for parenteral solutions is

A. 9–12

B. 7–11

C. 3–9

D. 1–3

Answer: C

   6. Which test detects bacterial endotoxins?

A. Sterility test

B. LAL test

C. pH test

D. Color test

Answer: B

   7. A large volume parenteral is usually more than

A. 5 mL

B. 10 mL

C. 50 mL

D. 100 mL

Answer: D

8. Ampoules are typically made of

A. Plastic

B. Paper

C. Glass

D. Aluminum

Answer: C

9. Which one is a multi-dose container?

A. Ampoule

B. Blister pack

C. Vial

D. Sachet

Answer: C

10. Which component maintains pH of parenterals?

A. Antioxidant

B. Preservative

C. Buffer

D. Solvent

Answer: C

11. What is used to remove microorganisms?

A. Oxidation

B. Pasteurization

C. Filtration

D. Sonication

Answer: C

12. Which is used to prevent oxidation in parenterals?

A. Glycerin

B. Citric acid

C. Sodium metabisulfite

D. Benzyl alcohol

Answer: C

13. Autoclaving is done at

A. $121\,^{\circ}C$

B. $100\,^{\circ}C$

C. $160\,^{\circ}C$

D. $140\,^{\circ}C$

Answer: A

14. Which parenteral route has the fastest onset?

A. Intramuscular

B. Subcutaneous

C. Intradermal

D. Intravenous

Answer: D

15. Multi-dose containers contain

A. Water only

B. Preservatives

C. Emulsifiers

D. Sweeteners

Answer: B

16. Total Parenteral Nutrition is given through

A. Oral

B. IM

C. IV

D. SC

Answer: C

17. Which container allows multiple withdrawals?

A. Ampoule

B. Tube

C. Vial

D. Strip

Answer: C

18. Preservatives are avoided in

A. Multi-dose

B. Eye ointment

C. Single-dose

D. TPN

Answer: C

19. Which test confirms sterility?

A. BET

B. LAL

C. Membrane filtration

D. TLC

Answer: C

20. Which is not a parenteral dosage form?

A. Emulsion

B. Eye drops

C. Syrup

D. Injection

Answer: C

21. What is the primary use of ophthalmic preparations?

A. Oral administration

B. Eye application

C. Injection

D. Nasal spray

Answer: B

22. What is lyophilization?

A. Dry heat sterilization

B. Freeze drying

C. Irradiation

D. Boiling

Answer: B

23. Which sterilization method is best for oily injections?

A. Filtration

B. Dry heat

C. Steam

D. Radiation

Answer: B

24. Which parenteral route is used for vaccines?

A. Oral

B. Intramuscular

C. Topical

D. Nasal

Answer: B

25. Prefilled syringes are

A. Reusable

B. Refillable

C. Single-use

D. Glass vials

Answer: C

26. WFI stands for

A. Washed Filtered Injection

B. Water for Injection

C. Wet Formulated Ingredient

D. White Fine Isomer

Answer: B

27. What is the volume limit for IM injection?

A. 1 mL

B. 5 mL

C. 10 mL

D. 20 mL

Answer: B

28. Which is used as a solvent in oily injections?

A. Olive oil

B. Alcohol

C. Water

D. Propylene glycol

Answer: A

29. A container made of soft plastic is called

A. Vial

B. Tube

C. Plastic ampoule

D. Glass bottle

Answer: C

30. The ideal sodium chloride concentration for isotonicity is

A. 0.9%

B. 5%

C. 1.5%

D. 2%

Answer: A

31. TPN provides

A. Vitamins only

B. Only electrolytes

C. Complete nutrition

D. Lipids only

Answer: C

32. Rubber closures allow

A. Light entry

B. Bacterial entry

C. Needle entry

D. Evaporation

Answer: C

33. Glass containers are preferred because

A. They are cheaper

B. They are soft

C. They are inert

D. They absorb drugs

Answer: C

34. Parenterals should be free from

A. Sugar

B. Flavor

C. Microorganisms

D. Color

Answer: C

35. SRP stands for

A. Sterile Ready Packaging

B. Sterile Ready-to-Use Products

C. Safe Repacked Product

D. Single-use Refill Pack

Answer: B

36. Which is an ophthalmic dosage form?

A. Suspension

B. Ointment

C. Tablet

D. Capsule

Answer: B

37. Sterile filtration uses pore size of

A. 0.45 µm

B. 0.22 µm

C. 1 µm

D. 0.5 µm

Answer: B

38. Dry heat sterilization is done at

A. 121°C

B. 100°C

C. 160°C

D. 50°C

Answer: C

39. What is added to parenterals to prevent microbial growth?

A. Color

B. Preservative

C. Flavor

D. Binder

Answer: B

40. What is the test for endotoxins?

A. LAL test

B. Sterility test

C. Disintegration

D. TLC

Answer: A

41. Why is visual inspection done?

A. To check pH

B. To ensure sterility

C. To detect particles

D. To remove air

Answer: C

42. Flash sterilization is mainly used in

A. Industrial plants

B. Emergencies

C. Autoclaves

D. Warehouses

Answer: B

43. Vials are sealed using

A. Aluminum caps

B. Plastic lids

C. Rubber bands

D. Glass covers

Answer: A

44. Aqueous parenterals must be

A. Preserved

B. Buffered

C. Colorful

D. Clear and sterile

Answer: D

45. In which product is depyrogenation most critical?

A. Capsules

B. Eye drops

C. Parenterals

D. Tablets

Answer: C

46. Eye drops should be

A. Colored

B. Viscous

C. Sterile

D. Non-isotonic

Answer: C

47. What is membrane filtration used for?

A. Filtering oils

B. Drying syrups

C. Coloring solutions

D. Sterilizing thermolabile solutions

Answer: D

48. Which dosage form must be isotonic?

A. Tablets

B. Lozenges

C. Parenterals

D. Capsules

Answer: C

49. Emulsions in parenterals are used to

A. Color the drug

B. Enhance viscosity

C. Deliver nutrients

D. Mask taste

Answer: C

50. What is used to maintain isotonicity in parenteral solutions?

A. Benzyl alcohol

B. Sodium chloride

C. Ethanol

D. Tween 80

Answer: B

CHAPTER SEVEN

Cosmetics

7.1 Lip and Skin Products

7.1.1 Lipsticks

Lipsticks are among the most widely used cosmetic products, serving both functional and aesthetic purposes. They are designed to enhance the natural appearance of lips by imparting color, texture, and shine while providing protection against environmental factors like dryness and UV rays.

Definition and Function

Lipsticks are **semi-solid cosmetic preparations** specifically formulated for application to the lips. They provide **color, gloss,** and **texture** to enhance the aesthetic appearance of the lips while also offering hydration and protection. The dual role of lipsticks as a beauty enhancer and a protective product makes them indispensable in the cosmetics industry.

Purpose:

To deliver long-lasting color and a smooth finish.

To provide hydration and protection against dryness and environmental stress.

To create a desired aesthetic effect, ranging from natural tones to bold, vibrant shades.

Lipsticks are designed to be easy to apply, non-toxic, and stable under varying environmental conditions.

Ingredients and Composition

Lipstick formulations consist of a balanced combination of ingredients, each contributing to specific properties such as texture, color, and stability.

1. Waxes

Waxes provide the structural integrity of the lipstick, allowing it to maintain its shape while ensuring smooth application.

Examples:

Carnauba Wax: Derived from palm leaves, it has a high melting point and imparts rigidity to the lipstick.

Beeswax: A natural wax that provides elasticity and ease of application.

Concentration: Typically constitutes **10–20%** of the formulation.

Role: Enhances hardness, stability, and smooth application.

2. Oils

Oils are responsible for the glossy finish, smooth texture, and spreadability of the lipstick.

Examples:

Castor Oil: Known for its high viscosity, it imparts shine and ensures uniform pigment dispersion.

Lanolin: Acts as a moisturizing agent and improves the emollient properties of the lipstick.

Concentration: Forms the major component, typically **50–70%** of the formulation.

Role: Provides hydration, gloss, and smoothness during application.

3. Pigments

Pigments impart color and opacity to the lipstick, ensuring a uniform and vibrant appearance.

Examples:

Titanium Dioxide: Provides opacity and brightness.

Iron Oxides: Commonly used for red, brown, and earthy tones.

Concentration: Typically comprises **5–10%** of the formulation.

Role: Determines the shade, depth, and vibrancy of the lipstick.

4. Preservatives and Antioxidants

Preservatives and antioxidants ensure the stability and safety of the lipstick by preventing microbial growth and oxidative degradation.

Examples:

Butylated Hydroxytoluene (BHT): Acts as an antioxidant, preventing rancidity of oils.

Parabens: Widely used as preservatives to inhibit microbial contamination.

Concentration: Typically used in trace amounts (<1%).

Role: Extends shelf life and ensures product safety.

Manufacturing Process

The production of lipsticks involves multiple steps to ensure uniformity, quality, and stability.

1. Melting and Mixing of Waxes and Oils

Waxes and oils are melted at temperatures between **80–85°C**, ensuring complete liquefaction.

The molten mixture is stirred continuously to achieve homogeneity.

Example: Carnauba wax and castor oil are melted together to form the base matrix.

2. Pigment Dispersion and Homogenization

Pigments are added to the molten base and dispersed uniformly using high-speed mixers or homogenizers.

This step ensures even color distribution and prevents clumping of pigments.

Example: Titanium dioxide and iron oxides are dispersed in the oil phase for vibrant and consistent shades.

3. Molding and Cooling Processes

The molten lipstick mixture is poured into preheated molds and allowed to cool gradually at temperatures below **25°C**.

The solidified lipsticks are removed from the molds, trimmed, and polished for a smooth finish.

Example: Lipsticks are often polished with a soft cloth to enhance their shine.

Testing for Quality

1. Melting Point

Lipsticks must have a melting point in the range of **55–75°C** to maintain structural integrity at room temperature while allowing smooth application.

Testing involves the use of melting point apparatus to ensure compliance with this range.

2. Color Stability

Lipsticks are tested for color stability under various conditions, including exposure to light, heat, and humidity.

Example: Stability studies at **40°C/75% RH** over a period of 12 weeks ensure no discoloration or pigment separation occurs.

Examples of Marketed Lipsticks

Lipsticks are available in a wide variety of formulations and shades to cater to different consumer needs.

Moisturizing Lipsticks: Contain higher oil content for enhanced hydration (e.g., lipsticks with lanolin for dry lips).

Matte Lipsticks: Formulated with more waxes for a non-glossy, long-lasting finish (e.g., products with high carnauba wax content).

Satin Finish Lipsticks: Balance gloss and opacity, using castor oil and beeswax as primary components.

7.1.2 Cold Creams

Definition and Purpose

Cold creams are **semi-solid emulsions** primarily designed for **cleansing and moisturizing the skin**. They consist of a blend of water and oil phases stabilized by emulsifiers. The "cold" in cold cream refers to the cooling sensation they provide upon application, resulting from the evaporation of water from the skin. These products are widely used as cosmetic formulations to remove makeup, dirt, and impurities while leaving the skin hydrated and smooth.

Primary Functions:

Cleansing: Effectively removes oil-based dirt, makeup, and environmental pollutants from the skin.

Moisturizing: Provides hydration and restores the skin's natural lipid barrier, especially during dry weather conditions.

Ingredients

The formulation of cold creams involves specific ingredients to achieve their characteristic emollient and cleansing properties.

1. Oil Phase

The oil phase provides the emollient and lipid-replenishing properties of the cold cream.

Mineral Oil:

A lightweight oil that forms a protective layer on the skin to prevent moisture loss.

Concentration: **10–15%**.

Lanolin:

A natural wax derived from wool, known for its moisturizing properties and ability to penetrate the skin.

Concentration: **5–10%**.

Role:

The oil phase helps dissolve oil-based impurities, providing a deep cleansing effect while leaving the skin soft and supple.

2. Water Phase

The water phase constitutes the bulk of the emulsion and provides a refreshing feel.

Purified Water:

Acts as the main vehicle for hydration and dispersion of other ingredients.

Concentration: **70–75%**.

3. Emulsifiers

Emulsifiers stabilize the oil and water phases to prevent separation and ensure a smooth, homogenous texture.

Borax:

Reacts with fatty acids to form a soap that stabilizes the emulsion.

Typical concentration: **0.5–1%**.

Cetyl Alcohol:

A fatty alcohol that thickens the formulation and imparts a creamy texture.

Typical concentration: **1–3%**.

Formulation

Cold creams are formulated as **oil-in-water emulsions,** where water forms the continuous phase and oil droplets are dispersed within it. This type of emulsion provides a light, non-greasy feel, making it suitable for regular use on the skin.

Oil-in-Water Emulsion System

Process:

The oil and water phases are heated separately to **70–75°C** and then blended together under constant mixing.

Emulsifiers like borax or cetyl alcohol are added during blending to stabilize the mixture.

Characteristics:

The water phase provides hydration, while the oil phase acts as a barrier to lock in moisture.

Emulsifiers prevent phase separation, ensuring a smooth and stable product.

Stability Considerations

Phase Separation:

Instability in the emulsion can lead to oil and water separating, causing the cream to lose its consistency.

To prevent this, the formulation must maintain optimal ratios of emulsifiers and a uniform mixing process.

pH:

Cold creams are formulated with a pH of **6–7**, which aligns with the skin's natural pH, minimizing irritation and ensuring compatibility.

Examples of Marketed Cold Creams

Cold creams are available in various formulations, each with unique selling points tailored to specific consumer needs.

Ponds Cold Cream:

Known for its deep cleansing and intense moisturizing properties.

Contains mineral oil and beeswax for soft, nourished skin.

Nivea Cold Cream:

Formulated with almond oil and vitamin E to provide long-lasting hydration.

Ideal for dry and sensitive skin.

Himalaya Nourishing Skin Cream:

Enriched with aloe vera and winter cherry extracts for natural hydration and soothing effects.

Marketed as a multipurpose cream for face and hands.

7.1.3 Vanishing Creams

Definition and Function

Vanishing creams are **light-textured, semi-solid emulsions** formulated to provide a non-greasy, matte finish on the skin. Their name originates from their ability to "vanish" or disappear upon application, leaving no oily residue. These creams are widely used for moisturizing, protecting, and enhancing the appearance of the skin without imparting a shiny look. Their lightweight texture and fast absorption make them suitable for daily use, particularly for individuals with oily or combination skin types.

Primary Functions:

Provides skin hydration and a smooth, matte appearance.

Acts as a base for makeup by creating a non-oily surface.

Protects the skin from dryness and environmental pollutants.

Composition

The formulation of vanishing creams involves a careful balance of ingredients that provide the desired texture, hydration, and stability.

1. Stearic Acid

Role:

Stearic acid serves as the primary base of the cream, imparting thickness and stability.

Upon saponification with alkali, it forms a soft soap that stabilizes the emulsion and gives the cream its characteristic light texture.

Concentration: 20–25%.

Significance: Ensures a smooth application and contributes to the matte finish.

2. Alkali

Role:

Alkali, such as **potassium hydroxide** or **sodium hydroxide**, is used to saponify stearic acid, forming a soap-based emulsion.

This process creates a stable cream structure and enhances spreadability.

Concentration: Added in small, stoichiometric amounts to balance the saponification reaction.

Reaction:

Stearic Acid + Potassium Hydroxide → Potassium Stearate (Soap) + Water.

3. Humectants

Role:

Humectants, like **glycerin**, are added to draw moisture from the environment to the skin, keeping it hydrated.

They improve the cream's moisturizing properties without adding greasiness.

Concentration: 5–10%.

Example: Glycerin is a common humectant used for its compatibility with most skin types.

4. Preservatives

Role:

Preservatives prevent microbial growth, ensuring the product's safety and stability over its shelf life.

Examples and Concentrations:

Methylparaben: Used at **0.2–0.3%.**

Propylparaben: Used at **0.02–0.05%.**

Significance: Extends shelf life and maintains product safety.

Manufacturing Process

The manufacturing process for vanishing creams involves the formation of a stable emulsion through controlled heating, mixing, and cooling.

1. Emulsion Formation

Heating Phase:

Stearic acid is melted and mixed with oils (if any) in one vessel, while water and humectants like glycerin are heated separately in another vessel.

The alkali solution (e.g., potassium hydroxide) is prepared by dissolving the alkali in water.

Blending Phase:

The melted stearic acid is slowly added to the water phase under constant stirring.

The alkali solution is introduced gradually to initiate the saponification reaction, forming a stable oil-in-water emulsion.

The mixture is homogenized to ensure uniform distribution of ingredients and prevent phase separation.

2. Cooling Phase

After emulsification, the cream is cooled gradually to room temperature while maintaining continuous stirring.

Cooling solidifies the structure, giving the cream its desired texture and spreadability.

3. Quality Control

Texture and Spreadability:

The cream is tested for a smooth, non-greasy feel.

Spreadability is assessed by applying a small amount on a smooth surface to ensure even application.

pH Testing:

The pH of the cream is measured to ensure it is within the skin-friendly range of **5–7**.

Examples of Marketed Vanishing Creams

Vanishing creams are available in various formulations, catering to different skin types and concerns.

Fair & Lovely Vanishing Cream:

Combines stearic acid and glycerin with additional skin-lightening agents to provide a matte finish while brightening the skin.

Nivea Soft Cream:

Enriched with humectants and vitamin E for lightweight hydration suitable for all skin types.

Pond's Light Moisturizer:

Contains stearic acid and glycerin, offering a non-oily moisturizing effect, ideal for everyday use.

7.2 Hair Care Products

7.2.1 Shampoos

Shampoos are essential hair care products formulated as cleansing agents for the **hair and scalp**. They are designed to remove dirt, excess oil, sebum, and environmental pollutants while maintaining the health of the hair and scalp. Modern shampoos often include ingredients that condition and nourish the hair, providing additional benefits such as dandruff control, scalp treatment, and enhanced hair texture.

Definition and Function

Shampoos are **aqueous formulations of surfactants and auxiliary ingredients** that clean the scalp and hair by emulsifying and removing accumulated oils and debris. They improve hair manageability, enhance shine, and maintain a healthy scalp environment.

Primary Functions:

Cleanse the scalp and hair of dirt, sweat, and oils.

Maintain scalp hygiene to prevent conditions like dandruff and infections.

Provide additional benefits such as moisturizing, conditioning, and treating scalp disorders.

Ingredients

Shampoo formulations consist of several key ingredients, each serving a specific role to achieve desired efficacy and aesthetic appeal.

1. Surfactants

Surfactants are the primary cleansing agents in shampoos. They lower surface tension, allowing water and oils to mix, enabling dirt and oils to be rinsed away.

Examples:

Sodium Lauryl Sulfate (SLS): A widely used anionic surfactant with excellent cleansing and foaming properties.

Cocamidopropyl Betaine: A milder surfactant often added to reduce irritation caused by primary surfactants.

Concentration: Typically **10–20%** of the formulation.

Role: Provides lather and emulsifies oils, dirt, and debris.

2. Conditioning Agents

Conditioning agents improve the texture, smoothness, and manageability of hair by forming a protective layer over the hair shaft.

Examples:

Silicones (e.g., Dimethicone): Provide a smooth, shiny finish and reduce frizz.

Panthenol (Pro-Vitamin B5): Improves hair elasticity, hydration, and appearance.

Concentration: Typically **1–5%**.

Role: Adds softness, prevents tangling, and protects hair from damage.

3. Preservatives

Preservatives prevent microbial growth, ensuring the safety and stability of the shampoo.

Examples:

Parabens (e.g., Methylparaben): Commonly used for their broad-spectrum antimicrobial properties.

Formaldehyde Donors (e.g., DMDM Hydantoin): Gradually release formaldehyde to inhibit microbial contamination.

Concentration: Typically less than **0.1–0.5%**.

Role: Extends shelf life and maintains product safety.

Types of Shampoos

1. Anti-Dandruff Shampoos

Formulated to address dandruff and flaking by incorporating active ingredients with antifungal and antibacterial properties.

Active Ingredients:

Zinc Pyrithione: Effective against Malassezia fungus, commonly associated with dandruff.

Ketoconazole: A broad-spectrum antifungal agent.

Example: Head & Shoulders Anti-Dandruff Shampoo, containing zinc pyrithione, is widely used for treating dandruff.

2. Medicated Shampoos

Specially designed to treat scalp conditions like psoriasis, seborrheic dermatitis, or eczema.

Active Ingredients:

Salicylic Acid: Reduces scalp flakiness by exfoliating dead skin cells.

Coal Tar: Slows skin cell turnover to alleviate scaling and itching.

Example: Neutrogena T/Gel Shampoo, formulated with coal tar for scalp treatment.

Formulation

Shampoo formulation requires precise adjustments to ensure performance, safety, and compatibility with the scalp and hair.

1. pH Adjustment

The pH of shampoos is adjusted to ~**5–7** to match the natural pH of the scalp and hair.

A balanced pH prevents scalp irritation and preserves the integrity of the hair cuticle.

Buffers like **citric acid** or **sodium hydroxide** are used to fine-tune pH levels.

2. Rheological Modifiers

Carbomers and other thickening agents are added to adjust viscosity, ensuring ease of application and controlled flow.

Typical viscosity for shampoos is maintained between **3000–5000 cps**, measured using a Brookfield viscometer.

Role: Ensures proper product consistency, prevents dripping, and enhances user experience.

Testing Parameters

Quality control tests are conducted to ensure that shampoos meet performance standards and provide a satisfactory consumer experience.

1. Foaming Index

The foaming index measures the shampoo's ability to create and sustain foam during use.

Method:

A standard volume of shampoo is diluted with water, agitated, and the foam height is measured.

Higher foam height indicates better cleansing performance.

2. Viscosity

Viscosity is a critical parameter influencing the shampoo's texture and usability.

Testing:

Measured using a Brookfield viscometer at room temperature.

Ideal viscosity: **3000–5000 cps**, providing smooth flow and easy application.

7.2.2 Hair Dyes

Hair dyes are cosmetic products formulated to alter the color of hair, catering to both aesthetic preferences and the need to cover gray hair. These products are available in various formulations and act through chemical or physical mechanisms to impart temporary, semi-permanent, or permanent color. The formulation of hair dyes involves precise ingredient selection and testing to ensure safety, stability, and effectiveness.

Types of Hair Dyes

1. Temporary Hair Dyes

Temporary hair dyes deposit color onto the surface of the hair shaft without penetrating the cortex. These dyes are ideal for short-term use, as the color is easily washed out with shampoo.

Mechanism: The dye molecules adhere to the hair cuticle but do not chemically react or bind.

Ingredients: Typically include large pigment molecules, such as FD&C dyes, which do not enter the hair shaft.

Longevity: Lasts for 1–2 washes.

Examples: Hair sprays or chalks used for vibrant, non-permanent color effects.

2. Semi-Permanent Hair Dyes

Semi-permanent dyes penetrate the outer layers of the hair shaft but do not reach the cortex. They provide a more lasting effect than temporary dyes but still fade over time.

Mechanism: The dye molecules are small enough to diffuse into the cuticle layers but do not involve oxidation reactions.

Ingredients: Include direct-acting dyes like nitro compounds (e.g., nitro-p-phenylenediamine).

Longevity: Lasts for 4–8 washes, depending on the hair porosity and washing frequency.

Examples: Products used for enhancing natural hair tones or adding subtle highlights.

3. Permanent Hair Dyes

Permanent hair dyes are the most enduring and involve chemical reactions to develop color within the hair cortex.

Mechanism: The dyes penetrate deeply into the cortex, where oxidative reactions lock the color in place.

Ingredients:

Para-phenylenediamine (PPD): A precursor that forms dye molecules through oxidation.

Hydrogen Peroxide (3–6%): Acts as an oxidizing agent and helps open the cuticle for deeper dye penetration.

Longevity: Permanent, with touch-ups required only as hair grows out.

Examples: Used in salon-grade hair dyes for complete gray coverage or dramatic color changes.

Mechanism of Action

The mechanism of hair dyeing varies based on the type of dye. For permanent hair dyes, the process involves the following steps:

1. Oxidation Reactions

Color Development:

PPD or related precursors undergo oxidation in the presence of hydrogen peroxide, forming larger dye molecules that develop color.

Example Reaction:

Para-phenylenediamine + Hydrogen Peroxide → Oxidized Dye Molecules.

Role of Hydrogen Peroxide:

Acts as both an oxidizing agent and a bleaching agent to lighten the natural hair color, creating a suitable base for the dye.

2. Penetration into the Hair Cortex

Cuticle Opening: Hydrogen peroxide lifts the cuticle layers, allowing dye precursors to enter the cortex.

Cortex Reaction: Inside the cortex, the precursors react to form large, colored molecules that cannot diffuse out, ensuring long-lasting color.

Safety and Regulations

The use of hair dyes involves potential safety concerns, particularly with permanent formulations, as some ingredients may cause skin irritation or allergic reactions. Regulations and testing protocols ensure consumer safety.

1. Allergic Reactions and Patch Testing

Allergic Reactions: Ingredients like PPD can cause contact dermatitis in sensitive individuals. Symptoms include redness, swelling, and itching at the site of application.

Patch Testing:

Recommended before use to identify potential allergic reactions.

Procedure: A small amount of dye is applied behind the ear or on the inner forearm and observed for 48 hours for any adverse reaction.

2. Regulatory Standards

EU Cosmetic Directive:

Limits the concentration of PPD in hair dyes to a maximum of **2%** when mixed with hydrogen peroxide.

Requires mandatory labeling of allergens and instructions for safe use.

FDA Regulations:

Mandates that hair dyes carry warnings for potential allergic reactions and include detailed instructions for patch testing.

Stability Testing

Hair dyes must undergo rigorous stability testing to ensure their efficacy and safety under various conditions.

1. Light Stability

Exposure to light can degrade dye precursors and oxidizing agents, reducing product effectiveness.

Testing Method:

Samples are exposed to UV and visible light in a controlled environment for specified durations.

Evaluated for changes in color intensity and chemical stability.

Example: Permanent dyes containing PPD showed a degradation rate of **5–10%** when exposed to UV light for 8 hours, emphasizing the need for UV-protective packaging.

2. Heat Stability

Heat exposure can accelerate oxidative degradation and alter product consistency.

Testing Method:

Samples are stored at elevated temperatures (e.g., **40°C ± 2°C**) for a minimum of 30 days.

Assessed for viscosity changes, phase separation, and active ingredient stability.

Example: Hair dyes stored at 40°C demonstrated consistent performance with no visible phase separation or significant loss of PPD activity.

7.3 Sunscreens

Definition and Purpose

Sunscreens are **topical formulations** designed to protect the skin from the harmful effects of **ultraviolet (UV) radiation** emitted by the sun. These products reduce the risk of sunburn, premature aging, and skin cancer by either reflecting or absorbing UV rays before they penetrate the skin. Sunscreens play a critical role in preventing both acute and chronic damage caused by **UV-A (320–400 nm)** and **UV-B (290–320 nm)** radiation.

Primary Functions:

Protect the skin from sunburn caused by UV-B rays.

Prevent premature skin aging, hyperpigmentation, and DNA damage caused by UV-A rays.

Reduce the risk of skin cancer by minimizing UV-induced cellular mutations.

Types of Sunscreens

Sunscreens are broadly categorized into **physical blockers** and **chemical absorbers** based on their mechanism of action.

1. Physical Blockers

Physical blockers work by reflecting and scattering UV rays away from the skin surface. These are composed of inert minerals that form a protective barrier.

Examples:

Titanium Dioxide (TiO$_2$): Effective against UV-B and short-wave UV-A radiation.

Zinc Oxide (ZnO): Offers broad-spectrum protection by blocking UV-B and UV-A rays.

Characteristics:

Non-irritating and suitable for sensitive skin.

Leave a whitish residue on the skin due to their reflective nature.

Usage: Found in sunscreens for infants, people with sensitive skin, and water-resistant formulations.

2. Chemical Absorbers

Chemical sunscreens absorb UV radiation and convert it into harmless heat, preventing it from damaging the skin.

Examples:

Oxybenzone: Absorbs UV-B and short-wave UV-A radiation.

Avobenzone: Provides broad-spectrum protection, particularly against UV-A rays.

Characteristics:

Lightweight formulations that are easily absorbed by the skin.

May cause irritation or allergic reactions in sensitive individuals.

Usage: Common in daily wear sunscreens for their cosmetically elegant finish.

Definition of SPF

SPF measures a sunscreen's ability to protect the skin from UV-B radiation, specifically the time it takes for the skin to burn when wearing sunscreen versus without sunscreen.

SPF Values for Different Skin Types

SPF 15: Blocks approximately **93%** of UV-B rays, suitable for individuals with darker skin tones or those exposed to minimal sun.

SPF 30: Blocks approximately **97%** of UV-B rays, ideal for fair-skinned individuals or moderate sun exposure.

SPF 50: Blocks approximately **98%** of UV-B rays, recommended for prolonged outdoor activities or intense sun exposure.

It is important to note that higher SPF values provide marginally increased protection but do not offer complete immunity from sun damage.

Formulation

Sunscreens are carefully formulated to ensure broad-spectrum protection, ease of application, and water resistance.

1. Emulsion Systems for Water-Resistant Sunscreens

Oil-in-Water (O/W) Emulsions: Commonly used in lightweight sunscreens for easy absorption and a non-greasy feel.

Water-in-Oil (W/O) Emulsions: Preferred for water-resistant formulations, as they form a hydrophobic layer that prevents wash-off during sweating or swimming.

Key Ingredients:

Film-Forming Agents: Silicones or polymers that create a protective barrier on the skin to enhance water resistance.

2. Antioxidants for Enhanced Protection

Vitamin E (Tocopherol): Neutralizes free radicals generated by UV exposure, reducing oxidative stress and skin damage.

Vitamin C (Ascorbic Acid): Protects against photoaging by boosting collagen synthesis and scavenging free radicals.

Antioxidants are often included in sunscreen formulations to complement UV filters and provide additional photoprotection.

Quality Control

1. UV Absorption Testing

UV absorption testing evaluates a sunscreen's ability to block or absorb UV radiation.

Method:

A thin layer of sunscreen is applied to a quartz plate and exposed to UV light.

The **spectrophotometer** measures the reduction in UV transmittance to determine the sunscreen's efficacy.

SPF Validation: Laboratory tests ensure the labeled SPF value matches the product's performance.

2. Water-Resistance Testing

Water-resistance testing assesses a sunscreen's ability to retain its protective properties after water exposure.

FDA Protocols:

Sunscreens labeled "Water-Resistant" must maintain their SPF level after **40 minutes** of water immersion.

"Very Water-Resistant" sunscreens must perform effectively after **80 minutes** in water.

Method:

Subjects apply the sunscreen and immerse themselves in water. Post-immersion, SPF is re-evaluated to confirm compliance with the claim.

Review Questions and Answers

1. What is the primary function of cosmetics?
To clean, beautify, and enhance the appearance of the body.

2. What are the key ingredients in a typical lipstick formulation?
Waxes, oils, pigments, and emollients.

3. Why is beeswax used in lipsticks?
It provides structure and rigidity to the stick.

4. Name two emollients used in lipsticks.
Lanolin and castor oil.

5. What is the function of cold cream?
It acts as a cleansing and moisturizing agent.

6. What are the main ingredients in a cold cream?
Water, mineral oil, beeswax, borax, and fragrance.

7. What distinguishes vanishing cream from cold cream?
Vanishing cream leaves a non-greasy film after application.

8. What are the active ingredients in vanishing cream?
Stearic acid, potassium hydroxide, and glycerin.

9. Why are preservatives added to creams?
To prevent microbial contamination and increase shelf-life.

10. What is the ideal pH range for facial creams?
Between 5 and 7 to match skin pH.

11. What is the function of shampoos?
To clean hair and scalp by removing dirt and oil.

12. Name a common surfactant used in shampoos.
Sodium lauryl sulfate.

13. What is the purpose of conditioning agents in shampoos?
To soften hair and reduce static.

14. Give an example of a conditioning agent.
Silicones like dimethicone.

15. What are the two main types of hair dyes?
Temporary and permanent.

16. What ingredient is common in permanent hair dyes?
Ammonia and hydrogen peroxide.

17. Why are stabilizers added in hair dyes?
To maintain color and prevent degradation.

18. What are sunscreens used for?

To protect the skin from harmful UV radiation.

19. Differentiate between physical and chemical sunscreens.

Physical sunscreens reflect UV rays, while chemical sunscreens absorb them.

20. Name two physical sunscreen agents.

Zinc oxide and titanium dioxide.

21. What is SPF in sunscreen products?

Sun Protection Factor, indicating protection level against UVB rays.

22. How is SPF calculated?

By comparing the time to sunburn with and without sunscreen.

23. Why is fragrance used in cosmetics?

To improve consumer acceptability and mask unpleasant odours.

24. What are the risks of using untested cosmetic products?

Skin irritation, allergic reactions, and long-term damage.

25. What is the role of emollients in skin care products?

To soften and hydrate the skin.

26. What is meant by comedogenicity?

The tendency of a substance to block pores and cause acne.

27. Name a non-comedogenic oil.

Sunflower oil.

28. Why is patch testing important?

To check for allergic or irritant reactions before full application.

29. What is the use of eye creams?

To reduce puffiness, dark circles, and hydrate the under-eye area.

30. What is the purpose of exfoliants?

To remove dead skin cells and improve skin texture.

31. What is the primary purpose of toners in skin care?

To remove residual impurities and tighten pores after cleansing.

32. Which ingredient is commonly used in astringents?

Alcohol or witch hazel.

33. What are anti-aging creams formulated to do?

To reduce wrinkles, fine lines, and improve skin elasticity.

34. Name a common anti-aging active ingredient.

Retinol or hyaluronic acid.

35. What are fairness creams claimed to do?

To lighten the skin tone or reduce hyperpigmentation.

36. What are natural or herbal cosmetics?

Products formulated using plant-based or naturally derived ingredients.

37. Give an example of a natural ingredient used in cosmetics.

Aloe vera, turmeric, or neem.

38. Why are antioxidants added to cosmetic formulations?

To prevent oxidative degradation and protect skin cells.

39. Name a common antioxidant used in cosmetics.

Vitamin E (tocopherol).

40. What is a BB cream?

Beauty Balm or Blemish Balm cream that combines skincare and makeup benefits.

41. What is the main benefit of using night creams?

To provide deep hydration and repair the skin overnight.

42. What is the function of scrubs in facial care?

To exfoliate and remove dead skin cells from the surface.

43. What is a clay mask used for?

To absorb excess oil and impurities from the skin.

44. What does hypoallergenic mean in cosmetics?

Formulated to minimize the risk of allergic reactions.

45. What are micellar waters?

Cleansing waters that remove makeup and dirt without rinsing.

46. Why are silicones used in skin and hair products?

To provide smoothness and shine.

47. What are serums in cosmetics?

Concentrated formulations for targeted treatment like hydration or anti-aging.

48. Name a cosmetic product used for nail care.

Nail polish or cuticle oil.

49. What is the role of humectants in cosmetics?

To attract and retain moisture in the skin.

50. Give an example of a humectant.

Glycerin or propylene glycol.

MCQs

Lip and Skin Products

1. Lipsticks are typically composed of waxes, oils, and which of the following components?
   A. Detergents
   B. Proteins
   C. Pigments
   D. Sugars
   Answer: C

2. Beeswax in a lipstick formulation serves to:
   A. moisturize the lips
   B. add flavor to the lipstick
   C. impart color to the lipstick
   D. provide hardness and shape to the lipstick
   Answer: D

3. Castor oil is often used in lipsticks to:
   A. harden the lipstick
   B. give a glossy shine and smooth application
   C. preserve the lipstick
   D. neutralize the lipstick's pH
   Answer: B

4. Lanolin (wool wax) in lip products acts as a:
   A. moisturizing agent
   B. colorant
   C. preservative
   D. cleansing agent
   Answer: A

5. Which of the following pigments, derived from insects, is used to give a red color in cosmetics like lipsticks?
   A. Chlorophyll
   B. Carmine
   C. Henna
   D. Tartrazine

Answer: B

6. To prevent the oils in lipstick from becoming rancid, manufacturers add a small amount of:

    A. an antioxidant

    B. a preservative

    C. a wax

    D. a sweetener

    Answer: A

7. Which wax, known for its high melting point, is added to lipstick to increase its hardness (especially in warm climates)?

    A. Beeswax

    B. Lanolin

    C. Paraffin wax

    D. Carnauba wax

    Answer: D

8. Cold cream is an example of a(n) __ emulsion.

    A. oil-in-water

    B. water-in-oil

    C. suspension

    D. solution

    Answer: B

9. What is a common use for cold cream?

    A. To cleanse the skin and remove makeup

    B. To protect the skin from UV rays

    C. To style hair

    D. To color the lips

    Answer: C

10. Which of the following is a common ingredient in cold cream formulations?

    A. Mineral oil

    B. Sodium hydroxide

    C. Talcum powder

    D. Sulfur

    Answer: D

11. The name "cold cream" comes from the cooling sensation it produces on the skin. This cooling effect is mainly because the cream:

    A. contains menthol or mint extracts

    B. causes evaporation of water from the skin

C. is stored at a low temperature

D. numbs the skin slightly

Answer: B

12. Which cream is more suitable as a nourishing night cream due to its high oil content?

A. Cold cream

B. Vanishing cream

C. Sunscreen lotion

D. Shampoo

Answer: A

13. Vanishing cream is an example of a(n) __ emulsion.

A. water-in-oil

B. suspension

C. gel

D. oil-in-water

Answer: D

14. Vanishing creams typically contain a high proportion of which fatty acid (that leaves a protective film on the skin)?

A. Oleic acid

B. Stearic acid

C. Palmitic acid

D. Acetic acid

Answer: B

15. Vanishing creams often include glycerin because it:

A. acts as a sunscreen

B. provides fragrance

C. helps keep the skin moist (as a humectant)

D. colors the cream white

Answer: C

16. Why is a vanishing cream so called?

A. Because it undergoes a chemical reaction and disappears

B. Because it leaves no greasy residue on the skin after application

C. Because it evaporates completely after application

D. Because it turns into a powder when applied

Answer: B

17. Vanishing cream is often used as a:

A. non-greasy daytime moisturizer or makeup base

B. heavy overnight cream for dry skin

C. hair styling gel substitute

D. lip balm for chapped lips

Answer: A

18. In vanishing cream formulation, a small amount of alkali is added to react with stearic acid and form soap. This soap functions as:

A. an antiseptic in the cream

B. a pearlescent agent for shine

C. an emulsifier to stabilize the mixture

D. a perfume to scent the cream

Answer: C

Hair Care Products

19. The primary cleansing agents in shampoos are:

A. detergents (surfactants)

B. oils

C. waxes

D. alkaline soaps

Answer: A

20. Which of these is a common detergent (surfactant) used in shampoos?

A. Sodium bicarbonate

B. Sodium lauryl sulfate (SLS)

C. Sodium chloride

D. Beeswax

Answer: B

21. Shampoos are often formulated to be slightly acidic (around pH 5–6) because this:

A. keeps hair cuticles smooth and reduces tangling

B. produces more lather during washing

C. helps hair absorb water

D. enhances the shampoo's fragrance

Answer: C

22. Some shampoos contain conditioning agents (e.g. silicones or quaternary ammonium compounds) to:

A. strip away all natural oils from hair

B. add color to the hair during shampooing

C. reduce static and make hair smoother and shinier

D. increase the shampoo's foaming power

Answer: D

23. An ingredient commonly added to anti-dandruff shampoos is:

    A. sodium hydroxide

    B. glycerin

    C. zinc pyrithione

    D. beeswax

    Answer: C

24. One major disadvantage of using soap instead of shampoo on hair is that soap:

    A. forms insoluble scum in hard water and can make hair rough

    B. produces no lather at all in water

    C. cannot clean oils and dirt from hair

    D. permanently damages hair color

    Answer: A

25. Temporary hair color preparations are characterized by the fact that they:

    A. penetrate the hair shaft and last for months

    B. wash out with the next shampoo

    C. chemically modify the hair's natural pigment

    D. must be mixed with a developer before application

    Answer: B

26. Unlike temporary dyes, permanent hair dyes work by:

    A. coating the hair surface with large pigment particles

    B. being completely natural with no chemicals

    C. simply staining the hair without any reaction

    D. undergoing a chemical reaction inside the hair to form color molecules

    Answer: D

27. In permanent hair dye kits, the "developer" is usually:

    A. water

    B. ammonia

    C. hydrogen peroxide

    D. alcohol

    Answer: C

28. Ammonia is often present in permanent hair dyes because it:

    A. opens up the hair shaft (cuticle) to help the dye penetrate

B. acts as the dye that gives color

C. works as a hair-conditioning agent

D. neutralizes the hydrogen peroxide

Answer: A

29. Para-phenylenediamine (PPD) is commonly used:

A. in sunscreens as a UV filter

B. in cold creams as an emulsifier

C. in shampoos as a thickener

D. in permanent hair dyes as a dye precursor

Answer: D

30. Which natural product is used to impart a reddish-brown dye to hair?

A. Henna (mehndi)

B. Aloe vera

C. Mint

D. Turmeric

Answer: A

31. The coloring compound present in henna leaves (Lawsonia) is called:

A. Indigo

B. Lawsone

C. Melanin

D. Carotene

Answer: B

32. A patch test is recommended before using a hair dye primarily to check for:

A. hair damage

B. proper color results

C. allergic reaction to the dye

D. even coverage on hair

Answer: C

Sunscreens

33. In the context of sunscreens, SPF stands for:

A. Sun Protection Factor

B. Skin Protection Formula

C. Sunburn Prevention Formula

D. Solar Product Factor

Answer: A

34. Which component of sunlight is mostly responsible for causing sunburn?

    A. Visible light

    B. UVA rays

    C. UVB rays

    D. Infrared rays

    Answer: C

35. Ultraviolet A (UVA) radiation is primarily associated with:

    A. no effect on the skin

    B. skin tanning and premature aging

    C. causing sunburn

    D. heating the skin

    Answer: B

36. Which of the following is an example of a chemical (organic) sunscreen ingredient?

    A. Zinc oxide

    B. Titanium dioxide

    C. Oxybenzone

    D. p-Aminobenzoic acid (PABA)

    Answer: D

37. Which of the following is a physical (inorganic) UV filter used in sunscreens?

    A. Oxybenzone

    B. Octyl methoxycinnamate

    C. Titanium dioxide

    D. PABA

    Answer: C

38. Physical sunscreen agents (like zinc oxide) protect the skin primarily by:

    A. reflecting and scattering UV radiation

    B. absorbing UV radiation chemically

    C. warming the skin to counteract UV effects

    D. staining the skin to block light

    Answer: A

39. A "broad-spectrum" sunscreen is one that:

    A. has SPF 50 or higher

    B. contains multiple vitamins for skin

C. is very water-resistant

D. protects against both UVA and UVB rays

Answer: D

40. Chronic unprotected exposure to UV radiation can lead to:

A. skin cancer

B. improved immunity

C. enhanced hair growth

D. vision improvement

Answer: A

41. Which SPF value indicates the highest level of UVB protection?

A. SPF 15

B. SPF 30

C. SPF 8

D. SPF 50

Answer: D

42. Bleaching hair with hydrogen peroxide primarily:

A. removes the natural pigment from the hair (lightens it)

B. coats the hair with a white dye

C. seals the hair cuticle completely

D. makes the hair more oily

Answer: A

43. Which of the following cosmetic products is typically **anhydrous** (contains no water)?

A. Cold cream

B. Vanishing cream

C. Lipstick

D. Sunscreen lotion

Answer: C

44. Shaving creams typically contain soap or surfactants to:

A. dye the facial hair for easier cutting

B. create a lather that softens the beard and lubricates the skin

C. harden the hair for a closer shave

D. cool the skin by evaporation

Answer: B

45. Antiperspirants help reduce sweating by using compounds (like aluminum salts) that:

A. add a strong fragrance to the skin

B. cool the skin surface

C. block sweat gland ducts temporarily

D. kill all bacteria on the skin

Answer: C

46. The primary solvent used in making perfumes is often:

A. Water

B. Glycerin

C. Acetone

D. Ethanol (alcohol)

Answer: D

47. In perfumery, the "top note" refers to:

A. the initial scent of a perfume that evaporates quickly

B. the main fragrance that lasts the longest

C. the fixative agent in the perfume

D. the base scent that remains after hours

Answer: A

48. Nail polish removers commonly contain which solvent?

A. Glycerol

B. Water

C. Benzene

D. Acetone

Answer: D

49. The film-forming ingredient in many nail polishes is:

A. Beeswax

B. Nitrocellulose

C. Silicone

D. Polyvinyl alcohol

Answer: B

50. Deodorants mainly work by:

A. masking odor with fragrance and reducing bacteria on the skin

B. blocking sweat glands from releasing sweat

C. absorbing all perspiration completely

D. cooling the skin to minimize sweating

Answer: A

Pharmaceutical Aerosols

8.1 Introduction to Aerosols

8.1.1 Definition and Components

Definition of Pharmaceutical Aerosols

Pharmaceutical aerosols are **pressurized delivery systems** designed to release drugs in the form of fine particles, droplets, or mist for therapeutic application. The unique advantage of aerosols lies in their ability to provide controlled, uniform, and targeted drug delivery, whether to the lungs, skin, or other surfaces. These systems ensure precise dosing and improved bioavailability of active ingredients, often bypassing systemic absorption and reducing side effects.

Key Characteristics:

1. Delivers drugs in finely dispersed forms for effective absorption.
2. Allows localized treatment with minimal wastage.
3. Ensures sterility and protection of the drug from external contamination.

Key Components of Aerosols

Pharmaceutical aerosols consist of several essential components, each playing a critical role in ensuring efficacy, stability, and controlled delivery of the formulation.

1. Active Ingredient

The **active pharmaceutical ingredient (API)** is the drug that provides the desired therapeutic effect.

Formulated as a solution, suspension, or emulsion within the aerosol system.

Example:

Salbutamol in inhalation aerosols for the treatment of asthma.

Lidocaine in topical sprays for pain relief.

2. Propellant

The propellant is a pressurized gas or liquid responsible for dispensing the drug in aerosol form. It creates the pressure required to expel the formulation and atomize it into fine particles.

Types of Propellants:

Liquefied Gases: Hydrofluoroalkanes (HFAs) are commonly used due to their low environmental impact.

Compressed Gases: Nitrogen, carbon dioxide, or air are used in certain formulations.

Function:

Expels the drug in the desired particle size and pattern.

Affects the spray characteristics, including velocity and droplet size.

3. Container

The container houses the aerosol formulation and must withstand high internal pressure while maintaining chemical compatibility with the formulation.

Materials:

Aluminum: Lightweight and corrosion-resistant.

Stainless Steel: Preferred for formulations requiring high stability.

Glass: Used for specific applications but requires protective coatings to enhance safety.

Significance:

Protects the formulation from external contamination and light exposure.

Ensures durability under pressurized conditions.

4. Valve and Actuator

The valve and actuator regulate the release of the aerosol and control the spray characteristics, such as the particle size, spray pattern, and dose per actuation.

Valve: Maintains a sealed system and allows controlled release of the formulation upon actuation.

Actuator: The user interface component that directs the spray to the intended area of application.

Example: Metered-dose inhalers (MDIs) use precision-engineered valves to deliver consistent doses.

Therapeutic Applications

Pharmaceutical aerosols are utilized across various therapeutic areas, providing efficient and targeted drug delivery.

1. Inhalation Aerosols

Inhalation aerosols are used for respiratory conditions, delivering drugs directly to the lungs for rapid onset of action and high local concentration.

Example:

Salbutamol Inhaler: A short-acting beta-agonist for asthma management, delivered via metered-dose inhalers (MDIs).

Advantages:

Immediate relief from bronchospasm.

Reduced systemic side effects due to localized delivery.

2. Topical Aerosols

Topical aerosols are applied to the skin or mucosal surfaces for localized therapeutic effects, often used for pain relief, wound care, or dermatological treatments.

Example:

Lidocaine Spray: A local anesthetic aerosol for pain relief during minor procedures or skin injuries.

Advantages:

Provides even application and uniform drug distribution.

Reduces the risk of contamination and enhances sterility.

8.1.2 Propellants, Containers, and Valves

The effectiveness and safety of pharmaceutical aerosols rely on the selection of suitable **propellants**, **containers**, and **valves and actuators**. These components work in harmony to ensure controlled drug delivery, product stability, and user convenience.

Propellants

Propellants are crucial components of aerosol systems, providing the pressure required to expel the formulation and disperse it into fine particles or droplets. Their selection depends on factors like safety, environmental impact, and compatibility with the formulation.

Types of Propellants

Hydrocarbons

Hydrocarbons such as **propane, butane,** and **isobutane** are commonly used due to their cost-effectiveness and excellent performance.

They are suitable for topical aerosols and other non-sterile applications.

Advantages:

Economical and readily available.

Good solvent properties for certain formulations.

Disadvantages:

Flammable, posing safety concerns.

Limited use in inhalation aerosols due to potential respiratory irritation.

Chlorofluorocarbons (CFCs)

Previously used extensively for their inertness and stability, **CFCs** have been largely phased out due to their harmful effects on the ozone layer.

Example: Dichlorodifluoromethane (CFC-12), once a primary propellant for inhalation aerosols, is no longer in use under global agreements like the **Montreal Protocol.**

Hydrofluoroalkanes (HFAs)

HFAs, such as **HFA-134a** and **HFA-227a**, are eco-friendly alternatives to CFCs. They are now the preferred choice for inhalation aerosols due to their environmental safety and non-flammability.

Advantages:

Non-ozone-depleting and environmentally sustainable.

Inert, ensuring stability with most drug formulations.

Disadvantages:

Higher production costs compared to hydrocarbons.

Physical Properties of Propellants

Vapor Pressure:

Propellants exhibit vapor pressures typically in the range of **30–70 psi** at room temperature, ensuring efficient expulsion of the formulation.

Higher vapor pressures result in finer particles, suitable for inhalation aerosols.

Boiling Point:

Propellants with lower boiling points vaporize easily, aiding in the dispersion of the drug.

Example: Propane has a boiling point of **-42°C**, while HFA-134a boils at **-26.3°C**.

Containers

The container houses the aerosol formulation and must withstand the high internal pressure generated by the propellant while maintaining the stability and sterility of the product.

Materials

Aluminum

Lightweight and corrosion-resistant, aluminum is the most commonly used material for aerosol containers.

It is compatible with a wide range of formulations, including those with organic solvents.

Stainless Steel

Preferred for products requiring high stability or extended shelf life.

Used in medical-grade aerosols and formulations with aggressive solvents.

Glass

Provides excellent visibility and inertness but is less common due to fragility.

Glass containers are often coated with plastic for added strength.

Features of Containers

Pressure Resistance:

Containers are designed to withstand internal pressures ranging from **140–180 psi**, ensuring safety under normal storage and usage conditions.

Chemical Compatibility:

The container material must not react with the formulation or propellant, preserving product integrity.

Valves and Actuators

The valve and actuator system regulates the release of the aerosol and controls the spray pattern, particle size, and dose.

Types of Valves

Metering Valves

Deliver a precise and consistent dose with each actuation.

Commonly used in inhalation aerosols for respiratory drugs like **salbutamol**.

Continuous Valves

Allow uninterrupted release of the formulation until the actuator is released.

Suitable for topical sprays, such as **lidocaine aerosols** for pain relief.

Actuator Design

The design of the actuator significantly impacts the characteristics of the spray.

Spray Pattern:

The shape and size of the actuator nozzle determine the spray pattern.

Wider nozzles produce coarse sprays, while narrower nozzles create finer mists.

Particle Size:

The actuator influences the particle size distribution, which is critical for inhalation aerosols.

Optimal particle size for pulmonary delivery ranges from **1–5 µm**.

8.2 Formulation and Manufacture

8.2.1 Types of Aerosol Systems

Pharmaceutical aerosols are formulated into different types of systems based on the physical state of the drug and the delivery requirements. These systems include **solutions, suspensions, emulsions**, and **foams**, each offering specific advantages and applications. The choice of the aerosol system depends on factors like the solubility of the drug, desired delivery site, and stability requirements.

Solutions

Description

In solution aerosol systems, the **drug is completely dissolved** in the propellant, a co-solvent, or a combination of both. These systems provide uniform drug delivery and are suitable for formulations where the drug has high solubility in the propellant or vehicle.

Mechanism: The propellant creates pressure, expelling the dissolved drug in fine droplets upon actuation.

Advantages: Provides consistent dosing and eliminates sedimentation issues found in suspensions.

Examples

Topical Anesthetics:

Benzocaine Aerosols: Formulated as solutions to deliver a uniform anesthetic effect over the skin or mucous membranes.

Formulation Considerations

Solubility Parameters:

The solubility of the drug in the propellant or co-solvent is critical. Solvents like **ethanol** or **propylene glycol** are often used to enhance solubility.

Example: Benzocaine's solubility in ethanol ensures uniform distribution within the system.

Interactions:

Compatibility between the drug, propellant, and solvent must be assessed to prevent precipitation or degradation.

Suspensions

Description

Suspension aerosol systems involve the **dispersion of solid drug particles** in the propellant or a non-volatile vehicle. These systems are ideal for drugs with poor solubility in common solvents, providing controlled delivery of the active ingredient.

Mechanism: Upon actuation, the propellant carries the dispersed drug particles in a finely atomized spray.

Examples

Steroid Inhalers:

Fluticasone Propionate: A corticosteroid used in metered-dose inhalers (MDIs) for asthma and COPD.

Formulation Considerations

Stability Concerns:

Sedimentation: The drug particles may settle at the bottom of the container. To prevent this, **suspending agents** like lecithin or sorbitan trioleate are added.

Particle Agglomeration: Fine particles may clump together over time. Particle size is typically maintained between **1–5 µm** to ensure proper dispersion.

Particle Size Control:

Fine particle size is critical for inhalation aerosols to ensure deep lung deposition.

Emulsions

Description

Emulsion aerosols are formulated as **water-in-oil (W/O)** or **oil-in-water (O/W)** systems, stabilized by emulsifiers. These systems are versatile and can deliver the drug as a spray, foam, or cream.

Mechanism: The emulsion is atomized upon actuation, forming a fine mist or foam depending on the nozzle design and pressure.

Examples

Foam Aerosols for Wound Care:

Foam-based emulsions are commonly used to deliver antiseptics, moisturizers, or wound-healing agents.

Formulation Considerations

Emulsifiers:

Stabilizers like **polysorbates** or **spans** are added to prevent phase separation.

Stability:

Phase separation can be a significant challenge. Proper emulsifier selection and homogenization ensure stability.

Foams

Description

Foam aerosols encapsulate the drug in a foam structure, providing **extended skin contact** and improved adherence to the application site. These systems are highly effective for dermatological applications requiring prolonged action.

Mechanism: Foams are dispensed when the propellant forces the formulation through a specialized nozzle, creating a light, airy structure.

Examples

Dermatological Foams:

Foams containing hydrocortisone or antifungal agents provide extended-release effects on the skin.

Physical Properties

Viscosity:

The viscosity of the foam determines its spreadability and adherence to the skin. Typical viscosity ranges from **10,000 to 100,000 cps**, depending on the intended application.

Foam Density:

Lighter foams are preferred for quick absorption, while denser foams are used for prolonged contact.

Manufacturing Process

The manufacturing process of pharmaceutical aerosols involves precise techniques to ensure the uniformity, stability, and efficacy of the product. The two primary methods of filling aerosol containers are **cold filling** and **pressure filling**, each with distinct steps, advantages, and limitations. The choice of method depends on the type of formulation, the propellant used, and the compatibility of components.

Cold Filling

Process Steps

Cold filling is a method where both the container and the propellant are chilled to extremely low temperatures before the filling process begins. This method ensures that the liquefied propellant remains stable and prevents evaporation during filling.

Chilling the Propellant and Container

The propellant is cooled to a temperature between **-30°C and -60°C** using specialized refrigeration systems.

Simultaneously, the aerosol container is chilled to similar temperatures to prevent thermal shock and ensure compatibility during the filling process.

Filling the Container

The chilled liquefied propellant is introduced into the container, usually in combination with the active pharmaceutical ingredient (API) and other excipients, depending on the formulation type.

Sealing and Testing

Once the propellant and formulation are filled, the container is sealed with a valve system to prevent leakage.

The sealed product is tested for leaks and pressure consistency.

Limitations of Cold Filling

Unsuitability for Aqueous Systems:

Water-based formulations are not compatible with this method, as the low temperatures used can cause freezing of the water phase, leading to phase separation or instability.

Energy Consumption:

The process requires significant energy to maintain the ultra-low temperatures, making it less efficient for large-scale production.

Thermal Stress on Containers:

Repeated chilling and warming can weaken some container materials, particularly those with lower thermal tolerance.

Pressure Filling

Process Steps

Pressure filling is a method where the liquefied propellant is added to the container under high pressure. This method is widely used in the pharmaceutical industry due to its compatibility with a broader range of formulations and reduced equipment costs.

Filling the Formulation

The active pharmaceutical ingredient (API) and excipients are first added to the container. Depending on the formulation type, this may include solutions, suspensions, emulsions, or pre-prepared foam bases.

Introducing the Propellant

The liquefied propellant is introduced under high pressure, typically ~**100 psi**, using a filling machine. This high pressure ensures that the propellant remains in a liquefied state during the filling process.

Sealing and Mixing

Once the propellant is filled, the container is sealed with a valve system. The sealed container is then agitated to ensure uniform mixing of the propellant and the formulation.

Quality Testing

After filling, the aerosol is tested for leak-proof sealing, accurate pressure levels, and uniform spray characteristics.

Advantages of Pressure Filling

Compatibility with Aqueous Systems:

Unlike cold filling, pressure filling is suitable for water-based formulations as it eliminates the risk of freezing.

Reduced Energy Requirements:

This method does not require chilling of the propellant or containers, reducing energy consumption and operational costs.

Cost-Effective Equipment:

The machinery used for pressure filling is simpler and more economical compared to the refrigeration systems required for cold filling.

Minimized Thermal Stress:

Since the process is conducted at ambient or slightly elevated temperatures, there is no risk of thermal shock to the containers.

8.3 Quality Control and Stability Studies

Quality control and stability studies are integral to ensuring that pharmaceutical aerosols meet stringent safety, efficacy, and performance standards. Various tests are conducted to evaluate the physical, chemical, and functional attributes of aerosol formulations. These tests are designed to maintain consistency, verify compliance with regulatory guidelines, and ensure that the product remains stable over its shelf life.

8.3.1 Quality Control Tests

Leak Testing

Leak testing ensures that the aerosol container is sealed properly and can withstand internal pressure without any leakage.

Methods:

Water Bath Immersion:

The filled and sealed aerosol is submerged in a water bath maintained at 50°C.

Any leakage is indicated by the escape of air bubbles from the container.

Pressure Decay Test:

The container is pressurized, and any reduction in pressure over a fixed period indicates a leak.

Acceptance Criteria:

No visible air bubbles or pressure decay over **30 seconds** at operational pressure.

Containers failing this test are rejected to prevent product failure or safety risks.

Valve Performance

The valve is a critical component of aerosols, and its performance must be thoroughly evaluated to ensure consistent delivery of the drug.

Parameters Tested:

Spray Rate: Measures the rate at which the formulation is expelled.

Delivery Dose Uniformity: Ensures that each actuation delivers a consistent amount of the drug.

Actuation Force: Determines the force required to activate the valve, ensuring it is user-friendly.

Example:

For metered-dose inhalers, the variability in metered dose delivery should not exceed ±**15%**.

Particle Size Distribution

Particle size distribution is a critical quality attribute for aerosols, especially for inhalation products, where particle size determines the deposition site within the respiratory tract.

Methods:

Cascade Impactors: Separate particles based on aerodynamic size to measure their distribution.

Laser Diffraction: Uses laser beams to measure particle sizes and distribution patterns.

Data:

For inhalation aerosols, the optimal particle size range is **1–5 μm** for effective deposition in the deep lungs.

Particles smaller than **1 μm** may be exhaled, while those larger than **5 μm** tend to deposit in the upper airways.

Spray Pattern and Plume Geometry

Spray pattern and plume geometry tests evaluate the distribution and directionality of the aerosol spray, which are critical for inhalation products and topical applications.

Parameters Evaluated:

Plume Width: Determines the breadth of the spray.

Plume Angle: Measures the angular dispersion of the spray upon actuation.

Testing Methods:

High-Speed Imaging: Captures the spray pattern in real-time to analyze its geometry.

Laser Diffraction: Provides precise data on plume characteristics and particle dispersion.

Importance for Inhalation Aerosols:

A properly directed plume ensures effective delivery of the drug to the targeted site, such as the deep lungs.

8.3.2 Stability Studies

Stability studies are essential to evaluate the performance, safety, and efficacy of pharmaceutical aerosols throughout their shelf life. These studies assess physical, chemical, and environmental factors that may affect the aerosol formulation and packaging components. Results from stability studies ensure compliance with regulatory standards and help establish product storage conditions and expiration dates.

Physical Stability

Physical stability focuses on the integrity of the formulation, particularly the interaction between the propellant, drug, and excipients. It also ensures the prevention of phase separation and sedimentation in complex systems like suspensions or emulsions.

Propellant-Drug Compatibility

Objective: Evaluate the miscibility of the propellant and formulation components to ensure consistent delivery and prevent instability, such as precipitation or phase separation.

Testing Methods:

Visual inspection for phase separation or settling of solid particles.

Measurement of propellant pressure to confirm that no propellant loss occurs during storage.

Phase Separation and Sedimentation

Suspensions and emulsions are prone to physical instability due to sedimentation of dispersed particles or phase separation.

Sedimentation Rate:

Sedimentation is measured over time to evaluate suspension stability. The sedimentation volume ratio is calculated.A value close to **1** indicates minimal sedimentation and good physical stability.

Example:

In salbutamol inhalers, sedimentation rates are monitored to ensure that the active ingredient remains evenly distributed.

Chemical Stability

Chemical stability evaluates the degradation of the active pharmaceutical ingredient (API) and excipients under different environmental conditions. This includes accelerated stability testing to predict long-term stability.

Drug Degradation

Accelerated Conditions:

Samples are stored at **40°C and 75% relative humidity (RH)** to simulate long-term storage conditions.

Chemical analysis is conducted at regular intervals to detect degradation products.

Testing Methods:

High-Performance Liquid Chromatography (HPLC) or Gas Chromatography (GC) to quantify API levels and identify degradation products.

Evaluation of pH, viscosity, and color changes in the formulation.

Example:

Salbutamol Stability:

At **25°C**, salbutamol maintains over **95% potency** after 12 months.

At **40°C**, degradation increases, with potency dropping to **85% after 6 months**, emphasizing the need for temperature-controlled storage.

Environmental Stability

Environmental stability studies test the performance of the aerosol formulation and packaging under extreme temperature and humidity conditions. These tests are critical to ensure the product's functionality in diverse geographic regions and storage environments.

Extreme Temperature Testing

Objective: Assess the aerosol's performance when exposed to extreme heat or cold, ensuring it remains functional across all conditions.

Conditions Tested:

Temperatures ranging from **-20°C to 50°C** simulate storage and transportation conditions.

Key Assessments:

Propellant behavior: Check for vapor pressure changes or loss of propellant at elevated temperatures.

Container integrity: Evaluate for deformation, leakage, or bursting under pressure changes.

Regulatory Requirements

Regulatory agencies require proof of the container and valve system's integrity under varying temperatures to prevent product failure during storage and use.

Testing Methods:

Aerosols are subjected to cyclic temperature changes, such as alternating between -20°C and **50°C** every 24 hours for a set duration.

Leakage, pressure changes, and valve performance are monitored to ensure compliance.

Example:

An aerosol for inhalation, like fluticasone, must demonstrate consistent spray characteristics and no leakage after exposure to temperature fluctuations.

MCQS

1. Pharmaceutical aerosols are administered via

A. Rectal route

B. Oral route

C. Ocular route

D. Inhalation route

Answer: D

2. Which component expels the drug from aerosol container?

A. Co-solvent

B. Actuator

C. Propellant

D. Solvent

Answer: C

3. In aerosol systems, liquefied gases are used as

A. Containers

B. Propellants

C. Valves

D. Preservatives

Answer: B

4. Which type of aerosol system uses compressed gas?

A. Solution

B. Two-phase

C. Three-phase

D. Foam

Answer: D

5. Actuator in an aerosol device helps in

A. Opening the valve

B. Pressurizing container

C. Releasing formulation

D. Measuring dose

Answer: C

6. The part of aerosol container that delivers the dose is

A. Cap

B. Actuator

C. Gasket

D. Dip tube

Answer: B

7. Which material is widely used in aerosol containers?

A. Aluminum

B. Copper

C. Plastic

D. Paper

Answer: A

8. Which is a suitable propellant for inhalation aerosols?

A. Butane

B. HFA-134a

C. Nitrogen

D. Carbon dioxide

Answer: B

9. In pharmaceutical aerosols, the function of the valve is to

A. Release contents evenly

B. Mix propellants

C. Heat the product

D. Cool the product

Answer: A

10. Which test checks the amount of drug emitted per actuation?

A. Dose content uniformity

B. Spray pattern

C. Leak test

D. Flame projection

Answer: A

11. Which part connects the formulation inside the container to the valve?

A. Dip tube

B. Actuator

C. Canister

D. Gasket

Answer: A

12. A dual-phase aerosol system contains

A. Drug and air

B. Propellant and product

C. Two containers

D. Two types of gases

Answer: B

13. The propellant used in metered dose inhalers is

A. HFA

B. Nitrous oxide

C. Carbon monoxide

D. Argon

Answer: A

14. Which is not a function of propellant?

A. Pressurizing the container

B. Delivering the drug

C. Increasing product viscosity

D. Creating spray force

Answer: C

15. Which type of valve is used in metered dose inhalers?

A. Open valve

B. Manual valve

C. Continuous spray valve

D. Metering valve

Answer: D

16. Which test evaluates the spray pattern of an aerosol?

A. Flame projection

B. Leak test

C. Spray pattern test

D. Content uniformity test

Answer: C

17. The leakage test for aerosols ensures

A. Proper labeling

B. Correct spray direction

C. Container integrity

D. Accurate formulation

Answer: C

18. The purpose of pressure testing in aerosols is to

A. Check fill volume

B. Verify container strength

C. Detect microbial growth

D. Measure drug content

Answer: B

19. The function of a crimping machine in aerosol production is to

A. Cool the container

B. Seal the valve

C. Mix the contents

D. Label the canister

Answer: B

20. Which is a commonly used liquefied gas propellant?

A. HFA-227

B. Hydrogen

C. Nitrogen

D. Methane

Answer: A

21. Why are co-solvents added to aerosol formulations?

A. For taste

B. To reduce toxicity

C. To dissolve active drug

D. To reduce can size

Answer: C

22. Which of the following gases is used in compressed gas systems?

A. Isobutane

B. Nitrogen

C. Propane

D. HFA-134a

Answer: B

23. What is the role of antioxidants in aerosol formulations?

A. Adjusting pH

B. Preventing oxidation

C. Coloring the product

D. Lowering pressure

Answer: B

24. HFA stands for

A. High Force Aerosol

B. Hydrofluoroalkane

C. Hydrogen Fluoride Acid

D. Hydro Forming Agent

Answer: B

25. The foam aerosol system typically contains

A. Compressed oxygen

B. Surfactants and hydrocarbons

C. Inert gas

D. Organic acids

Answer: B

26. The product fill method for aerosols includes

A. Dry powder loading

B. Cold fill and pressure fill

C. Drop method

D. Liquid phase transfer

Answer: B

27. Which device is used to deliver measured doses of aerosol drugs?

A. Nebulizer

B. Inhaler

C. Dropper

D. Capsule

Answer: B

28. Aerosols for dermatological use are mainly applied

A. Intramuscularly

B. Orally

C. Topically

D. Rectally

Answer: C

29. A typical canister used in aerosol packaging is made of

A. Tin

B. Aluminum

C. Glass

D. PVC

Answer: B

30. Which formulation is suitable for respiratory tract delivery?

A. Metered dose inhaler

B. Cream aerosol

C. Powder puff

D. Topical gel

Answer: A

31. Which component in an aerosol ensures accurate dosing?

A. Canister

B. Metering valve

C. Gasket

D. Cap

Answer: B

32. The force that expels the product in an aerosol comes from

A. Gravity

B. Hand pressure

C. Propellant pressure

D. Atmospheric suction

Answer: C

33. Which of the following is used as a hydrocarbon propellant?

A. Carbon dioxide

B. Butane

C. Nitrogen

D. Helium

Answer: B

34. In a two-phase system, the formulation exists as

A. Solid and gas

B. Solution and vapor

C. Liquid and propellant gas

D. Cream and foam

Answer: C

35. Inhalation aerosols must be

A. Sterile and isotonic

B. Non-sterile and thick

C. Syrupy and acidic

D. Opaque and viscous

Answer: A

36. Which device turns liquid medication into a fine mist?

A. Nebulizer

B. Capsule

C. Tube

D. Spray gun

Answer: A

37. The main drawback of chlorofluorocarbon propellants is

A. Low pressure generation

B. Toxic to humans

C. Ozone layer depletion

D. High cost

Answer: C

38. Aerosol foams are commonly used for

A. Oral administration

B. Eye treatment

C. Skin application

D. Injections

Answer: C

39. Which test is done to check for blockage in the actuator or valve?

A. Spray pattern

B. Leak test

C. Valve performance

D. Crimp test

Answer: C

40. The ideal particle size for lung deposition in aerosols is

A. 10–20 microns

B. 5–10 microns

C. 1–5 microns

D. 0.1–1 micron

Answer: C

41. Which of the following is NOT an advantage of pharmaceutical aerosols?

A. Sterile delivery

B. Localized action

C. Low manufacturing cost

D. Ease of administration

Answer: C

42. Which formulation is ideal for nasal delivery?

A. Foam aerosol

B. Nasal spray aerosol

C. Transdermal aerosol

D. MDI

Answer: B

43. The main component of a spray system that determines the spray quality is

A. Cap

B. Dip tube

C. Orifice

D. Label

Answer: C

44. The propellant that is least toxic and most environmentally friendly is

A. Butane

B. HFA-134a

C. CFC-11

D. Freon

Answer: B

45. What does the term "burst pressure" mean in aerosol testing?

A. Maximum usable dose

B. Lowest operating pressure

C. Maximum internal pressure container can tolerate

D. External sealing pressure

Answer: C

46. A proper crimp seal ensures

A. Color stability

B. Mechanical strength

C. Valve leakage prevention

D. Aesthetic packaging

Answer: C

47. Aerosol containers should be stored at

A. Below -10°C

B. Any temperature

C. Below 30°C

D. Above 50°C

Answer: C

48. Primary benefit of topical aerosols is

A. Extended systemic effect

B. Non-contact application

C. Rapid injection

D. Internal cleansing

Answer: B

49. Which term describes the uniformity of aerosol spray over time?

A. Valve resistance

B. Spray repeatability

C. Actuator speed

D. Emission rate

Answer: D

50. What is the function of a mounting cup in an aerosol can?

A. Controls pressure

B. Attaches valve to container

C. Filters impurities

D. Adds fragrance

Answer: B

Review Questions and Answers

1. What are pharmaceutical aerosols?
Pharmaceutical aerosols are pressurized dosage forms that release active ingredients as fine particles, sprays, or foams through a valve system.

2. How are aerosols administered?
They are mainly administered by inhalation, nasal, topical, and occasionally rectal or vaginal routes.

3. What is the main advantage of aerosol formulations?
They allow rapid onset of action and avoid first-pass metabolism.

4. Name the key components of a pharmaceutical aerosol system.
The main components include the container, propellant, valve, actuator, and the drug formulation.

5. What is the role of a propellant in an aerosol system?
The propellant expels the drug from the container and may also help dissolve or suspend the drug.

6. Mention two types of propellants used.
Liquefied gases such as HFA (hydrofluoroalkanes) and compressed gases like nitrogen.

7. What is an actuator?
It is the part pressed by the user to release the contents in a desired form like spray or mist.

8. What is a metered-dose inhaler (MDI)?
It is a type of aerosol device that delivers a fixed amount of drug with each actuation.

9. What is the function of the valve in aerosol systems?
It regulates the release of formulation and can be continuous or metered.

10. What is the use of a dip tube?
It connects the formulation inside the container to the valve for delivery.

11. What is a two-phase aerosol system?
It consists of a liquid phase (drug + propellant) and a vapor phase.

12. Define a three-phase aerosol system.
It contains a water phase, a propellant phase, and a vapor phase.

13. What are compressed gas systems?

These use gases like nitrogen or carbon dioxide as the propellant, stored under pressure.

14. What is spray pattern testing?

It is used to evaluate the uniformity and shape of the spray discharged.

15. What is the importance of valve crimping?

It ensures the valve is tightly attached to the container, preventing leakage.

16. Name one environmentally safe propellant.

HFA-134a is considered safe and ozone-friendly.

17. Why are co-solvents used in aerosols?

They improve solubility of the drug in the formulation.

18. What is flame projection testing?

It determines the flammability and projection of flame when the aerosol is sprayed near a flame.

19. What is the function of leak testing?

It checks for any leakage in the sealed container to ensure product stability.

20. What is dose content uniformity?

It confirms that each actuation delivers a consistent amount of drug.

21. Why is particle size important in inhalation aerosols?

Optimal particle size (1–5 microns) ensures deposition in the lungs.

22. What is burst pressure?

It is the maximum pressure a container can withstand before failing.

23. What is the role of antioxidants in aerosol formulations?

They prevent oxidation and degradation of active ingredients.

24. What are topical aerosols used for?

They are used for skin conditions, wound care, and cosmetic applications.

25. Define foam aerosol systems.

These produce foamy products using surfactants and propellants, often for topical use.

26. What is the cold fill method?

In this method, both product and propellant are cooled and filled under low temperatures.

27. What is the pressure fill method?

The formulation is filled first, and then propellant is added under pressure.

28. Which materials are commonly used for aerosol containers?

Aluminum, stainless steel, and coated glass.

29. What are the regulatory requirements for aerosols?

They must be tested for valve integrity, leakage, spray pattern, and content uniformity.

30. What is a dual-chamber aerosol system?

It separates two incompatible components and mixes them upon actuation.

31. Why is HFA preferred over CFCs?

HFA does not deplete the ozone layer, unlike chlorofluorocarbons.

32. What are nasal aerosols?

They deliver drugs to the nasal cavity for local or systemic effect.

33. What are the applications of rectal aerosols?

They are used for local delivery of anti-inflammatory or anesthetic agents.

34. What determines the quality of the emitted spray?

Valve design, actuator orifice size, and propellant pressure.

35. How is sterility ensured in aerosol packaging?

Through aseptic filling or terminal sterilization depending on formulation.

36. What is inhaler priming?

Releasing a few test sprays to ensure the device delivers a full dose.

37. What is the significance of surface tension in aerosols?

It affects droplet formation and spray characteristics.

38. What is crimp diameter testing?

It checks the mechanical fit of the valve to the container.

39. What does the term "sprayback" refer to?

Unwanted splash-back of product during actuation.

40. What is emitted dose?

The amount of drug that exits the device and is available for inhalation.

41. What is tail-off in aerosol performance?

A drop in dose delivered as the container nears empty.

42. What are the uses of water-based aerosols?

They are used in cosmetics and medical applications with reduced flammability.

43. Define valve delivery rate.

The rate at which a valve dispenses the formulation per unit time.

44. What is the significance of actuator geometry?

It determines the spray angle, droplet size, and plume shape.

45. What is the function of mounting cups?

They hold the valve in place and seal the container top.

46. What is the importance of overfill testing?

To confirm that excess product does not cause malfunction or container rupture.

47. How do barrier-type aerosols work?

They use bags or bladders to separate product from propellant.

48. What is the risk of using flammable propellants?

Potential explosion hazard if handled near heat or flames.

49. How is valve clogging prevented?

By using suitable solvent systems and filtration of the formulation.

50. What is the primary requirement for pulmonary aerosols?

They must generate respirable-sized particles for lung delivery.